Etiquette Bibliography

ETIQUETTE

*An Annotated Bibliography of Literature
Published in English in the United States,
1900 through 1987*

by

Deborah Robertson Hodges

McFarland & Company, Inc., Publishers
Jefferson, North Carolina, and London

British Library Cataloguing-in-Publication data available

Library of Congress Cataloguing-in-Publication Data

Hodges, Deborah Robertson.
 *Etiquette : an annotated bibliography of literature published in English
in the United States, 1900 through 1987* / by Deborah Robertson Hodges.
  p. cm.
 Includes index.
 ISBN 0-89950-429-9 (lib. bdg. : 50# alk. paper)
 1. Etiquette—Bibliography. I. Title.
 Z5877.H6 1989
 [BJ1853]
 016.395—dc20   89-42724
                                                                      CIP

Printed in the United States of America

McFarland & Company, Inc., Publishers
 Box 611, Jefferson, North Carolina 28640

Dedicated
with thanks to Pat,
my very special Mom and Dad,
Mom and Dad H.,
and especially to Mary Brooke,
for all those long hours spent
roaming dark library stacks
when you'd have rather been playing.

Table of Contents

Foreword

The distinction between etiquette (rules of behavior) and manners (method or mode of action) is discussed in the introduction to many etiquette books. This distinction was not considered relevant when selecting materials for this bibliography, however. In fact, "etiquette" was interpreted broadly in terms of materials selected for inclusion.

Books (including some text books), parts of books, periodical and journal articles, government publications, pamphlets and other material published in English in the United States between January 1, 1900, and December 31, 1987, are included in this work.

Juvenile literature, reprints, book reviews and excerpts from books reprinted in periodicals were generally not included.

Overview of the Literature

Widespread American interest in correct behavior at the beginning of the twentieth century is indicated by the great number of books and magazine articles written about etiquette. As a popular writer of the time, Florence Howe Hall explains, "Natural prosperity has enabled a large portion of our people to pay more attention to the grace of life."[1] During the Age of Opportunity, when the "fast train, the automobile, the telegraph, the telephone, annihilate space and time and bring people into daily, not to say hourly touch and communication,"[2] etiquette writers worked to improve the manners of the masses in America. The changing times, brought about in part by the influence of immigration, new technologies, the real possibility for upward mobility and the changing position of women in society, challenged etiquette writers to explore the answers to questions posed by this changing society.

There were two basic types of magazine articles about etiquette written during the first years of the twentieth century. One type was primarily instructional in nature, setting forth the rules for proper conduct. The other type of article was concerned with the nature of manners and the function of good manners in society. The more prominent writers during this decade included Julia Ward Howe, and her daughters, Florence Howe Hall, and Maud Howe. Florence Howe Hall gave advice through numerous articles and books, and was the most prolific of the three. Mrs. Sherwood, an active social arbiter in the nineteenth century, continued to be an influential writer. And Mrs. Albert Payson Terhune, writing under the pseudonym Marion Harland, was author of Everyday Etiquette, probably the most popular etiquette book of the time.

The instructional articles outlined clearly for the reader social obligations such as calling, the use of cards, how a gentleman should behave at his club, automobiling and the more traditional concerns such as table manners. New technologies challenged social arbiters to forge new paths in defining correct behavior, a challenge readily accepted by Ladies' Home Journal in an editorial called "Kodak Manners," which

1

explains the correct way to use that newly available camera
when taking pictures. Before automobile manners were legis-
lated, Florence Howe Hall included automobiling as one of
the sports discussed in her article, the "Etiquette of Sport,"
which appeared in Harper's Bazaar. Mrs. Hall gives this practical advice: "As the machine creates a tremendous wind
of its own, no headgear should be worn which carries any
sort of sail...."[3] Articles instructed readers in the "Etiquette
of Towns and Villages," and readers were reminded of "Minor
Table Manners," as well as advised "What Not to Do in Society."
Disappearing customs, "The Decay of the Chaperone" (which
never really firmly took hold in this country) and the "Vanishing
Curtsey" are lamented by still other writers.

   Articles entitled "Has the American Bad Manners," "Modern Manners in the Unmannerly Age," "The Passing of Good
Manners," and the almost wistful "Memories of Manners"
are indicative of the concern etiquette writers had about
what they perceived to be as a decline in American manners.
The discussions about this decline provide insight into the
relationship between the democratic society and manners
which writers observed. One writer, identified as an American
Mother, concerned about the unmannerly appearance of Americans in high ranking political positions declares: "In no other
country is such ignorance found in high places simply because
in no other country are high places open to men ignorant
of these things." She asks, "why, in the name of common
sense, should the desire for social equality make us shrill
and rude and vulgar?"[4] Maud Howe, discussing the "Importance
of Good Manners," writes "Republican manners ought surely
to be the best; we have no privileged class which must be
deferred to, we all have an equal right to courteous treatment
to each other."[5] An editorial appearing in the Independent
presents this perspective: "When political creed...extols
freedom and equality while in practical fact inequality and
dissimilarity are everywhere conspicuous, the conflict between
the actualities, and the idealistic is too acute to make the
problem of manners a simple one to solve." The editorial
provides insight to the social environment in turn-of-the-cen-
tury America: "As yet no set of connections has been worked
out to apply to men and women in a heterogenous population—a
population in which there are distinctions of nationality,
of education, of religion and above all of wealth."[6]

   The integral relationship between morals and manners
is discussed frequently in the literature, the writers' attitudes
reaffirming those of innumerable philosophers, such as Goethe,
Plato and Cicero, who had come before. The Golden Rule
lies at the root of all good manners; "being kind—in the last
analysis it always comes down to that."[7] "All we can safely

say is that at the bottom the causes of good manners lie in
those principles...of fraternity and equality."[8] "The best manners are founded on a consideration of others...this is the
point at which we must take refuge in good morals. Goethe
told us long since that good manners were good morals."[9]
Good form is discussed in these terms: "its ethical element
rests upon those changeless laws which define the moral
obligation of the individual to his fellow man and to the community at large."[10] The relationship between manners and
morals is explained: "true good form is based upon certain
essential qualities of the heart, without which it is a body
without a soul...."[11]

Marion Harland puts the philosophical point of view to
work practically when she writes in "Minor Table Manners,"
"I have no moral right to disgust my neighbor at a feast by
supping my soup as a pig swallows his swill, or to smack my
lips over a toothsome morsel," and she declares herself to
be "preaching the gospel of conventionality as a natural out-
come of the Golden Rule, and a direct means of grace to
those who practice it."[12] The editorial "Leagues for Courtesy,"
in the Outlook, suggests, "conventions are not arbitrary social
requirements; they are almost always based on sound principles."[13]

Women's manners are the focus of a significant number
of magazine articles written during this decade. The role
of the woman in America has been one of sovereignty in the
social realm, social arbiters being predominantly female,
interpreting social codes for fellow women. However, as
opportunities for women to venture into the business and
sporting realms begin to occur, so does concern for the decline
in women's manners. Until this decade, the prevailing attitude
could be summarized as: "The test of the quality of a society
everywhere is the respect paid to women."[14] But, as Florence
Howe Hall explains in an article significantly asking "Are
American Women's Manners Deteriorating?": "The changed
position of women has had an immense effect on our manners.
Now that a woman can hold property...and can earn her own
living...she feels an independence that shows itself in her
behavior and bearing."[15] Mrs. Sherwood offers her own explanation, "The advent of women into new fields, and the feministic
agitation to widen their paths still further, and the active
opposition or indifference of men toward them, are responsible,
it is often explained, for a deterioration in manners."[16] In
her popular book, Everyday Etiquette, Marion Harland specifically addresses the women who have risen from "decent poverty
to actual wealth." Mrs. Harland also encourages women to
shape themselves independently, as "men...do not take polish
readily." In fact, she lists as her clientele "women, in particu-

lar—to whom changed circumstances...involved the necessity of altered habits of social intercourse."[17]

Books published during the first decade of the twentieth century still maintained a traditional approach to etiquette, renumerating advice offered by arbiters from centuries past. For example, chapters on cards and calling, and the chaperone, were included in most of the books, even though indications were that these practices were no longer followed by the majority of Americans. Emily Holt, author of the Encyclopaedia of Etiquette, succinctly stated the prevailing attitude among arbiters, "Etiquette in its principles and practice is ever the same and almost as old as civilization."[18]

Interestingly, the titles to books published during this time usually do not refer to society in the way they had during the nineteenth century. Indeed, some nouveau-riche displayed their wealth with such vulgarity that good marketing techniques indicated a dissociation with "Society," because the reference was offensive to many Americans. Titles appeared to take on a practical tone, with titles like Everyday Etiquette and Good Morals and Gentle Manners typifying the etiquette-book marketing approach.

Mrs. Sherwood makes some interesting predictions about what manners will be like in post-World War I America. She suggests that Americans, because of their contacts with the rest of the world as a result of World War I, will be more egalitarian in their approach to manners. "The ideals of the new society will be more democratic than aristocratic; not 'noblesse oblige', but 'let us work and play together as brothers'." She also predicts that "The formal condescension shown by those of the so-called upper classes to those below them is likely to become largely a thing of the past."[19]

Her predictions were amazingly accurate in that there is general agreement among social observers that the twenties heralded the turning point in the development of American etiquette. The twenties were a time of considerable change in the American social scene, and one of the most influential changes continued to be that of the role of women in society. Interestingly, as women gained yet greater independence during the twenties, the alarm continued to sound among social arbiters about the decline in the manners of the American woman. The independence gained by women at this time has in part been attributed to the advancing technologies which were able to free her from some of the drudgeries of housekeeping. Surely the affluence of the times afforded some women greater freedom as well.

Some young women were obvious in their disregard for social conventions, causing great consternation for one writer who asks, "Where Are Our Manners?" and says, "The girls

these days do not walk; they lope. They do not sit; they wriggle.
They do not talk; they chatter...to be tough and mannerless
is up-to-date." The author does not hesitate to link this undesirable behavior with the morals of those she is critcizing, "The
undesirable morals are to a great extent the result of very.
bad manners."[20]

Another author maintains that the young women of the
times were declaring, "We don't want chivalry; we want equality."[21] A female world traveler tells readers "You Get What
You Expect from Men," and an article called "Motoring Manners" is addressed to women, who are told how to drive without
offending their passengers, and passengers are instructed
in the least offensive behavior towards the driver. Articles
like "Country Club Manners," "Vacation Manners," "The Ideal
Guest," and "Telephone Temper" are exemplary of both the
technological advances and new lifestyle of the twenties.

Certainly not all arbiters of it were dismayed by the
changing social scene. Mrs. Ludwig Hoyt, in telling readers
"How to Avoid Social Blunders" writes:

> Older people complain that the present generation
> is careless about social observances, but I think it
> is an excellent thing we have discarded some of the
> tiresome formalities. Think of the dreary hours our
> mothers and grandmothers spent in making and receiving
> perfunctory calls which were a bore to everybody.
> We are emancipated from that slavery now.[22]

H.I. Phillips, the humorist, asks "Are You the Master of Your
Forks, the Captain of Your Spoons?" and declares, "There
is too much etiquette in the ballrooms and not enough in
the revolving doors.... The tendency today is to put on etiquette
too thickly on some spots, and skip more noticeable ones
entirely."[23]

The concern about the lack of manners exhibited by the
general populus leads to demands for the implementation
of programs in the schools which would teach the social graces.
"A Course in Manners" reviews the success of one such program
in Cleveland, saying, "Through the country educators are
talking about teaching character, manners, and morals."[24]
An educator provides "A Laboratory Method for Social Guidance," to be used in the schools, and says, "Much time and
thought are being devoted to the consideration of giving to
pupils of high school age a knowledge of the fundamental
principles in social relations."[25] "A High School Course in
Social Training" was implemented in one school because
of "the necessity of having the school do what the home was
not doing in training the girls for social contacts."[26] In an
article called "Social Training for Our Boys" the author declares
the need for mothers to train boys for business success by

providing them with the necessary social training, and "failing that, to send them to a good school, where the training may be procured."[27]

C.H. Towne offers his view of the times:

Immediately following the World War, and up to and through Prohibition, young people in America became almost impossible, socially. An era came in which might be called, not the Age of Innocence, but the Age of Impudence.[28]

Mary Borden sums up the problems of manners in a modernizing America:

And so the elaborate decorative standards of the leisured nineteenth century have been replaced by a simplicity, a severity, and a brevity befitting a hurried world of dust and crowds and snorting machines. Motors and aeroplanes, undergrounds, elevators and telephones have designed our clothes for us and our manners...and the problem of decent, becoming, agreeable behavior becomes a problem more serious than that of the curve of a bow or the pattern of a greeting...Manners must adapt themselves to the paraphernalia and tempo of life.[29]

And so the stage was set in the twenties: the backdrop—a society in search of its own culture in a technologically advancing country; the actors—those newly arrived into a rapidly expanding middle class; the script—Etiquette: The Blue Book of Social Usage; and the director—Mrs. Emily Price Post. Before Emily Post appeared to serve as America's premier social director, etiquette books reflected social customs which were held over from the nineteenth century, and "etiquette" was a word not used in polite company. The phenomenal success of Etiquette can be measured by the fact that it was published in July 1922, and by August 1923 it had been reprinted eight times, and was said to be, with the Bible, the largest-selling book in America at the time. There can be no doubt about the significance of this book, since the name Emily Post is virtually synonymous with etiquette in America (even three decades after her death). There is some irony that an etiquette book, setting forth codes of social convention, enjoyed such success at the same time that American literary classics were being written by expatriates such as T.S. Eliot and Ernest Hemingway.

Emily Post's biography establishes her credentials as America's premier arbiter of the social graces. She was born into a wealthy family in 1872, the daughter of Brice Price, a successful architect. Emily Post made her debut into New York society in 1892, and married Edwin Main Post shortly thereafter. Unfortunately, the marriage ended in divorce in 1904, amidst a scandal. As unusual as divorce was at this time, Post's position in society remained unaffected. She had two sons, whom she was able to support by writing novels, and she had as a life-long interest architecture.

Had it not been for Richard Duffy of Funk & Wagnalls, Etiquette might never have been written. Mr. Duffy initially requested Emily Post to write an etiquette book, and the story goes that she declined fervently. However, after her friend, Frank Crowninshield, editor of Vanity Fair, sent her a copy of an unidentified etiquette book, she read it and changed her mind. Apparently Emily Post felt the tone of the book was condescending and realized the need for a sensible etiquette book.

The first edition of Etiquette had a wonderful cast of characters, their role defined by name—Mrs. Toplofty, The Worldlys, The Notquites, Mr. Clubwin Doe—each serving his own purpose. The first edition was also full of aristocratic luxuries such as butlers, maids and footmen, so much so that many Americans wrote Mrs. Post frantically wanting to know how to entertain without any servants. Mrs. Post, always conscious of the necessity for etiquette books to address the changing times, came out with Mrs. Three–In–One in her second edition, published in 1937. Mrs. Three–In–One was the wife who had no servant, but she was able to be cook, waitress and charming hostess at once. Mrs. Post also conceded to the Vanishing Chaperone in her second edition. On manners, Mrs. Post says, differentiating from manner:

> Manners are made up of trivialities of deportment which can be easily learned if one does not happen to know them, manner is personality—the outward manifestation of one's innate character and attitude toward life.[30]

Her philosophy of the basic nature of the role of manners in society is:

> Best society is not a fellowship of the wealthy, nor does it seek to exclude those who are not of exalted birth; but it is an association of gentle-folk, of which good form in speech, charm of manner, knowledge of social amenities, and instinctive consideration for the feelings of others, are the credentials by which society the world over recognizes its chosen members.[31]

Most of the colorful characters of the first edition have long since disappeared, and during Mrs. Post's lifetime Etiquette went through ten revisions and eighty-nine printings. Her wonderful success was also enhanced by a daily newspaper column and daily radio broadcast, both starting in the early 1930's. Elizabeth L. Post, her granddaughter-in-law, has carried on the tradition. Emily Post died at the age of 87 in 1960.

The social changes in the twenties were met by equally
dynamic changes in the thirties, heralded with the arrival
of the Depression. According to one arbiter of etiquette,
"a new book on etiquette needs no excuse," and cites numerous
changes to be addressed by arbiters such as the earning capacity
of both men and women, the shift from rural to urban populations, and changes brought about by the telephone, car and
radio.[32]
    The large number of articles written during the thirties
about business etiquette indicate the regard for economic
conditions held by social observers. The luxury of examining
the relationship between morality and manners, or between
democracy and manners, seems to give way to a practical
interpretation of the social codes within a business context,
in order to help people get jobs, or help businesses attract
or keep much needed patronage.
    Women were also notably visible in the work force, and
the need for arbitration for women in a formerly predominately
male world is met by two women in particular. Elizabeth
MacGibbon suggests that the new working woman "understands
the business world better, she comes to feel that she would
rather be accorded a square deal by men than be placed on
a pedestal merely because she happened to be born a woman."[33]
Joan Wing, an enterprising telephone operator, saw a need
for more courteous behavior in the business world and established her own business to meet that need. She became a business-
courtesy expert, lecturing around the country and advising
people to hold onto their jobs during hard times by "doing
them in the spirit management likes."[34] Wing created a niche
for herself by proving that improved manners among employees
would mean improved efficiency in business. She demonstrated
that by improving the manners of switchboard operators,
the operators improved their efficiency as well.
    Male social arbiters were also concerned about courtesy
in the business world. Robert Coates asks "Do You Offend?"
and relates courtesy in business to the Depression in a very
direct way: "With millions of men out of work, there is no
reason why a poorly-qualified person should hold a job. And
discourtesy is a poor qualification for any work."[35] The article
"Bad Times, Better Manners" echoes this sentiment, acknowledging that "fear of losing one's job and the cupidity that
now must conciliate every possible customer are not the
noblest reasons for courtesy." However, the author continues,
"life in the city is in many casual ways far pleasanter than
when there were plenty of jobs and plenty of money."[36] Even
the railroads jumped on the courtesy bandwagon, as the article
"Smile School: Teaching Courtesy and Service to Railroaders,
U.P. Trouble-Shooter's Job" would indicate. The trouble-

shooter's job is "instructing railroad employees on the best
ways to avoid getting angry at finicky passengers."[37]
Apart from the profit or "job security" motives promoted
by business etiquette arbiters, Frances Maule sees "Office
Etiquette" somewhat differently. "Business etiquette is determined...simply and solely by rank, exactly as it is in the
government service, the Army and the Navy." Maule maintains
that neither personal wealth nor social position are determining
factors in the world of business etiquette.[38]

If social position had no place in the business world, some
were asking if the gentleman as an institution was outmoded
in the social world. Articles proclaimed "Gentlemen Wanted"
and reminisced about "What a Gentleman Was," contending
that "the elimination of the gentleman that is and for some
time has been taking place under the stress of alien forces..."
may disappear.[39] Another article laments "The Vanishing
Gentleman," and questions the motives which "induced democracy to reject the institution by so overwhelming a majority."[40]

In the same way that the Depression focused attention
on business etiquette in the thirties, World War II focused
arbiters' attention on the lack of courtesy found among service
workers. While the lack of courtesy among public servants
was not a new topic for arbiters, the shortages of goods available and of services caused by the war made discourtesy
from public servants even less acceptable.

Struthers Burt, writing "Manners Maykth Man" describes
the situation saying, "When manners break down, anarchy
begins; and anarchy always ends eventually in force and tyranny
of some kind...Fascism and Nazism are modern examples."
He expressed the concern shared by many authors that "it
is upon a breakdown of manners, civic and personal, that
all the dangerous people in this country, the marplots, the
demagogues, the haters of democracy, are banking in their
search for personal power...." Burt does offer an explanation
for why the social climate is the way it is, "war is a dislocating
business. People are hurried, crowded, over-worked, each
with his private worry. For a while manners, like everything
else, get along as best they can. But peace is different. Peace
is civilization..."[41]

In somewhat vengeful tones, in an article called "After
the War the Worm May Turn," an author offers his analysis
of the stateside social situation: "The fact that we are at
war has become the blanket alibi for every variety of bad
service and bad faith...the shortage of manpower has given
many wage earners the green light for slackness and insolence."
The author threatens these wage earners in no uncertain
terms, "Enraged customers are writing down names in little
black books for future boycotting."[42]

Another writer laments, "no matter how much I modulate
my voice, keep my elbows in, and refrain from blowing bubbles
in my milk, I seem to arouse wrath and antagonism on every
side..."[43] The offenders are actually listed by another victim
of them:
> scarcely a day passes in the life of a shopper or traveler
> in which he doesn't at least once long to murder a
> pugnacious bus driver, a waspish salesperson, a huffy
> hotel clerk, a quarrelsome railway employee, a nasty
> theater attendant or an insolent waiter.[44]

All the criticism of the service workers did generate some
backlash by those choosing to focus on their more positive
experiences. The Rotarian published letters from people relating anecdotes of courteous service encountered during war
time. Emily Post published a wartime supplement in Etiquette
to guide people through problems peculiar to the times, and
several articles dealt with the presence of the extra woman
in social functions.

One forecast of what American influence would be in
the world after the war suggested that "with an age of travel
and increased trading setting in, there is every advantage
in the world in taking time individually and nationally to
figure out how not to give offense and how to make foreigners
like us."[45] Concerned about the role of the United States
as a democracy which other countries may wish to emulate,
the author maintains that "at its highest point of clarity and
development, human conduct is attracted toward democracy...if
we want to improve democracy, we must improve personal
conduct."[46]

The Rotary Club set about to teach courtesy to Filipinos
in Manila after the war by distributing 25,000 posters throughout the city which listed some points of courtesy. "Seven
Points of Courtesy" were also outlined for employees in government offices, commercial firms, factories, stores and
educational institutions.[47]

Writers about etiquette during the forties also showed
great interest in teaching manners to children. Articles like
"Manners in the Making" by Eleanor Boykin set out to help
adolescents who appeared to be "in a welter of bewilderment
and self-consciousness over behavior puzzles," and she encourages fortifying through role play those children who are accus-
tomed to maidless meals, so they will not suffer "service
jitters" when they are waited upon.[48]

Several articles promoted teaching manners as a function
of the school systems, as "A Good Way to Develop Leaders,"
or incorporated in the language curriculum, as the title "Social
Forms of Oral Language" would suggest. Most social arbiters,
however, encouraged and directed parents in teaching manners

to their children. Articles such as "Teaching the Small Child
Table Manners," "Thank You, Baby," and "Your Manners Are
Catching" were written solely for this purpose. Advising parents
how to "Teach Your Boy or Girl Good Manners," one writer
feels that teaching girls is easier because they are willing
to learn to "be sweet, polite and courteous." However, she
says, "boys are wary...you must appeal to their manhood,
develop his pride."[49] "This Way to Courtesy" urges parents
to begin early in helping children learn just what is expected
of them in social situations. "Is there any one trait which
we can cultivate in our children that will pay greater dividends
than instinctive courtesy?" she asks.[50]

Two articles surfaced in the forties which foreshadow
the social-political climate of coming decades. "Courtesy
Across the Color Line" concerns itself with forms of address
between blacks and whites. J.H. Marion, a southerner, is
"disturbed and saddened by this tradition of racial discourtesy
that is unworthy of the best in southern people.... [T]he most
cultured and law abiding Negroes among us are usually
compelled to endure the same searing and contemptuous
indignity..." as that of the prostitute or prisoner.[51]

The second article sets forth one man's protestations
about the expectation women have for courteous treatment.
"Down with the Little Things" may have been written partially
in jest, but his protests are heard from women in the decades
to come. "Ever since the turn of the century women have
continued their gradual encroachment on man's position in
the world of business, the arts, and even politics." He objects
to the little courtesies men show women such as lighting
the ladies' cigarettes, serving ladies first, and helping ladies
out of cars![52]

The literature following the war years raises some new
concerns among social observers as the era of casual living—the
fifties—unfolds. At least one observer is led to wonder "if
the price of the new informality has to be messiness."[53] Examining the cause for the state of manners in the fifties, Russell
Lynes, suggests that conventions of earlier times no longer
seem applicable because of all the changes brought about
by modern conveniences. Lynes cites changes in food service,
the thaw and serve meal, houses designed in the open plan,
the permissiveness of the "child-centered curriculum" which
dealt the imposition of manners on children a hard blow and
the general leveling of society as factors affecting changes
in social conventions.[54] Book titles such as Short Cut to
Etiquette and Simplified Guide to Table Setting reflect this
fast and easy attitude towards living.

Lynes believes that even amongst all the social changes
and the adoption of a relaxed social standard, cries could

be heard for some convention, and that young people, having grown up in an age where social codes have not been clearly defined, will formalize their own. Lynes states, "in the process of levelling the classes of America we have not yet managed to decide what the manners of such a society should be." He concludes with the prediction that "it will be the formality of democratic self-respect, the manners of a people so sure of its national freedom that it will respect the freedom of every individual in it."[55]

The new informality did not go unnoticed by <u>Rotary Magazine</u>, which sponsored a debate-of-the-month about the ready use of first names among strangers. The question "Can We Cope with Comfort?" is asked by Kenneth Sellers, who contends that modern culture in America is a cult of "informalism." The "cult" views social convention "as outmoded relics of the past" and "equates sloppy manners with modernity and comfortable informality." Sellers takes exception to the "informalists'" view that anything which is "casual and informal must automatically represent the best expression of sincerity and tact."[56]

The child-rearing practice of nonintervention was a focal point of etiquette writers during the fifties as well. The notion that discipline for children goes against nature was declared invalid, and parents are told that "Children Can Have Manners." One mother confesses that not all courtesies came naturally to her children, that children do not inherently acquire good manners, and that by failing to teach her children good manners she had failed to give the children the ability to cope with the "natural awkwardness most children feel in some social situations." The mother continues, "Looking back, it seems clear I was so concerned in my early years of motherhood about developing inner emotional security for my children, that I overlooked the contribution of outer social security."[57]

Articles outlining successful programs instituted in the public schools to teach manners to children are plentiful as well. Educators tell each other how to "Improve Your Pupils' Cafeteria Manners" and how "Our Eat-and-Learn Program Works."

The question of democracy and manners also surfaces again in the fifties. One explanation of the relationship between the two is that: "We distrust fancy manners because they seem to us affected, but we have a hankering for conventions, and when old ones go out of date we make up new ones."[58] Another interesting explanation of this relationship appears in an article written by Morton Cronin called "The Tyranny of Democratic Manners":

American manners...decree egalitarian behavior in a hierarchical society. The result is that the subordinate,

compelled to behave formally and superficially in
a democratic way, is forced in making his adjustments
to the facts of life to behave informally and profoundly
in a hierarchical way.[59]

Cronin calls for a sensible system of manners, with formalities
which "allow the individual to acquiesce in the social order
while reserving his final judgment of it."[60]

Of particular importance among the etiquette books
published in that decade is Amy Vanderbilt's Complete Book
of Etiquette, published in 1952 "after five years of writing
and research." The book is notable at least in part because
of Vanderbilt's social position, descending from the "Staten
Island Vanderbilts." In fact, she outlines the line of descent
in the introduction to her book, and explains the need for
etiquette, "For we must all learn the socially acceptable
ways of living with others...." The traditional aristocratic
topics—staffing a mansion, or dressing for an evening horse
show—are generously covered. However, the scope of the
book is broad enough to acknowledge the changing times
by interpreting social codes for religions other than mainstream
Protestant, recognizing that there were women in the work
force, and that people even buy on credit. The success of
her book can best be measured by the fact that five editions
were published between 1952 and 1958.[61]

Any noticeable trend in the etiquette literature written
in the 1960s and early 1970s is difficult to define. This is
significant because it is a reflection of the lack of definition
in the social codes of the time because of the social upheaval
America was experiencing during this time. During the "Age
of the Party Dip and Casserole,"[62] when people were letting
it ALL hang out, social conventions were neither easily determined nor generally adhered to. Social arbiters were not
readily recognized, and American youth was rebelliously
redefining social code.

Dismay for the dismantled family relationships which
were part of the social revolution was expressed readily by
some of the more conservative members of society. Mary
Guitar, in an article ruefully entitled, "Can't the Pendulum
Swing This Way?" laments, "We have moved so far in the
direction of casual living, self-expression, and spontaneity
that we are in danger of losing something equally precious—
namely civilized family life." Guitar continues to describe
the American way of life as "20th century motel style."[63]

Many children were reared with the theory that serious
discipline might interfere with the free flowering of the
creative child. One hopeful, if not premature, article declared
"Manners Are Back in Style," maintaining:

In spite of the cherished notion of a few years back
that burdening a child with the baggage of social good
form was repressing him and therefore harmful, many
parents have apparently - on the sly - been teaching
their children manners, anyway.[64]

Amy Vanderbilt seems to remain optimistically philosophical
about it all: "Most of today's fashion-setting is observation
of sociological change, and a lot of it is common sense." She
does, however, concede that society is "rapidly leveling," so
that it is hard "to know what's correct any more..."[65]

Amidst all the social awareness of the times racial etiquette
does not go unnoticed in the literature. One article, "Interracial
Etiquette," declares that "Good manners...are nowhere more
pressingly needed today than in the realm of interracial relations...," and the author sets forth five basic rules of communications etiquette to use in establishing good relationships.[66]
Another author expresses concern with the form of address
using contemptuous familiarity when addressing Negroes,
which is "deeply resented by Negroes, not merely because
of the personal affront but also because such derogatory
titles symbolize the whole racial caste system. In racial
encounters politeness is both inexpensive and precious."[67]

If the nonconformists of the sixties scoffed at social conventions observed by the Establishment, then society as a whole
must have been at least a bit distracted from them by the
social crusades of the times. At a time when some women
were in public outcry against what they saw as sexist behavior,
the social rituals observed by men toward women were called
into doubt. These are the very conventions which at one time
showed deference to the position of women in society, and
were expected by women. As Letitia Baldrige explains, "The
women's movement called a world of once reflexive rituals
into doubt...whether to rise or open a door for a woman...Would
the courtesy offend her?"[68]

Dating customs, and the way in which men and women
interact would never be the same. Amy Vanderbilt writes
in the preface to the 1971 edition of her Etiquette:

I have certainly had to consider the Sexual Revolution
which in many cases merely reflected what people
were doing all along but were not prepared publicly
to admit...I have had to take cognizance of new, and
rather general forms of expression which have had,
to say the least, a leveling effect upon upper-class
speech.[69]

Indeed, the topic of sexual etiquette which was openly
discussed during this era, is one which was certainly not written
about in the days of Mrs. Sherwood and Mrs. Hall. The Sexual
Revolution threw the door to life's most intimate relationships

wide open, and there were social arbiters at the ready with
advice. The Cosmo Girl's Guide to the New Etiquette, edited
by Helen Gurley Brown, includes a section called the "Libidinal
You," which includes chapters such as "How Sexually Generous
a Girl Should Be," "A Philosophy of Considerate Adultery,"
and "The Etiquette of Not Getting Pregnant." An article
called "Sexual Courtesy: The New Rules" implies in the title
that there were old rules...
    Advice about the Sexual Revolution was not limited to
women. Playboy Press published The Single Man's Indispensable
Guide and Handbook, by Paul Gillette, in 1973. Although
etiquette books exclusively for men were not new, one with
a chapter called "The Single Man on the Make, with the A
to Z of Sex," certainly was. The author sought to concentrate
"on the how rather than the whether of pleasurable living."[70]
    Without a doubt, as Elizabeth Post describes in the 1975
preface to Emily Post's Etiquette:
> our life-style is new. Yesterday, privacy, self-discipline,
> and formality were the rule. Today, openness, freedom,
> and informality are the qualities that we live with...Man-
> ners evolve of their own accord.[71]

One consequence of the sky-rocketing divorce rate was
remarriage, and several arbiters were willing to set forth
some guidelines for those needing assistance. "Remarriage:
Survival Manual" is an article in which the author begins
to explore the need for the evolution of an etiquette to guide
families through a remarriage. Another author suggests, in
"The New Etiquette, How to Survive a Second Marriage," that
the woman keep the same name as the children, and that
it is ill-advised to get too friendly with the "ex" and his new
wife. Susan Fields, author of Getting Married Again, suggests
that people may encounter difficult receptions when announcing
a forthcoming second marriage. "If you're planning to get
married for the second time, probably you have already run
head on into a painful paradox: all the world may love a lover,
but nobody likes a loser...."[72] Delia Brock writes in "Twice
Is Nice" that "What the etiquette books say is only good for
a laugh...The problem the writers of these books have is that
they can't quite forgive you for having failed the first time
around."[73] (She failed to consider the marital histories of
some very prominent arbiters.) Books such as The New
Etiquette Guide to Getting Married Again, The New Etiquette:
How to Survive a Second Marriage and the Second Marriage
Guidebook were all written to help define the social codes
for a relatively new social phenomenon.
    The transition out of the era of the late sixties and mid-
seventies and into the eighties is highlighted by a renewed
interest in etiquette. The literature focuses upon etiquette

as a positive factor in social and business relationships. Although there can be little doubt that me-ism was a primary factor in the social development of many people coming out of the seventies, the awkwardness of self-expression which left little regard for the sensitivities of others appears to have taken its toll on society. The rudeness which was a result of asserting oneself, or telling it like it is, was met by a number of arbiters in the eighties ready to fill the void left by fifteen years of undefined social convention.

This renewed interest in manners is evidenced by the popularity of etiquette advice columns like those of Miss Manners (Judith Martin) or Charlotte Ford, the success of classes which teach manners to children, and even the increase in formal wear rentals! Marjabelle Stewart has 420 franchised White Gloves and Party Manners schools throughout the country, enjoying great success while teaching propriety to youngsters.

The return to an interest in manners may tie in with economic hard times felt by some industries, as it has in the past. However, where the literature of the thirties was concerned with how the business owner could improve his business with courteous employees, the literature of the eighties focuses upon etiquette as a tool to develop one's own success. Moving up the corporate ladder by knowing how to behave seems to be the issue in the business etiquette of the eighties.

Entire etiquette books, such as The Professional Image: The Total Program for Marketing Yourself Visually by Susan Bixler, are devoted to details of how one should appear in order to promote an image of power. Much of the current literature equates a person's success in business with achieving a particular state of "class." A book entitled Class Acts offers advice to those subscribing to the successful lifestyle of the upwardly mobile. An article asks, "Do You Have Working Class?" and lists those attributes necessary for an individual to be able to acquire that particular state of being.

The need for guidance in the codes of the business world is explained by one author: "Amid the social and economic tumult of the past 20 years, some of the signposts of business civility have been twisted around and others uprooted entirely."[74] Letitia Baldrige's Complete Guide to Executive Manners emerges as a comprehensive tome to direct lost executives down that signless road. The book is subtitled: The Ultimate Guide; Everything People and Their Companies Need to Know to Do the Right Thing at the Right Time in Every Business Situation. Baldridge's credentials include experience as social secretary to ambassadors in Paris and Rome and as Jacqueline Kennedy's chief of staff during the Kennedy

administration. She also authored the revised edition of <u>Amy</u>
<u>Vanderbilt's Complete Book of Etiquette.</u>
    Judith Martin, a.k.a. Miss Manners, has also enjoyed tremen-
dous popularity as a social arbiter in the eighties. She has
written several books in addition to her syndicated newspaper
column. <u>Miss Manners' Guide to Excruciatingly Correct</u>
<u>Behavior</u> is currently a favorite. Martin maintains, "I am
not the only crank who is being driven mad by the abrasiveness
of modern America.... The modern etiquette problem...is
that the citizens are screaming at one another in the streets."[75]
    Elizabeth Post sets out to address the etiquette problems
particular to the eighties by including in the 1984 edition
of <u>Emily Post's Etiquette</u> "new tools...to cope with new
situations. Since the last revision of this book, two things
have occurred which have profoundly affected modern society
and our manners. They are the growth of women in the work
force...and the way society views single people."[76]
    As Charlotte Ford explains in the introduction to her
<u>Book of Modern Manners,</u> the challenge to arbiters of etiquette
is "to help answer the whys and hows of situations for which
there are no longer exact standards of proper behavior."[77]
In what directions society will challenge arbiters into the
twenty-first century remains to be seen. If the literature
of the past is any indication, however, there will be continued
efforts to define those codes of behavior which are uniquely
American, and to examine the relationships between manners
and a democratic society.
    The literature of the past has explored the need for stan-
dardized codes of behavior in society, and surely these philosophical discussions will continue.
    Etiquette for virtually every human situation has been
set down by arbiters through the years, and as new situations
arise in an ever-changing society, arbiters will be there to
both establish and record the codes of behavior.
    And as it always has been, the foundation upon which
these codes have been built, that basic premise of the Golden
Rule—do unto others as you would have them do unto you—will
continue to be the source of inspiration for social arbiters.
    Perhaps Dr. Norman Vincent Peale best summarized what
etiquette writers throughout years past are proposing:
        Life is full of minor irritations and trials and injustices.
        The only constant, daily, effective solution is
        politeness—which is the golden rule in action.[78]

Notes

1. Hall, Florence Howe. "Are American Women's Manners Deteriorating?", Harper's Bazaar, Vol. 40, Jan. 1906, p. 19.
2. West, Mrs. George Cornwallis. "Modern Manners and the Unmannerly Age", Cosmopolitan, Vol. 37, Aug. 1904, p. 394.
3. Hall, Florence Howe. "Etiquette of Sport", Harper's Bazaar, Vol. 42, Nov. 1908, p. 1130.
4. "Has the American Bad Manners?", Ladies' Home Journal, Vol. 17, Nov. 1900, p. 19.
5. Howe, Maud. "Importance of Good Manners", Harper's Bazaar, Vol. 41, Dec. 1907, p. 1233.
6. "Causes of Manners", Independent, Vol. 58, Jan. 19, 1905, p. 159.
7. Howe, p. 1234.
8. "Causes of Manners", p. 159.
9. "Good Manners", Harper's Weekly, Vol. 50, Sept. 8, 1906, p. 1270.
10. Good Form. Monroe, Mich., St. Mary's College, 1915, p. 2.
11. Good Form, p. 2.
12. Harland, Marion. "Minor Table Manners", Good Housekeeping, Vol. 49, Nov. 1909, p. 528.
13. "Leagues for Courtesy", Outlook, Vol. 77, May 7, 1904, p. 15.
14. "Leagues for Courtesy", p. 15.
15. Hall, "Are American Women's Manners Deteriorating?", p. 20.
16. Sherwood, Mary Elizabeth. Manners and Social Usages. New York, Harper, 1918. p. xi.
17. Harland, Marion, and Ven De Water, Virginia. Everyday Etiquette, A Practical Manual of Social Usages. Indianapolis, Bobbs-Merrill Co., 1905. p. iii.
18. Holt, Emily. Encyclopaedia of Etiquette. Garden City, N.Y., Doubleday, Page & Co., 1923. p. v.
19. Sherwood, p. xii.
20. Marbury, Elisabeth. "Where Are Our Manners?", Collier's, Vol. 75, May 9, 1925, p. 25.
21. Borden, Mary. "Manners, American and English", Harpers, Vol. 160, Dec. 1929, p. 78.
22. Hoyt, Mrs. Lydig. "How to Avoid Social Blunders", American Magazine, Vol. 93, Jan. 1922, p. 34.
23. Phillips, H.I. "Are You the Master of Your Forks, The Captain of Your Spoons?", American Magazine, Vol. 100, Sept. 1925, p. 98.
24. "Course in Manners; John Adams High School of Cleveland", School Review, Vol. 35, Apr. 1927, p. 249.

25. Hunter, Lucretia P. "Laboratory Method for Social Guidance", Educational Review, Vol. 75, Jan. 1928, p. 31.
26. MacNachtan, Ethel R. "High School Course in Social Training", Journal of Home Economics, Vol. 20, July 1928, p. 473.
27. Ewertsen, Lillian. "Social Training for Our Boys", National Education Association Journal, Vol. 14, Apr. 1925, p. 116.
28. Towne, Charles Hanson. Gentlemen Behave: Charles Hanson Towne's Book of Etiquette for Men. New York, Julian Messner, Inc., 1939. p. ii.
29. Borden, p. 81.
30. Post, Emily. Etiquette; The Blue Book of Social Usage. New York, Funk & Wagnalls Co., 1927. p. 2.
31. Post, p. 3.
32. Richardson, Anna Steese. The Bride's Book of Etiquette. New York, Harper & Brothers, 1930. p. vii.
33. MacGibbon, Elizabeth Gregg. Manners in Business. New York, Macmillan Co., 1936. p. x.
34. "Presenting the Courtesy Expert", Reader's Digest, Vol. 35, Sept. 1939, p. 95.
35. Coates, Robert M. "Do You Offend?", New Republic, Vol. 86, Apr. 8, 1936, p. 246-7.
36. Wynkoop, Eliza. "Bad Times, Better Manners", Atlantic, Vol. 150, Sept. 1932, p. 381.
37. "Smile School: Teaching Courtesy and Service to Railroaders", Literary Digest, Vol. 123, May 29, 1937, p.5.
38. Maule, Frances. "Office Etiquette", Literary Digest, Vol. 123, May 8, 1937, p. 33.
39. Sedgwick, Henry Dwight. "What a Gentleman Was", Atlantic, Vol. 155, Mar. 1935, p. 261.
40. Sedgwick, Henry Dwight. "Vanishing Gentleman", Atlantic, Vol. 155, Apr. 1935, p. 419.
41. Burt, Struthers. "Manners Maykth Man", Ladies' Home Journal, Vol. 63, May 1946, p. 6.
42. Pollock, Channing. "After the War, the Worm May Turn", Rotarian, Vol. 66, Feb. 1945, p. 14.
43. Smith, Elinor Goulding. "The Rebel", Atlantic, Vol. 177, May 1946, p. 144.
44. Beatty, Jerome. "Salespeople Drive Me Nuts!", American Magazine, Vol. 140, Sept. 1945, p. 46.
45. Banning, Margaret Culkin, and Culkin, Mabel Louise. Conduct Yourself Accordingly. New York, Harper & Brothers, 1944. p. 170.
46. Banning, p. 186.
47. "Manila Takes a Lesson in Courtesy", Rotarian, Vol. 74, June 1949, p. 15.

48. Boykin, Eleanor. "Manners in the Making," Parents Magazine, Vol. 18, Jan. 1943, p. 5.

49. Ahern, Nell G. "How to Teach Your Boy or Girl Good Manners," Better Homes and Gardens, Vol. 27, Mar. 1949, p. 175.

50. Hodge, Harriet Mason. "This Way to Courtesy," Parents Magazine, Vol. 15, June 1940, p. 24.

51. Marion, J.H. "Courtesy Across the Color Line," Christian Century, Vol. 57, May 15, 1940, p. 638.

52. Rosenfield, Loyd. "Down with the Little Things," Collier's, Vol. 124, Nov. 19, 1949, p. 36.

53. Lynes, Russell. "We Are Fashioning a New Formality," House and Garden, Vol. 111, Mar. 1957, p. 56.

54. Lynes, p. 56.

55. Lynes, p. 160.

56. Sellers, Kenneth. "Can We Cope with Comfort?," American Mercury, Vol. 83, Nov. 1956, p. 17-20.

57. Puner, Helen. "The Habit of Courtesy," Parents Magazine, Vol. 32, Jan. 1957, p. 90.

58. "Automatic Thank You, Mr. Harper," Harpers, Vol. 211, Aug. 1955, p. 86.

59. Cronin, Morton. "The Tyranny of Democratic Manners," New Republic, Vol. 138, Jan. 20, 1958, p. 12.

60. Cronin, p. 14.

61. Vanderbilt, Amy. Complete Book of Etiquette; A Guide to Gracious Living. New York, Doubleday and Co., Inc., 1952, p. iii.

62. Guitar, Mary Anne. "Can't the Pendulum Swing This Way?," American Home, Vol. 68, Mar. 1965, p. 8.

63. Guitar, p. 8.

64. "Manners Are Back in Style," House and Garden, Vol. 122, Sept. 1962, p. 146.

65. Vanderbilt, Amy. "Modern Manners, the Newest Status Symbol," Coronet, Vol. 48, Oct. 1960, p. 113.

66. "Interracial Etiquette," America, Vol. 112, May 29, 1965, p. 796.

67. "Respecting People and Titles," Christian Century, Vol. 81, Feb. 19, 1964, p. 229.

68. "America's New Manners; Views of L. Baldrige," Time, Vol. 112, Nov. 27, 1978, p. 64.

69. Vanderbilt, Amy. Amy Vanderbilt's Etiquette. New York, Doubleday and Co., Inc., 1972. p. vii.

70. Gillette, Paul. The Single Man's Indispensable Guide and Handbook. New York, Playboy Press, 1973. p. ix.

71. Post, Elizabeth L. The New Emily Post's Etiquette. New York, Funk & Wagnalls Pub., 1975. p. v.

72. Fields, Susan. Getting Married Again. New York, Dodd, Mead & Co., 1975. p. 9.

73. Brock, Delia. "Twice Is Nice: A Guide to Your Second and Most Important Wedding", Esquire, Vol. 86, July 1976, p. 69.

74. "Office Etiquette", Time, Vol. 121, June 13, 1983, p. 52.

75. Martin, Judith. "The Pursuit of Politeness", New Republic, Vol. 191, Aug. 6, 1984, p. 31.

76. Post, Elizabeth L. Emily Post's Etiquette. New York, Harper & Row, 1984. p. xiv.

77. Ford, Charlotte. Charlotte Ford's Book of Modern Manners. New York, Simon and Schuster, 1980. p. 25.

78. Peale, Norman Vincent. "Courtesy: Key to a Happier World", Saturday Evening Post, Vol. 247, May 1975, p. 37.

The Bibliography

1 Abbott, Lawrence F. "Good Manners." Outlook, 144:45, Sept. 8, 1926.
Expresses concern about the lack of good manners exhibited by Americans, and cites Thomas Jefferson and Charles William Eliot, educator, as exemplary role models for Americans.

2 Abeel, Erica. I'll Call You Tomorrow, and Other Lies Between Men and Women. New York: Morrow, 1981.
Examines relationships between men and women, considering the "New Morality" in discussion. Chapters called "Manspeak," "Sexual Etiquette" and "Divorce Fever" are included. Also offers advice on possible hazards of intimacy, coping with parental advice and how to use "niceness" selectively.

Abel, Theodora Mead, joint author See Mead, Elsie C.

Abrams, Ray, joint author See Bell, Mary L.

3 "Academic Courtesies." Atlantic, 114:141-2, July, 1914.
Author compares experience at a Spanish university to that of an American male institution where she was denied access to a classroom because of her gender.

4 Adler, Jerry. "Miss Manners' Right Stuff." Newsweek, 100:77, July 5, 1982.
Describes Judith Martin's views about manners.

5 Aflalo, F.G. "Lost Art of Behaving Well." Living Age, 277:125-6, April 12, 1913.
Contrasts the "revulsion of feeling against good manners..." of contemporary youth to a courtesy manual written in 1803 which gives "Instructions Peculiarly Adapted to Young Women," and exhorts men to avoid kissing the ladies or punching anyone in conversation. Author maintains his right to have "moments of doubt as to whether the demagogues are right when they shout that good manners necessarily mean bad morals."

6 Ahern, Nell G. "How to Teach Your Boy or Girl Good Manners." Better Homes and Gardens, 27:174-5, March, 1949.
Suggests that parents begin teaching manners when children are toddlers, saying, "You have to teach good manners at home."

7 Alihan, Milla Aissa. Corporate Etiquette. With foreword by Franklin M. Jarman. New York: Weybright and Tally, 1970.
"addressed to the young executive straddling two cultures:...the business confines permeated by the traditional...and the explosive, high-geared, contagious turmoil of today's youth in action." Covers topics ranging from business meetings, communication, the executive fashion look, entertaining, international business situations, to yachting and the country clubs. Includes examples from real-life situation.

8 Allen, Frederick L. "How to Behave in Society." Harpers, 149:800-
   1, Nov., 1924.
   Spoof of an unnamed etiquette book. According to Allen,
   "Etiquette is coming down..." in price—author was able to pur-
   chase this particular book for only 25 cents....
9 Allen, Jennifer. "Are You a Manners Machine?" Seventeen, 37:98,
   Aug., 1978.
   Allen discusses her childhood training in manners, and defines
   that behavior exhibited by "manner machines."
10 Allen, Lucy G. Table Service. Boston: Little, Brown, 1915.
   Intended "to be a guide to the teacher and the waitress and
   a reference book for the hostess...." Describes all the functions
   involved in serving dinners, both formal and informal, and includes
   how-to's for serving wines and cordials, cheeses and caviar.
   Also covers setting the table for all types of dining, table equipment, care and serving of fruit and salads. Details functions
   of the maid, and describes the duties and requisites of a waitress.
   Illustrated with photographs.
11 _____. Table Service. New ed., completely rev. Boston: Little,
   Brown, 1940.
   Contends the trend in formal service has been toward "greater
   simplicity and less display...." Differs in content from earlier
   edition by including notes on table appointments, and advice
   on the home breakfast and home dinner. Lists service for various
   types of luncheons and dinners, and is illustrated.
12 Allen, Willis Boyd. "Etiquette of Humor." Nation, 96:570-1, June
   5, 1913.
   Maintains the "cannons of good taste which are universally
   accepted by well-bred people..." should govern humor, both
   in spoken jest and in print.
13 Alsop, Gulielma Fell, and McBride, Mary Frances. She's Off to
   College. New York: Vanguard Press, 1940.
   Suggestions as to appropriate dress for class and dates, how
   to get along with others and what to look for when choosing
   a college.
14 _____, and _____. She's Off to Marriage. New York: Vanguard
   Press, 1942.
   Outlines proper etiquette for weddings, including the proposal,
   the fiance's duties, and advice for war brides. Also offers advice
   on how to adjust to marriage, homemaking and motherhood.
15 "American Manners." Harper's Bazaar, 41:299-300, March, 1907.
   A discussion of the state of American manners, concluding
   "we have no doubt that considerate manners would in time tend
   to the development, in part, of the inward gentleness of which
   some of us still stand somewhat in need."
16 "American Manners." By an American woman. Outlook, 115:510,
   March 21, 1917.
   An American woman relates "real courtesies and kindnesses"
   she has received, and encourages other American women to
   be careful and gracious in the acceptance of a courtesy.
17 "American Manners." By a lame man. Outlook, 115:278-9, Feb.
   14, 1917.

Having been on crutches for a considerable time, he observes
that "no matter what appears on the surface, the American
of every class has indeed kindliness of heart, which is the root
of good manners." He relates several stories to support this.
18 "America's New Manners; Views of L. Baldrige." Time, 112:64-6,
Nov. 27, 1978.
Reviews the changes in the American social scene brought about
by the "Me Decade" of the sixties, and relates influences such
as women's liberation, gay liberation, and the anti-war movement
to the "craving for social standards."
Ames, Elinor, pseudonym See Durning, Julia Addis.
19 Ames, Louis Annin. Etiquette of Yacht Colors; a Treatise on
Yacht Flags and Their Use. New York: Annin and Co., 1902.
Tells what different colors of nautical flags mean, and when
and how they should be flown. Illustrated with some color.
20 Anderson, Dave. "Gentlemen Prefer Golf." New York Times
Magazine, 72, March 9, 1986.
Gives examples of gentlemanly behavior shown by golf
professionals, and compares their behavior to those of other
sports. Author believes the gentlemanly nature of golf players
endures "because of its solitary nature, which is enforced by
nature itself."
21 Anderson, Harriet. "Books for Good Manners." Woman's Home
Companion, 63:52, May, 1936.
Annotated list of etiquette books which generally agree that
"the best manners are those of sincerity and thoughtfulness
for others...manners are essentially the outward result of an
inward attitude."
Anderson, Robert Helms, joint author See Shapiro, Norman.
22 "Annoying Mannerisms." Harper's Bazaar, 43:692-3, July, 1909.
Editorial reminds readers to be aware of the "little irritating
habits" at the table, in appearance, use of language, or fussiness
which we inflict upon one another.
23 Antoine-Dariaux, Genevieve. Accent on Elegance; Etiquette
at Home and Abroad. Garden City, New York: Doubleday, 1970.
Arranged in alphabetical order, written by a "Frenchwoman
who is very much at home throughout the world." This dictionary
is addressed to Americans. Topics covered range from accents,
cocktails, and foreigners to sulkiness. "Habitual sulkers are
totally lacking in a sense of humor and they should never get
married." Includes chapters on foreign countries and travel
as well.
24 Ardman, Harvey, and Nadeau, Gisele. Woman's Day Book of
Weddings. With an introduction by Letitia Baldrige. Indianapolis:
Bobbs-Merrill, 1982.
Discusses both pre-wedding and wedding details. Tells how to
decide upon a style of wedding, who to invite, set the date and
organize a schedule. Gives proper etiquette for issuing invitations,
making announcements, and other publicity. Advises on selecting
and receiving wedding gifts, the functions of all parties associated
with the wedding. Concludes with discussion of wedding reception
traditions and what the proper attitude is should the wedding

be canceled. Appended with wedding checklist and the actual wording of some traditional wedding ceremonies. Illustrated, has an index.

25 "Are Good Manners Important Today?" Ladies' Home Journal, 74:74-5, Nov., 1957.
   Reports on a forum sponsored by Ladies' Home Journal to discuss manners, including questions about which country has the best manners and whether manners are changing under the American democratic system. People attending included Emily Post, Paul Hyde Bonner and Ogden Nash.

26 "Are We Ashamed of Good Manners?" Century, 79:310-12, Dec. 1909.
   Explores causes for deteriorating public manners, declaring that Americans who do have good manners act as though they are ashamed of them. Encourages society not to submit to ill treatment from private and public servants without protest.

27 Argyle Publishing Corporation. How to Use a Business Telephone. New York: Argyle, 1968.
   Self-instruction manual covers all aspects of telephone operation, from how to take messages to correct answering procedures.

28 Aridas, Chris. Your Catholic Wedding: A Complete Plan-Book. Garden City, New York: Image Books, 1982.
   Aridas hopes this book will "help you wind your way through the labyrinth of details, questions, and preparations which engaged couples usually encounter." Begins with discussion of the sacrament of marriage, and describes the couple's meeting with the priest. The liturgy is described, and advice on how to choose appropriate scripture passages for the ceremony is given. There are checklists for all aspects of planning such as for the preparation of the church, the people in attendance, and other names and phone numbers which may be needed. Includes an appendix telling how to have booklets for the wedding printed.

29 Aristides. "Greetings and Salutations." American Scholar, 47:16, Winter, 1977.
   Discusses changes in salutations and correspondence in light of changes in society brought about by feminism, and "instant intimacy."

30 Astor, David. "Her Feature Provides a Decorum Forum." Editor and Publisher, 62, Aug. 3, 1985.
   Biographical highlights of Judith Martin and her career as Miss Manners.

31 "Automatic Hat-Raiser." Atlantic, 108:714-6, Nov., 1911.
   Contends the "automatism" of raising one's hat to a woman may or may not be good, but the "symbolism of the act..." is "worth the very slight risk of a cold in 'one's valuable head'."

32 "Automatic Thank You, Mr. Harper." Harpers, 211:86-7, Aug., 1955.
   Reflects on America's need for books of etiquette because of a need "to do the right thing..." and "a hankering for conventions." Focuses on an automatic thank-you sign at the Saw Mill River Parkway toll booth.

33 "Automobile Manners." Independent, 55:1281-2, May 28, 1903.
Editorial decries the lack of manners exhibited by "automobilists."
Axtell, Roger E., editor and compiler, See Do's and Taboos Around
the World.

34 "Ayatollah's Book of Etiquette." Harpers, 21, June, 1985.
Excerpts 17 points from A Clarification of Questions by Ayatollah
Ruhollah Khomeini, in which his position on questions of everyday
life (including when it is lawful to eat locusts) is outlined.

35 Aywyos. "Hints on Etiquette, 1834." Reader's Digest, 60:117-18,
Feb., 1952.
Excerpts from a book by Aywyos written in 1834.

36 Babson, Roger W. "Good and Bad Manners in Business." American
Magazine, 89:28-9, April, 1920.
Statistician advises that good appearance and courteous behavior
help gain employment and further advancement.

37 Bacharach, Bert. Bert Bacharach's Book for Men. New York:
A.S. Barnes, 1953.
Book is "a compendium of all things to all men...." Includes
chapters on dress and clothing, exercise and diet, travel and
how to pack, and personal grooming. There are chapters called
"The Handyman Stag" and "The Social Stag," and there is advice
on weddings, dining out, tipping and being a good guest.
Illustrated, and has diagrams and an index.

38 Backus, William Vernon. Making Happiness Epidemic. New York:
Henry Holt, 1916.
Backus' discourse on courtesy suggests practicing appreciation
in everyday living, the "science of appreciation" and how to
spread this attitude among others.

39 Bacmeister, Rhonda W. "Saying I'm Sorry Is Not Enough." Parents
Magazine, 38:60-1, March, 1963.
Suggestions on how to teach a child to make up for a wrong
perpetrated on another, and how to learn to take responsibility
for his behavior.

40 "Bad Manners." Delineator, 88:10, Feb., 1916.
Winning letters of a contest which answer these questions:
"What...has been the value of good manners as an aid to happiness
and success?" and "Have you...found the cultivation and practice
of good manners of definite value in business or social life?"

41 Badenoch, Nena Wilson. "Teach Courtesy Toward the Disabled."
Parents Magazine, 20:30, Nov., 1945.
Encourages parents to turn negative perceptions of the disabled
into positive ones by helping children make disabled people
feel "comfortable, capable, and well-adjusted to our normal
scene."

42 Bailey, Margaret Emerson. "Country Club Manners." Women's
Home Companion, 50:56, July, 1923.
The country club should be "joined and used in proper spirit..."
so that all members will enjoy it. Considers manners which
can make the club a congenial place, and discusses the role
of managers in enforcing good manners. Describes manners
members should exhibit toward managers and servants.

43 _____. "Ideal Guest." Woman's Home Companion. 50:72, Aug., 1923.
Discusses what company manners really should be. Tells how to accept invitations, and advises on the propriety of an "appreciative word of praise." Suggests guests should be neat and prompt, and come "provided."

44 _____. "Motoring Manners." Woman's Home Companion, 50:50, May, 1923.
Describes types of discourtesies drivers inflict upon their passengers, and tells of the driver who is glad of the guest "who gives us the full measure of her confidence."

45 _____. "Telephone Manners." Women's Home Companion, 50:41, Nov., 1923.
Proper use of the telephone is outlined.

46 _____. "Vacation Manners; Two Questions of Week-end Etiquette Answered." Woman's Home Companion, 50:49, June, 1923.
Answers the question of table etiquette at a wealthy friend's house, and the question of how a single woman should behave when visiting a fashionable weekend resort.

47 _____. The Value of Good Manners, Practical Politeness in the Daily Concerns of Life. Garden City, N.Y.: Doubleday, Page, 1922.
Dissertation on "courtesy in the daily concerns of life." The "value of good manners" is applied to the family, husband and wife relationships, parent and child relationships, "Master and Servant" relationships, and that of host and guest. Contends that a scant measure of manners "means not only the loss of business opportunities and the respect of the community, but the forfeiture of friendship, of affection, and of self-esteem."

Bailey, N.B. See McLean, Nemadji Beth (Bailey).

48 Baker, Russell. "Decline of Manners." New York Times Magazine, 12, Jan. 25, 1981.
Describes the social awkwardness experienced by numerous innocent pedestrians which was caused by two men arguing loudly on a public street. "They were presumptuously exercising their presumed right to express themselves freely in public."

49 _____. "A Matter of Timing." New York Times Magazine, 20, March 13, 1983.
Humorous anecdote about the author's difficulties in arriving at the proper time for dinner parties.

50 _____. "Seaside Cover-up." New York Times Magazine, 14, Aug. 14, 1983.
Discusses the rights of nudists on beaches in terms of courteous behavior. "Common courtesy should restrain others from flaunting their good fortune on the beach in front of the unhealthily repressed...."

Baker, Thomas, joint author See Bennett, Marilyn.

Baldrige, Letitia See Amy Vanderbilt's Complete Book of Etiquette, 1978; and Amy Vanderbilt's Everyday Etiquette, 1981.

51 Baldrige, Letitia. "Christmas-giving Etiquette." Essence, 15:118, Dec., 1984.
Advice on gift-giving, focusing on the holidays.

52 _____. Letitia Baldrige's Complete Guide to a Great Social
Life. New York: Rawson Assoc., 1987.
Encourages the reader to think positively in working toward
having a better social life and being better liked. Chapters
offer advice on how to meet people, make proper introductions,
and the many different ways to make new friends. The chapter
on "Conversation" suggests that good conversation has structure
characterized "by clarity of content and clarity of voice" and
lists do's and don'ts for developing this skill. There are chapters
called "Looking the Best You Can," "Making Friends at Work"
and "Men and Women Getting Together Nicely." Also offers
advice on learning how to appreciate "the time spent alone
in your home." Tells what to do after a spouse dies, or after
a divorce. Concludes with a discussion of "Creative
Manners"—those manners which are good manners can be turned
into creative manners with a little thoughtfulness. Includes
index.

53 _____. Letitia Baldrige's Complete Guide to Executive Manners.
Edited by Sandi Gelles-Cole. New York: Rawson Assoc., 1985.
"For this book, I made the decision to approach executive social
behavior from two perspectives: as an interpersonal human
relationship and as protocol-governed ritual." The book is comprehensive, and divided into two parts. Part I is called "Human
Relations at Work," and is concerned with relations between
men and women at work, personal qualities, communications,
dress and international business manners. Part II is "Business
Protocol," and meetings, conferences, visual communication,
business entertaining, invitations and replies, forms of address,
receptions and assistants are among the topics dealt with. Public
relations with the nonprofit sector, retirement and death, and
business gift giving are additional topics covered. Includes numerous lists, diagrams and charts as well as a Meeting Manager's
Notebook. Also featured are new business etiquette for women,
25 hallmarks of a polished executive, and rules of deference
that can make or break a career. Includes index.

54 _____. "Manners Maketh Man; Etiquette Quiz." Saturday Evening
Post, 250:48-9, April, 1978.
The test is intended to prove that "manners are very relevant
today." Contains questions with multiple choice answers about
topics such as weddings, entertaining and business etiquette.

55 _____. "Who Says Manners Are Out of Style?" Seventeen, 36:142-
3, May, 1977.
Discusses the importance of good manners, and explores the
distinction between etiquette manners and real manners.

56 "Ballroom Bores." Coronet, 32:16-7, May, 1952.
Illustrates, with photos, behavior which qualifies people as ball-
room bores, such as the smoking dancer, the death grip partner
and those cavorting athletes.

57 Banashek, M.E., and Calvert, C. "New Man/Woman Etiquette."
Mademoiselle, 85:103, July, 1979.
Pot-pourri of advice meant to encompass new situations not
referred to in the etiquette books, such as new rules in dating.

58 Banning, Kendall. "Some Hints on Business Good Manners." System,
    33:370, March, 1918.
    Advises salesmen to avoid "the outward appearance of that
    easy familiarity that a tilted hat gives." Also discusses the
    adverse effect on business which overstaying a leave, bad tele-
    phone manners, and entering a buyer's office with a lighted
    cigar can have.
59 Banning, Margaret Culkin, and Culkin, Mabel Louise. Conduct
    Yourself Accordingly. New York: Harper & Brothers, 1944.
    Divided into three parts: Part I discusses the "Importance of
    Conduct" by examining American manners abroad and judging
    the general behavior of Americans. Part II describes "The Training
    and Acquisition of Good Behavior" and considers whether manners
    are inherited and the teaching of democratic conduct. Part
    III describes "The Effect of the War on American Conduct,"
    including a discussion of international behavior and a prediction
    of what the conduct of Americans will be like after the war.
    Deals directly with World War II and its impact upon American
    conduct.
    Banta, K., joint author See Demarest, M.
60 Barber, Edith Michael. Short Cut to Etiquette. N.Y.: Sterling, 1953.
    Topics covered range from introductions and hospitality to
    proper conduct in public places and etiquette of travel. Includes
    advice on telephone manners, and considers the smoking, alcohol
    and driving problems of youth.
61 Barclay, Dorothy. "Manners That Help to Make the Man." New
    York Times Magazine, 54, Dec. 7, 1952.
    Discusses current trends in child rearing and teaching children
    manners. Parents' concern should be "on youngsters' feelings
    in social situations...." Suggests emphasizing form taught by
    example, rather than "hammering" children about manners.
62 Barker, Mary Perin. Good Manners for Young Women. New York:
    John Wiley, 1935.
    "It is my conviction that a young woman should deliberately
    develop her talents, her abilities, and her avocations with the
    main idea of making herself worthy of, and desirable to, the
    kind of man she wants to marry." Includes brief discussions
    of the usual topics such as personal appearance, table manners,
    introductions and conduct with men.
63 _____. The Technique of Good Manners, a Handbook for College
    Men. New York: John Wiley, 1935.
    Originally written as a course of study and guide to efficient
    living for college men. The booklet briefly covers topics such
    as introductions, table manners, dances, and attitudes and rules
    towards women.
64 Barry, Joseph A., and Barry, Naomi Jolles. "Primer on Etiquette
    for Innocents Abroad." New York Times Magazine, 12, July
    23, 1950.
    Describes European manners for the American traveler. Proper
    deportment on an oceancraft, and on a train is given. Includes
    advice for the young girl traveling alone, and the type of enter-
    tainment to be found in French or Italian society is described.

65 Barry, Les. "Mind Your Travel Manners." Popular Photography,
61:46, July, 1967.
Tells how to be polite and stay out of trouble while accumulating
a good set of travel pictures. Suggests researching possible
restrictions in an area, communicating with the subject and
being inconspicuous to insure success.
Barry, Naomi Jolles, joint author See Barry, Joseph A.
66 Bashkirtseff, Marie. "Log-cabin Lady." Delineator, 99:4-5, Dec.,
1921; 100:15-6, Feb., 1922; 100:19-20, March, 1922.
Story (in installments) of a woman who was raised in the wild
west without knowledge of the social amenities, and how she
rose to social prominence.
67 "Basic Rules of Holiday Etiquette." Good Housekeeping, 157:179,
Dec., 1963.
Do's and don'ts of gift etiquette, including tips on appropriate
presents, thank-you notes and employer/employee gift giving.
68 Beattie, Barbara. "Teach Your Child Manners." Good Housekeeping,
96:106, May, 1933.
Concrete advice on teaching manners to children from a very
young age, covers the **what** to teach and the **how** to do it.
69 Beatty, Jerome. "Salespeople Drive Me Nuts!" American Magazine,
140:46-7, Sept., 1945.
Anecdotes about the uncivil war being waged in the States
between the buyer and the seller. "How many times have you
wanted to sink ten strong fingers into the throat of a sulky
clerk...?"
70 Beaulac, Carole. "I Can Put a Man in His Place." Saturday Evening
Post, 225:32-3, March 14, 1953.
Wife of the ambassador to Cuba discusses why she thinks protocol
is important. She maintains that protocol is a force for peace
and requires respect for other people's customs. Illustrated
with photos.
71 Becker, Esther R., and Lawrence, Richard L. Success and
Satisfaction in Your Office Job. New York: Harper, 1954.
Advice includes establishing the right attitude and techniques
in work situations. Uses everyday situations as a means of illustrating how to apply the techniques to uncomfortable situations
which may arise.
72 Beeckman, Mrs. Cornelius. Common Sense in Etiquette.
Philadelphia, David McKay, 1938.
"Etiquette...is a logical method; a system of behavior that
governs...the daily contacts of civilized people." Chapters offer
advice on manners at home, in public, and at ceremonies such
as weddings, Christenings, and funerals. The use of cards, invitations and letter writing are also covered. Discusses courtesy
as a lubricant to good business as well as offering advice on
dress, travel and "The Woman and Her Club." Includes lists,
charts and an index.
73 _____. Etiquette Up-to-date. New York, Southern Publishers,
1938.
Substantially the same book as that published by McKay, **See**
Common Sense in Etiquette.

74 Beery, Mary. Manners Made Easy. New York, McGraw-Hill, 1949.
Intended for use in the classroom as a tool to teach manners,
includes a list of filmstrips to use in conjunction with the text.
Text covers social poise, home and school manners, posture
and health, grooming and clothes, conversation, social functions,
table manners, travel and correspondence. Each chapter ends
with a quiz "to enable the student to test his awareness of points
of etiquette."

75 Bell, Louise Price. "Good Manners Are Taught; Correct Eating
Habits." American Home, 38:112-13, Nov., 1947.
Suggests parents teach table manners when children are very
young. Includes specific techniques for parents to use.

76 Bell, Mary L., and Abrams, Ray. Business Behavior, a Series
of Lessons Planned for Commercial Students, Dealing with
Problems of Human Relationships That Will Be Met in Initial
Clerical and Selling Positions. Cincinnati: South-western, 1937.

77 _____. Business Behavior; Personality Training for Businessmen
Women. 2nd ed. Cincinnati, South-western, 1956.
"As the office becomes mechanized, the relative importance
of personality may be even greater in initial employment and
promotion than it is today." Lists goals in business behavior,
suggests a personal regimen for use in business settings and discusses in detail techniques used in business contacts such as
introductions, telephone use and the sales office. Discusses
"trait training" such as adaptability, appreciation, honesty,
industry, self-control and sociability as positive traits to acquire
to insure success in business. Includes bibliography and index.
Uses practice exercises and case conference problems which
give business situations for students to learn from.

78 Benjamin, Louise Paine. "Mind Your Manners!" Ladies' Home
Journal, 54:69, Nov., 1937.
Pointers from men who are in service to women, i.e., waiters,
hairdressers, shoe sales clerks, which tell how they would like
women to behave. Suggestions include being generous with tips,
making up one's mind clearly, and watching lipstick smudges
on linen.

79 _____. "Mind Your Manners, Other People Do." Ladies' Home
Journal, 65:214, May, 1948.
Suggests that how manners are used in the home is the quickest
way to discover the kind of manners people really have.

80 _____. "What Price Manners?" Ladies' Home Journal, 61:150,
Dec., 1944.
Contrasts/compares manners of male and female teen-agers,
as seen through their own eyes and told to the author.

81 _____. "When She Can and When She Can't." Ladies' Home
Journal, 63:116-7, Jan., 1946.
Advises young women how they can meet a nice young man
and maintain their respectability.

82 _____. Why Men Like Us; Your Passport to Charm. Illustrated
by Jean Sage. New York: Stackpole Sons, 1937.
First chapter includes views of confirmed bachelors (men past
thirty) about what kind of women they like and why. Other

chapters offer advice on what women should do to be attractive to men, and how men should be treated. There are chapters called "The Young Idea About Women," and "What Your Employer Has On His Mind." Discusses attributes of a good wife, and lists behaviors men do not like. There is a section on self-improvement. The end of each chapter has a list of tips called "What To Do About It."

Bennett, Dorothy Blanchard, joint author **See** Muller, Gladys Blanchard.

83 Bennett, Marilyn; Judge, Lucille; Pawlas, George; and Baker, Thomas. "Where Have All the Manners Gone?" Instructor, 132, Oct., 1984.
Suggestions for teachers to use in teaching manners in the classroom. Includes books to read, bulletin board ideas, and techniques developed by these teachers.

84 Bentley, Marguerite. "Good Manners for Happy Living." Woman's Home Companion, 80:10, Oct.; 80:10, Nov.; 80:6, Dec., 1953; 81:93, Jan.;81:10, Feb.; 81:26, March; 81:22, May; 81:6, June; 81:71, July; 81:12, Aug.;81:22, Oct.; 81:52, Dec., 1954.
Question/answer format column discusses a variety of etiquette problems.

85 _____. Wedding Etiquette. Philadelphia, Winston, 1947.
"Written...as a handbook for brides in all circumstances of life." Includes the details for all aspects of the wedding, from the engagement to the honeymoon. Lists procedures for the announcement of the engagement. Tells how to make the wedding list, and describes a variety of wedding showers. There is a chapter for the groom which has a buying guide for the groom's outfit, luggage and his expenses for the wedding. There are chapters called "Your Wedding Silver" and "Your Kitchen and Laundry Outfits." Advice is given on the form of invitations and announcements, and how to recall invitations if necessary. Music for the ceremony, the photographs, bridal party gifts and wedding rehearsal are all discussed. Detailed procedure for religious ceremonies, military ceremonies and the Canadian wedding is listed. Includes index and numerous photos.

Benton, Frances, editor **See** Etiquette; the Complete Modern Guide for Day-to-day Living the Correct Way.

86 Berenberg, Samuel R. "I Wish He'd Mind His Manners!" American Home, 42:46-7, July, 1949.
Contends children learn manners gradually by observing others, and suggests that families which practice courtesy and respect in the home will be most successful in teaching manners to children. Illustrated with photos.

Bernstein, Sandra, joint author **See** Jankowic, Elena.

86a Berg, Barbara. "On the Training Table." New York, 19:15, Jan. 13, 1986.
Describes several different classes which are offered in New York and designed to teach table manners to children.

87 Berry, Elizabeth. Our Flag and Its Uses; Genesis—History—Etiquette... Boston, Mass.: National Association of Patriotic Instructors, 1914.

Manual describes the origin and history of the American flag as well as the etiquette of raising and lowering the flag, using it as a cover, in decoration, and in the salute.

88 Bevans, Margaret (Van Doren). McCall's Book of Everyday Etiquette; a Guide to Modern Manners. Illustrated by Mircea Vasiliu. New York: Golden Press, 1960.

The "important part of etiquette...is consideration." Includes sections outlining general manners for men, women, teen-agers and married couples which includes introductions, calling, visiting, public manners, correspondence, entertaining at home and in public and covers household equipment and the bed and bath. Advice also is given about chewing gum and smoking. The etiquette of formal situations such as coming out, weddings, funerals, and christenings is included. Advice about travel manners, gift giving and tipping is given. Illustrated and includes charts, diagrams and an index.

89 Bicknell, Frank M. "Hats Off or On?" Lippincott's Magazine, 91:634-5, May, 1913.

Examines the logic of the custom of removing one's hat in the public library, elevators and churches. "To doff one's hat to a collection of books...seems not of vital importance...," there is "little reason in some of our strictest unwritten laws."

90 Billingsley, Sherman. "How to Behave in a Night Club." Good Housekeeping, 125:40, July, 1947.

The author lists points of etiquette to follow when visiting a night club so that young men may avoid criticism, i.e., don't comb your hair at the table.

91 Birmingham, Frances, and Birmingham, Frederic A. The Wedding Book, a Complete His and Her Guide. Illustrated by Jon Buelow. New York: Harper & Row, 1964.

Begins with general discussion of love and marriage customs. Follows the sequence from announcing the engagement, to the duties of the bride and groom in preparation for the wedding. Detailed discussion of all facets of preparation, such as the order for leaving the church, the receiving line and different types of weddings. Also includes advice on living "Happily Ever Afterward." Illustrated, has numerous lists and diagrams and an index.

Birmingham, Frederic A., joint author See Birmingham, Frances.

92 Birnbach, Lisa. Etiquette for the Preferred Lifestyle; an Official Preppy Handbook. New York: Workman, 1983.

93 Bixler, Susan. The Professional Image: The Total Program for Marketing Yourself Visually. Illustrated by Linda Haas Baliko, photographs by Kerry Hackney. New York: Putnam, 1984.

Discusses visual appearance in detail and relates it to one's marketability. Raises points of corporate etiquette as a part of the image projected, including discussion of shaking hands, body language, and professionalism during pregnancy. Includes illustrations, photographs, and charts.

94 Black, David. "Sign of the Times: Etiquette '79." Feature, 82, Feb., 1979.

Believes the current interest in etiquette books is "signs of great social insecurity...survival manuals for the 1980's." Examines the need for gross behavior in order to provide a basis for comparison with good behavior.

95 Black, Kathleen. Manners for Moderns. Illustrated by North Young. Boston: Allyn and Bacon, 1938.
Addressed to young men "to encourage an ever-increasing respect for the common sense of courtesy." Gives the history of manners briefly, and a general discussion relating cheerfulness and manners. Table manners are discussed in specific terms, with advice on how to eat difficult foods. Also included are "certain things a guest owes his host." Introductions, dance etiquette, personal appearance and manners on the job are topics included. Includes lists of do's and don'ts, illustrations and an index.

96 Blackett, William C. "Courtesy First!" System, 37:985-9, May 1920.
Through narration of a particular incident the author illustrates how a rude receptionist can cause actual dollar loss to business. How a caller is greeted in business can adversely affect the underlying principles of a company. Believes the motto of every business organization should be "Courtesy first."

97 Bleecker, Katharine. Business Etiquette: the ABC of Making Good. New York: G.P. Putnam's Sons, 1942.
Chapters discuss appearance, job hunting, office relations, private lives and public relations, office manners, and manners in sports. Lists Ten Commandments for Business, i.e., "Thou shalt rise from thy chair to greet the caller in thy office." Also gives advice on tipping, and gives the advantages of belonging to a club.

98 Bloom, Vera. Entertaining Lady, an Informal Guide to Good Living. Decorations by Sari. New York: Putnam, 1949.
Instructions for the hostess about planning a successful party, including the type of food to serve, decorations, and conversations. Also offers advice on letters and travel.

99 Boggs, Barbara; Poston, Gretchen; and Proxmire, Ellen. The Wonderful Wedding Workbook. Washington: Robert B. Luce, 1971.
Covers all aspects of wedding etiquette. Includes tear-out calendars, planning schedules and worksheets. Advises on different types of receptions and honeymoon arrangements. Numerous time schedules can be used for arranging the wedding with time management maximized. Tells how to announce engagements, send invitations and give pre-nuptial parties. Describes proper attire, flowers, music, liquor, catering, photography and gift display. Outlines different ceremonies, the efficient rehearsal and types of receptions.

100 Booher, Dianna Daniels. The New Secretary: How to Handle People as Well as You Handle Paper. New York: Facts on File, 1985.
Divided into three parts: the Team; the Relationship to Clients and Customers; and One's Own Image. Addressed to those "who are spending most of their time shuffling people rather

than paper." Uses experiences of secretaries to offer advice about good manners, covers many aspects of office etiquette, with particular emphasis on interpersonal relationships.

101 Booysen, C. Murray. "Courtesy." Rotarian, 87:1, Dec., 1955. "I believe that the salvation of the world lies in being courteous to one another."

102 _____. "Courtesy Costs Nothing; Special Week in South Africa." Rotarian, 84:34-5, Feb., 1954.
Outlines the program of events for the annual Courtesy Week sponsored by the Rotary Clubs in South Africa, with the intention "of molding public opinion on the side of the principles of right living."

103 Borden, Mary. "Manners, American and English." Harpers, 160:77-81, Dec., 1929.
After comparing present manners with those of the past, author decides they are merely changed as opposed to deteriorated. Also maintains that Americans tend to have "too much manner," whereas the "English have too little."

104 Borrus, Amy. "Treating Clients to Some Splendor on the Grass." Business Week, 49, July 1, 1985.
Discusses companies' demand to entertain their clients at Wimbledon, and the strict rules of decorum which are observed.

105 Boykin, Eleanor. "Manners in the Making." Parents Magazine, 18:24-5, Jan., 1943.
Addresses the etiquette questions which puzzle adolescents the most, including introductions and table manners.

106 Bracken, Peg. "Etiquette, the Social Whirl, and All That Jazz." Ladies' Home Journal, 80:28, Dec., 1963.
Gives the ground rules for parties, including dinner schedules, invitations, guests of honor and the extra woman.

107 _____. "How to Cope with the Social Tangle." Ladies' Home Journal, 81:26, March, 1964.
Humorous discussion of using the "social lie," making introductions, avoiding bores, and topics suitable for conversation.

108 _____. I Try to Behave Myself; Peg Bracken's Etiquette Book. Drawings by Hilary Knight. New York: Harcourt, Brace and World, 1964.
The author feels manners are good breeding, a show of warmth of heart and concern for people. Book covers the usual topics, i.e., guests, table manners. Lists three things not to talk about: age, ailments and children. Uses symbolic names as a means of illustration. Last chapter is called, "Lord Chatterly's Mistress: Men and Women and What to Do About It."

109 _____. "Toast to Victor Goodhost." Ladies' Home Journal, 81:20, Jan., 1964.
Discusses the etiquette of smoking and drinking. Tips for the host include how to keep from running out of ice and what to do if a guest gets "slugged."

Braddy, Nella See Henney, Nella (Braddy)

110 Bradford, Barbara T. How to Be the Perfect Wife: Etiquette to Please Him. New York: S & S, 1969.
Topics include the etiquette of introductions, use of titles,

invitations, cards, party dress, table manners, problems with foods, dining out, letter writing, good telephone manners, hostess and travel manners. Illustrated with diagrams and line drawings and sample forms. "Today's successful wife is the first to appreciate the importance of correct etiquette."

111 Braganti, Nancy L., and Devine, Elizabeth. The Travelers' Guide to European Customs & Manners: How to Converse, Dine, Tip, Drive, Bargain, Dress, Make Friends and Conduct Business While in Europe. Deephaven, MN: Meadowbrook, 1984.
Designed as the how to of travel in Europe "to avoid being rude inadvertently and embarrassing yourself or others." Covers topics for countries from Austria to Yugoslavia. Each country is divided into sections which cover aspects of life such as greetings, conversation, tipping, dress, meals, key phrases and pronunciation.

112 Brant, Ethel Cushing. Standard Etiquette for All Occasions. New York: J.H. Sears, 1925.

113 Brasier, Virginia. "Thank You, Baby." Hygeia, 27:692-3, Oct., 1949.
Suggests teaching courtesy to children by example in the home, gives specific instructions to parents.

114 Bride's Magazine. Bride's Book of Etiquette. New York: Grosset and Dunlap, 1948.
Guide begins with correct way to announce the engagement, and continues by describing different types of weddings and ceremonies. Includes reminder lists for the bride and groom. "The Whys and Wherefores of Wedding Customs" are given, and specific chapters are devoted to the informal, formal, ultra-formal, and special wedding. Etiquette for invitations, announcements and gifts is discussed. Concludes with advice about types of receptions, and "Going Away." Illustrated, diagrams, lists and index included.

115 _____. Bride's Book of Etiquette. Revised and updated. New York: Grosset and Dunlap, 1973.
"Concerned about what will make everyone involved in an important event happy, comfortable and thoroughly able to enjoy this great celebration in your life." Substantially the same as earlier edition, with advice updated where needed, includes a list of expenses and index.

116 _____. Bride's Book of Etiquette. New York: Perigee Books, 1984.
Published as the Golden Anniversary edition, newly updated text intends to address modern day brides. Editors try to avoid cliches and rigid texts, and depend upon common sense and good taste instead.

117 _____. New Bride's Book of Etiquette. New York: Grosset and Dunlap, 1981.
Substantially the same as earlier editions. Includes advice on remarriage and unexpected situations which may arise. Concludes with a chapter on reaffirmation of wedding vows.

118 Brock, Delia. "Twice Is Nice: a Guide to Your Second and Most Important Wedding." Esquire, 86:68-70, 1976.

Suggestions for the second time around include, "invite only
people you like...," "white gloves are definitely declasse...,"
and "you are a grown up now...."
119 Broderick, Robert C. The Catholic Layman's Book of Etiquette.
St. Paul: Catechetical Guild Educational Society, 1957.
"Our purpose in preparing this book is to offer to the Catholic
laity a book of manners and Practice." The chapters are "The
Church and Her Authority," "The Commands of the Church,"
"Holy Mass, Devotions and Pious Practices," "The Church Calendar," "The House of God," "Catholic Reading and Education,"
"Catholic Organizations," and "Miscellany." Also includes a
dictionary and index.
120 Brody, Rosalie. Weddings. New York: Simon and Schuster in
association with the Emily Post Institute, 1963.
Ten chapters offer advice about weddings from announcing
the engagement, wedding invitations, showers, flowers, and
music to photographs. Different religious ceremonies, wedding
receptions and guests are also topics covered. Illustrated with
photos, includes charts and diagrams.
121 Brooks, Mel. "Mel Brooks' Six Rules of Dining Etiquette." Feature,
28, April, 1979.
Spoof on table manners.
122 Brossard, Chandler. "Children Can Have Manners." Look, 22:111-
14, June 24, 1958.
Illustrated with photos of situations showing the exemplary
life of the well-mannered family.
123 Brown, Charlotte (Hawkins). Correct Thing to Do—to Say—to
Wear. Boston: Christopher, 1941.
"The practice of fine manners is an art, but it should always
be so natural that there be nothing of affectation about it."
Chapters cover mealtime, teas, behavior at school, church,
concerts, theater, movies and dances. Proper deportment when
travelling, making introductions, using the telephone or attending
a wedding is outlined. The "Earmarks of a Gentleman" are
given, and a catch-all chapter called, "Helpful Hints for Correct-
ness" is included. Format of chapters is general discussion
with numbered points to follow. There are also questions/answers
at the end of each chapter.
Brown, Helen Gurley, editor See Cosmo Girl's Guide to the
New Etiquette.
124 Brown, John Mason. "How to Go to the Theatre." Good Housekeeping, 123:39, Dec., 1946.
Directions are given for correct behavior at the theater, offering
advice on dress, and leaving during a performance. Philosophical
discussion of the joys of theater going and audience participation
ensues.
125 Bryan, Dawn. The Art and Etiquette of Gift Giving. New York:
Bantam Books, 1987.
Written to address a void in information on gift protocol, and
"to the gift exchange as a mode of international communication."
Discusses "issues of propriety and protocol...," beginning with
examination of the art of gift giving and receiving. Suggests

easy ways to make gift giving special, i.e., start a collection
for someone. Lists numerous gift suggestions for every possible
circumstance. Concludes with a chapter on gift wrappings,
cards and includes index.

126 Bryant, Flora F.T., and Bryant, Kendall S. It's Your Wedding:
a Complete Wedding Guide for Making the Most Important
Day of Your Life the Most Beautiful and Memorable. New
York: Cowles Book, 1970.
The book "is meant to delineate in detail all the steps necessary
from the moment a girl becomes engaged to the end of her
wedding reception." Advises on cost, budgets, type of wedding,
invitations, clothing for all parties, the trousseaux, catering
and rental services. Also discusses different types of receptions,
decorations, music, and photography. Appendices include her-
aldry, a sample budget and chronological checklist.

Bryant, Kendall S., joint author See Bryant, Flora F.T.

127 Buchanan, Wiley T. "It's the Most Fascinating Job in Washington."
Life, 58:74-5, March 12, 1965.
Reminiscences of former Chief-of-Protocol, defining the true
function of the Chief as that of personal diplomacy.

128 Buck, Joan Juliet. "In a Rude World—the Joys of Following
Form." Vogue, 172:342, Feb., 1982.
"Only within a formal structure can one go about one's business
efficiently, without offending others or leaving chunks of one's
deeper being lying around in shreds."

129 Buckley, William F. "For Moderation in Osculation." National
Review, 36:54, March 23, 1984.
Tongue-in-cheek article about the protocol of bussing among
world leaders.

130 _____. "Reflections on the Presidential Style." National Review, 29:512, April 29, 1977.
Discusses President Jimmy Carter's informal style. "It is, really,
an effort to stage an unreal situation, to breed a synthetic
equality."

131 _____. "Silver Lining." National Review, 26:391, March 29,
1974.
Relates story of the numerous courtesies enjoyed by a Spanish
woman travelling on the East Coast.

132 Burger, Chester. Executive Etiquette. N.Y.: Collier Books, 1969.
"The purpose of this book...is to encourage you to do the right
thing, the considerate act, the courteous act." Advice starts
with the first day on the job and covers introductions, lists
of information to tell the new person, and telephone etiquette.
Also covers correspondence, business luncheons, dress, what
to do when you make a mistake, promptness, and office parties.
Topics such as going through channels, money, business trips,
secretaries, personal lives, and rivalry are also included.

133 Burgess, Gelett. "Have You an Educated Heart?" American
Magazine, 94:23, Sept., 1922.
Describes the educated heart in terms of human kindness,
the "Educated heart is rare enough...but it is found quite as
often among those who know not your artificial social code...."

134 _____. "Invisible Eating." Reader's Digest, 39:1-4, Aug., 1936.
Gives specific advice on how to eat, urging readers not to
commit Vegicide, "the wanton cutting of the innocent tender
leaves of lettuce with a knife." Defines other crimes such
as the Divorced Digit, Loading, Elbow Eating and the Bust
Hug.

135 _____. "Telltale Table Manners." Literary Digest, 77:38-42,
May 26, 1923.
Describes assorted offenders at the table, i.e., Harpooners,
Cup-cuddlers and Lizzies-Lick-the-Spoon. Burgess finds these
"Egoistic Eaters" not only offensive but ethically objectionable.

136 Burt, Emily Rose. "Other Times, Other Manners." Woman's
Home Companion, 50:41, Nov., 1923.
Comparison of some principles of correct conduct set forth
in an 1885 Ladies' Home Companion, with those of current
practice, including discussion of the chaperone.

137 Burt, Struthers. "Manners Makyth Man." Ladies' Home Journal,
63:6, May, 1946.
Examines the difference between manners and polish, saying
that manners "are the simplest application of the Golden Rule."
Also discusses manners and democracy.

138 Burton, Sara R. Good Manners Pay Off. New York: Vantage,
1954.
Topics are listed alphabetically, and instructions are listed
under appropriate topic. Information ranges from acceptance,
boarding places, calls, dining, employment, funerals, gifts,
host and hostess, introductions, table service, and visits to
weddings. Also includes charts for wedding anniversaries, wedding superstitions and the language of flowers. Has index.

139 Byrne-Dodge, Teresa. "The Write Stuff." Savvy, 70, Jan., 1986.
Detailed advice on paper selection, and includes examples
of stationery used by famous people.

140 Cadden, Vivian. "Your Manners Are Catching." Parents Magazine,
24:38, Feb., 1949.
Contends that adults have a double standard in the manners
they show other adults and those they show children. Encourages
parents and other adults to be polite toward children as a way
to teach children good manners.

141 Cades, H.R. "Companion Way to Make Them Say, Isn't She Charming!" Woman's Home Companion, 77:138-9, Nov., 1950.
Suggests one common denominator in different kinds of charm
is the desire to put people at their ease. Offers tips on developing charm which include being neat, being yourself, and being
nice on the telephone.

Calvert, C., joint author See Banashek, M.E.

Campbell, Jean See Vermes, Jean Campbell.

142 Campion, Rosamond. "Why Not Hit Him While He's Down?"
Vogue, 161:113, Jan., 1973.
Decries present state of manners. "Cheapness breeds cheapness,
and few of us can withstand the temptation to respond rudely
to the rude."

143 Card, Emily. "Tips on Tipping." Ms., 14, Aug., 1985.
Paying special attention to women in male dominated services,
offers specific guidelines for tipping everyone from the Maitre
d' to the hairdresser.

144 Carlson, Judy. "Am I Eating with the Right Fork, Mabel?" Seventeen, 40:146-7, Oct., 1981.
Questions about table etiquette are answered, particularly
how to eat difficult foods.

145 Carney, Marie L. Etiquette in Business. Illustrated by Vida Carney. New York: Gregg, 1948.
"Etiquette is an important essential in the conduct of modern
business...within the business organization it promotes pleasant
and productive working relationships among employees." Written
as a guide for secretaries, clerical workers, salespersons, and
junior executives. Parts 1 and 2 are addressed to the new employee. Parts 3 and 4 cover topics of interest to an experienced
employee. Part 5 is concerned with social life in business.
Chapters end with questions for discussion. Illustrated.

146 Cartland, Barbara. Barbara Cartland's Etiquette for Love and
Romance. New York: Pocket Books, 1984.
Discusses the etiquette of dating, dining, office romance,
living together, weddings, honeymoons, marriage, home life,
and birth. Written in question/answer format. Maintains that
"Good manners in marriage are absolutely essential...."

147 Case, Carleton Britton. Etiquette for Every Occasion; a Guide
to Politeness and the Customs of Good Society. Adapted from
standard authorities by Mortimer Chesterfield (pseud.) Chicago:
Shrewesbury, 1927.
Advises on public behavior, dress, travel, salutations, hand-shak-
ing and kissing. Letters of introductions are covered, and one
chapter is called "Gallantry and Coquetry." The correct use
of cards is detailed, and there is advice on the propriety of
calling. The chaperone in America is discussed, as are weddings.
Concludes with a list of rules to remember, a list of do's and
don'ts and a discussion of the current social revolution, "changes
that are directly traceable to the influence of modern inven-
tions."

148 Casey, Thomas Francis, and Gainor, Leo C. Social Manual for
Seminarians. Forward by Richard Cardinal Cushing. Milwaukee:
Bruce, 1963.
"It is an essential part of your apostolate that you acquire
good manners in order to secure the respect of the public and
the confidence of the laity." Directly relates aspects of etiquette
such as conversation, table manners, tipping sports, sickness,
correspondence and introductions to the life of the seminarian.
Includes chart of ecclesiastical forms of address, a bibliography
and an index.

149 "Causes of Manners." Independent, 58:158-9, Jan. 19, 1905.
Editorial discusses the assimilation of immigrant populations
in America and the establishment "of fraternity and equality..."
in relations with them as essential to good manners in America.

150 Chambers, Mary Daveron. <u>Breakfasts, Luncheons and Dinners;</u>
<u>How to Plan Them, How to Serve Them, How to Behave at</u>
<u>Them.</u> Boston: Boston Cooking-School Magazine, 1926.
Discusses in great detail innumerable types of meals, correct
service, with detail given to every type of plate, pot, pitcher,
utensil, glassware and napkin. Sample menus for every occasion
with instructions on correct service techniques are given. Conduct at mealtime is outlined. Tables at the end of the book
outline the nutritional values of foods. Illustrated with photos,
diagrams and line drawings.

151 Chaneles, Sol. <u>The New Civility.</u> Illustrated by Claudie Chaneles
Grandberg. New York: Grossman, 1973.
Introduction defines civility. Lists 75 topics in alphabetical
order ranging from admiration, assertiveness, clothing, decorum,
drugs, food, gentleness, honesty, lying, praise, smoking to
work. Each topic includes pertinent quotations from famous
people, as well as the author's advice.

152 Chase, Fannie Dickerson. <u>Good Form and Social Ethics.</u> Washington, D.C.: Review and Herald, 1913.
"We must admit with regret that the present age is lacking
in kindly, courteous attention to others." Chapters discuss the
qualities of the gentleman, and give advice to the home girl,
i.e., "Acquaint yourself early with high ideals of womanhood."
There is also advice for the schoolgirl, the business girl and
the social girl. Etiquette for children, in the home, at church,
and on the street is given. The use of visiting cards is outlined.
Other topics include introductions, kindness in speech, invitations, guests and hostesses, weddings, trains, telephone etiquette,
punctuality, borrowing and when not to laugh. Anecdotes and
numerous quotations are used to enrich the text.

Chesterfield, Mortimer, pseudonym **See** Case, Carleton Britton.

153 "Chivalry: Shall We Give It Back to King Arthur?" <u>Scholastic,</u>
53:16-7, Dec. 15, 1948.
Discusses the pros and cons of chivalry in 1948. Pro contention
is that chivalry is an attitude of courtesy towards others. Con
maintains that women are waging a campaign for equal rights
in intellectual, social and business fields so that society should
cease to superimpose old fashioned notions of chivalry on the
20th century world.

154 Clark, Janet. "Tips on Table Manners." <u>Better Homes and Gardens,</u>
35:204, May, 1957.
Addresses some of the more common perplexities of table
manners in light of changing customs.

155 Clausen, Christopher. "On Manners; a Decent Impersonality."
<u>Current,</u> 15, Feb., 1986.
Examines the "tendency toward indiscriminate informality
and the public exhibition of personality," and the result that
"Meaningful ritual has virtually vanished from public life."

156 Clift, Eleanor. "Is Chivalry Dead?" <u>McCall's,</u> 101:35, June, 1974.
Results of a test engineered by two university professors,
and those of an informal test on car door opening conducted
by <u>McCall's.</u>

157 Coates, Robert M. "Do You Offend? Efforts of Advertisers
    to Teach Us Good Manners." New Republic, 86:246-7, April
    8, 1936.
    Correlates all the offenses advertisers name in order to sell
    their products and their efforts to teach good manners to the
    public by naming "dozens of ways of offending."
158 "Coats On? Coats Off?" Woman's Home Companion, 74:7-8,
    July, 1947.
    Results of a poll which asked women when they objected to
    men not wearing a coat.
159 Cocke, Zitella. "Dress and Address." New England Magazine,
    n.s. 39:483-91, Dec., 1908.
    Discusses morality and manners, maintaining that the conven-
    tions of politeness represent the moral ideas. Chastises the
    "ambitious and pretentious class..." saying "mannerism is fatal
    to good manners." Also discusses the moral aspects of decorum
    and attire.
160 "Coffee Ranks Tea; Instructions to R.O.T.C. Students." Time,
    65:50, March 7, 1955.
    Details protocol at a tea, i.e., coffee is served by the top-ranking
    officer's wife.
161 Coggins, Carolyn. The Book of Etiquette and Manners. New
    York: Pyramid Books, 1961.
    Part one discusses the courtesies due in family, social and
    business relationships. Tells how to encourage children to learn
    manners, advises on the "Knotty Problems of Teenagers," and
    offers tips about neighbors, clubs and jobs. Part two illustrates
    matters of custom such as tipping, restaurants, travelling,
    telephone use, gift-giving, clothes and grooming. Part three
    discusses "Your Spiritual Life," the solemn moments such as
    wedding and funerals.
162 Cole, Duane. "Do Unto Others..." Flying, 110:20-1, Jan., 1983.
    Addressed to air pilots, says courtesy, thoughtfulness, awareness
    and respect are necessary for safety's sake as well as to insure
    that the airports run smoothly. Suggests that when on the
    ground, courtesy should be extended to the ground crew.
163 _____. "The Niceties of 9 to 5." Mademoiselle, 90:222-3,
    Aug., 1984.
    How to behave appropriately in a variety of office situations.
    Written to help women understand "the rules—and be able
    to adjust them to the situation...."
164 Cole, Emma Aubert. The Modern Bride Book of Etiquette and
    Entertaining. New York: Ziff-Davis, 1961.
    "This book is intended as a practical and comprehensive refer-
    ence work that covers the general rules of social behavior."
    Part One is "Etiquette for the Bride," and offers advice to
    the single woman about basic social etiquette, i.e., introductions,
    correspondence, planning and executing the wedding. Part
    Two is concerned with "Your Married Life" and addresses issues
    such as the bride in business, running a household, being a
    successful hostess and table settings. Includes diagrams, sample
    correspondence and an index.

165 Cole, Harriette. "Tips for Table Etiquette." Essence, 15:104, Feb., 1985.
   Illustrated with diagrams of utensils at the table setting describing their functions. Gives how-to's for dining out as well.
166 Cole, Joanna. "Oops! I'm Sorry!" Parents, 58:56-60, Sept., 1983.
   How to teach children manners using methods such as instruction, reminding and correction, praise and encouragement, feedback, and setting an example. Discusses developmental stages of children to help parents understand an occasional lapse of manners.
167 Collins, Clella Reeves. Army Woman's Handbook. New York: McGraw, 1943.
   Advises army wives on social problems peculiar to an army post, and on army post decorum. Also gives financial advice about insurance, tax returns and pensions.
168 _____. Navy Woman's Handbook. New York: McGraw, 1943.
   "The life of a Navy wife is so like that of her Army sister that much of this book is an exact counterpart of the Army Woman's Handbook!"
169 Colton, Helen. "How Do You Do on Introductions?" Coronet, 33:107-8, March, 1953.
   "Good introductions can be a real asset...." Tells how to make introductions to everyone's advantage.
   Colton, Jennifer, pseudonym See Moltke, Mab Wilson.
169a Comer, James P. "Public Conduct." Parents Magazine, 62:216, Oct., 1987.
   Author expresses concern about youth who display a lack of respect for "themselves, their families and their communities." Compares past social environments, where authority figures commanded respect, with present situations, where "the number of close and guiding relationships our youngsters have with adults who are important role models..." has been reduced by the busy lifestyle of the eighties. Advises parents to establish standards in order to instill respect in youth, and to get involved in school programs in order to develop desirable standards for public conduct.
170 "Company Manners in the Seventeenth Century." Hobbies, 54:63, Aug., 1949.
   Highlights some points of etiquette prescribed by 17th century arbiters, including the propriety of drinking from a common goblet and using a common dish.
171 "Complete Etiquette of Eating Awkward Foods." Good Housekeeping, 143:52-3, Nov., 1956.
   Tells how to eat asparagus, peel apples and pears, and use croutons and oyster crackers. Awkward foods such as watermelon and corn-on-the-cob (which should be buttered two or three rows at a time, eaten, and repeated) are included.
172 Comstock, Sarah. "Are You a Lady?" Delineator, 130:24-5, Feb., 1937.
   Compares advice of 19th century authors with that of 20th century arbiters.

173 Conant, Luther. "How to Make an Exit." Reader's Digest, 57:38,
    Sept., 1950.
    Outlines exactly what to do in order to leave without unduly
    delaying the process. Encourages guests "to spare your hostess
    one of those prolonged hallway farewells."
174 "Confessions of an Etiquette Teacher." Saturday Evening Post,
    202:37, June 7, 1930.
    Relates experience as an etiquette teacher, including some
    humorous questions which have been submitted. Maintains,
    however, that people trying to improve themselves by learning
    etiquette is honorable.
175 Conger, Ella R. "How Are Your Medical Manners?" Today's
    Health, 44:8-10, Sept., 1966.
    Tells how to be a courteous patient, i.e., be prompt for appoint-
    ments, and call if you can't make it.
176 Copeland, Lennie, and Griggs, Lewis. Going International: How
    to Make Friends and Deal Effectively in the Global Marketplace.
    New York: New American Library, 1985.
    "Our ability to remain in the world economic major league
    will depend on the competence of our players...And competence
    must now be defined in terms of cultural savvy as well as busi-
    ness skills." Advises Americans against going native. Outlines
    how to get started in the foreign market, i.e., learn the rules
    of government, the business and social etiquette, and how
    to deal with headquarters. Offers suggestions for managing
    personal and family life abroad. Describes entertaining and
    protocol abroad. Features a country-by-country guide to leading
    trade partners, and offers special advice for women in the
    international marketplace. Includes index.
177 Cornell, Richard D. "Examining Our Telephone Manners." Super-
    visory Management, 7, March, 1986.
    The way to significantly affect business is by using good tele-
    phone manners. Offers advice on training employees, handling
    difficult people, and "telephone tennis."
178 Correct Social Usage, a Course of Instruction in Good Form,
    Style, and Deportment. By eighteen distinguished authors. New
    York: Society of Self-Culture, 1906.
    Two volume set includes photos, glossary and index. Writings
    collected from contributors belong to the New York Society
    of Self-Culture, which "aims to thoroughly teach the underlying
    rules which govern good society." Scope of the subject matter
    "includes everything which could be rightly placed between
    the covers of a practical work on etiquette...." Among the
    authors contributing are Mrs. Burton Kingsland, Margaret
    Watts Livingston, Marion Harland, Mrs. Sherwood, and Christine
    Terhune Herrick. Topics include discussions of social self-
    culture, everyday etiquette, conventional requirements, ceremo-
    nious occasions and home and family.
179 "Correct Thing." Harper's Bazaar, 39:71-3, Jan., 1905.
    Discusses passing fashions; "the introduction of debutantes
    is no longer a simple affair...the affair is a vastly greater
    undertaking than the popular receptions of a year or two ago."

Also disconcerted that teas are no longer kept simple, but that some entertainment must now be provided, and describes fashionable entertainment.

180 The Cosmo Girl's Guide to the New Etiquette. Edited by Helen Gurley Brown. New York: Cosmopolitan Books, 1971.
"Etiquette could be defined as intuition, empathy, thoughtfulness, as well as self-confidence and poise." Divided into three parts: The Private You; The Public You; and The Libidinal You. The Private You describes ways to take care of personal appearance, dress, and make-up. The Public You describes what constitutes classy behavior, from conversation, tactfulness and dating expertise to being a hostess. The Libidinal You discusses aspects of sexual behavior such as "A Philosophy of Considerate Adultery."

181 Costello, Joan. "Fresh Kids." Parents Magazine, 160, April, 1986.
Fresh kids are those aged 7 to 10, and "refers to (the) verbal bantering with elders that becomes mildly rude and edges on disrespect." Offers advice to parents for coping with the behavior.

182 _____. "In Praise of (a Little) Brattiness." Parents Magazine, 57:96, April, 1982.
Describes the self-image of children who are socialized to be too good, and suggests it is best for children to strike a balance between being good and being bad.

183 _____. "When Company Comes." Parents Magazine, 59:156, Dec., 1984.
"Including children in meeting and household customs teaches them valuable lessons in how to cope with strangers in ways that may smooth their paths in future relationships...." Offers concrete suggestions such as letting the children take coats or pass snacks.

184 Coudert, Jo. "Excuse Me, Your Manners Are Missing." Reader's Digest, 127:148, Oct., 1985.
Coudert intends to fight back against the extent of the breakdown in manners in today's society, insisting that simple courtesy makes life easier. "We're learning the hard way that manners aren't merely decorative but serve to keep the foundations of society intact."

185 "Course in Manners; John Adams High School of Cleveland." School Review, 35:249-50, April, 1927.
Reviews the first year of an experiment in teaching manners, in which the "outward signs of character and good breeding are taught."

186 "Courteous Fault-finding." Living Age, 264:118-20, Jan., 1910.
"We believe that the real way to reprove effectually...is...simply by taking refuge in officialism.... An official rebuke gives the minimum of personal pain, and creates as a rule a maximum renewal of effort."

187 Courtesy as an Asset." Outlook, 140:446-7, July 29, 1925.
Describes Minneapolis' system of traffic courtesy and the pay off in goodwill toward the city.

188 "Courtesy Begins at Home." Practical Home Economics, 5:8, May, 1960.
    The importance of maintaining good manners in the home is discussed, and a variety of authors are cited who support this premise.

189 "Courtesy en Route." Atlantic, 161:699-700, May, 1938.
    Relates story of a Don Quixote observed by the author, whose courteous behavior caused a traffic jam.

190 "Courtesy from Employees on the Hoboken Tunnel Railroad." Outlook, 91:861-3, April 17, 1909.
    Gives the railroad president's views on courtesy as it pertains to profit oriented management.

191 "Courtesy in Business." Scientific American, 99:134-5, Aug. 29, 1908.
    Focusing on the directives of a New York railroad company, editorial relates the advantage courteous employees give a business.

192 "Courtesy in Japan." Literary Digest, 51:1244-5, Nov. 27, 1915.
    The experience of Reverend Walter Weston as a traveler to Japan is narrated. He encountered courteous treatment everywhere he went.

193 "Courtesy of Mind." Atlantic, 103:713, May, 1909.
    Suggests conversational skills such as knowing when to be quiet, and how to listen, are an often overlooked phase of unselfishness.

194 Coville, Alice Perkins. "Use of the Old Hero Stories in Teaching Courtesy." Home Progress, 5:183-6, Dec., 1915.
    "True courtesy will ever be a mean between seeming and being.... In no way, perhaps, can a child's mind be so easily disabused of this idea that manners are effeminate or weak than by acquainting him with persons, or the old heroes, in whom the greatest strength is usually accomplished by the greatest gentleness...."

195 Coville, Frederick V. "Courtesy of the Camp." Playground, 18:223, July, 1924.
    Defines courtesy of the camp as those principles of behavior which are essential to the general enjoyment of outings.

196 Crane, Frank. "Are You Well Bred?" American Magazine, 92:47, Oct., 1921.
    Provides a test for readers to use as a guideline for defining qualities they may possess which are universally admired.

197 Craster, Elizabeth. "George Washington Ate Here!" Better Homes and Gardens. 38:75, Feb., 1960.
    Question/answer format about table manners. The author cites George Washington's appreciation of good manners as inspiration for readers.

198 _____. "Manners for Men." Better Homes and Gardens, 38:113-4, Sept., 1960.
    Question/answer format for the man with questions about the correct ways of "escortmanship."

    Crawford, Miriam, joint author See Mothershead, Alice.

199 Crews, Edna. Mrs. Lieutenant—Air Force Customs and Protocol. Chuluota: Beau Lac, 1968.

"Written for...wives who would like a direct answer to the many questions pertaining to military life." Topics covered include social functions, cards and calling, teas, invitations, luncheons and dinners, receptions, dress, flag courtesy, children, clubs and miscellaneous customs. Chapters begin in question/answer format, and continue with general discussion. Includes diagrams.

200 Crisp, Quentin. Manners from Heaven: a Divine Guide to Good Behavior. New York: Harper and Row, 1984.
Describes his view of the world with humor, relating past experiences which brought him to his present conclusions. Offers advice such as, "You've got to make yourself likeable enough to join the world in spite of your vice. Thus my interest in manners was born."

201 Cronin, Morton. "Tyranny of Democratic Manners." New Republic, 138:12-4, Jan. 20, 1958.
Discusses the democratization of manners which "decree egalitarian behavior in a hierarchical society."

202 Crosse, Theodosia. Social Customs; the Art of Gracious Manners. Philadelphia: J.B. Lippincott, 1938.
"This book is offered to the nursing profession." Topics cover social customs, introductions, entertaining, invitations, table conversation, dress, wedding, friendship, correspondence, birth, mourning, travel and a final chapter called "The Portrait of an Ideal Nurse." The chapter devoted to friendship discusses the wise selection of literature, social contacts and friends as an important part of the career of the modern nurse. All chapters relate aspects of etiquette to nurses specifically, discussing particular situations which those in nursing may encounter and the correct behavior they should exhibit. The author concludes, "In the dark pathways of life you be the light."

203 Crowninshield, Francis Welch. Manners for the Metropolis; an Entrance Key to the Fantastic Life of the 400. Decorations by Louis Fancher. New York: D. Appleton & Co., 1908.
A parody of social life, Crowninshield's advice ranges from visiting country houses to "Newport" to dances. "In giving a dance, avoid, if possible, sending invitations to bores—they come without them." A list of General Rules is also included, covering situations such as church going ("no longer considered fashionable....") to motoring ("avoid running over hens, dogs,...").

204 Crowther, Mary Owens. Book of Letters. New York: Doubleday, 1922.
Handbook covers etiquette of personal and business letters, using numerous examples. There are also chapters on children's letters, telegrams, stationery, crests and monograms and the cost of letters.

205 "Cruelty to the Timid." Nation, 92:644-5, June 29, 1911.
Exclaims that there is "ceaseless harping on the disadvantages of shyness," and encourages arbiters to "refrain from the condescending sympathy that makes the timid soul turn in pale terror upon itself."

206 Culbertson, Josephine. "Manners at the Bridge Table." <u>Good
Housekeeping</u>, 110:152-3, June, 1940.
According to the author, manners at the bridge table comes
down to the "simple matter of kindness." Advises on how to
give a bridge party which is conducive to peace and good
manners.
Culkin, Mabel Louise, joint author **See** Banning, Margaret Culkin.

207 Culver, D. Jay. "Voice with a Smile Won a Business for Joan."
<u>American Magazine</u>, 112:74, Dec., 1931.
Tells how Joan Wing started her own business teaching others
in business that courtesy pays.

208 Cuming, Luella. <u>The Luella Cuming Studio Course in Social
Awareness, Poise, and Gracious Living</u>. New York: Parker,
1965.
Home study version of course offered by Cuming in her private
studio. Arranged in lessons beginning with an evaluation of
"Your Present State of Social Awareness." Other chapters
include "How to Create and Project the Correct Social Image,"
"Develop Savoir Faire," and "The Lifetime Plan for Personal
and Social Growth." Advice on entertaining, correspondence,
special occasions, and conversations is also given.

209 _____. <u>Social Awareness: Your Guide to Today's Manners</u>.
Edited by Mary Milo, illustrated by Maribeth Olson. New York:
Family Circle, 1967.
Discusses broad aspects of social awareness including advice
on how to avoid awkward moments, build self-esteem or "sweeten
your personality." Topics covered include social awareness
in the family, the neighborhood and the office. Tells how a
wife can add to her husband's prestige. Telephone manners,
money matters, social emergencies, correspondence, parties
and other forms of entertaining are also discussed. Illustrated,
has index.

210 Curtis, Charlotte. "Importance of the Right Fork." <u>McCall's</u>,
103:168-9, April, 1976.
Gives historical perspective to table etiquette: "In another
hundred years, the finger bowl may go the way of the lorgnette,
and it's always possible that there is no such thing as the eter-
nally correct fork."

211 Curzun, Daniel. <u>The Joyful Blue Book of Gracious Gay Etiquette</u>.
San Francisco: D. Brown, 1982.
Spoof of "the best advice about...manners and agreeable social
behavior..." in the gay lifestyle.

212 Dale, D. "Mediaeval Courtesy." <u>American Catholic Quarterly</u>,
32:123-37, Jan., 1907.
Includes excerpts from English mediaeval Books of Courtesy,
with discussion of customs of the times, and the note that
these books were "intended for the use of the upper classes."
Daly, Maureen **See** McGivern, Maureen (Daly).
Dame, Curtsey **See** Glover, Ellye H.
Darieux, Genevive **See** Antoine-Darieux, Genevive.

213 Darling, Jan. <u>Outclassing the Competition: The Up & Comer's
Guide to Social Survival</u>. New York: St. Martin's Press, 1985.

After reading this book "you'll soon feel devastatingly self-assured around impossible clients, your affluent company president, even your wealthy prospective in-laws." Advice covers "Restaurant Resourcefulness," "Dining, Decorum, Delicacies, and Dilemmas," "Giving to the Rich," "Wing Tips to White Tie," "The Silk Stocking Set" and "The Beautiful Person's Bar Guide." There are also suggestions for entertaining, including recipes. Includes a vocabulary guide for foreign words and phrases, wines and related terms and French food. Pages called "Class Notes" cover a variety of topics from limousines, tipping, catalog shopping and house guesting. Illustrated with photos, has bibliography and index.

214 Davidson, Judith. "Let's Go Dutch." Good Housekeeping, 136:13, Jan., 1953.
Seven hints on how to share an evening's expenses so that "the delicate male ego has survived the ordeal."

215 Davis, Lydia. "Teaching the Small Child Table Manners." Better Homes and Gardens, 26:176, Nov., 1947.
Detailed instructions for teaching children table manners, has photos.

216 Davis, Mrs. N. "Courtesy Builds Mail Orders." Profitable Housekeeping, 10:58, Nov., 1954.
Tells how courteous treatment of customers is good business. Includes advice on correspondence.

217 "Dear Miss Manners..." Redbook, 166:112-3, Dec., 1985.
Judith Martin discusses her philosophy of gift-giving and gives concrete suggestions for getting the gift list down to the appropriate size.

218 DeArmond, Fred. "Matter of Courtesy; Good Business Relations." Rotarian, 89:12-3, Dec., 1956.
Discusses what he considers to be a double standard of courtesy in business and illustrates with examples this double standard in face-to-face contacts, telephone communications and answering letters.

219 Debrett's Etiquette and Modern Manners. Edited by Elsie Burch Donald. New York: Viking Press, in association with Debrett's Peerage, 1981.
Describes formalities such as introductions to the Pope, how to address one's butler, and technicalities in dealings with royalty. Includes tables of correct forms of address. Procedures for traditional ceremonies such as christenings, weddings and funerals. Proper methods for issuing invitations, sending thank-you notes, and making introductions are given. Also covers business manners, sports, running a household, entertaining, single motherhood, unmarried couples, women in business, drugs at a party and table manners. Ends with a table of Precedence in Scotland. Illustrated, with index.

220 DeLee, Dolores. Etiquette of Flowers. Chicago: Allied Florists' Association of Illinois, 1939.
Tells the when, where and how of using flowers. Includes suggestions for the use of flowers "for beautifying the home" as well.

221 Demarest, M., and Banta, K. "Crusader for Couth." Time, 118:89,
    Dec. 21, 1981.
    Profiles the work of Marjabelle Stewart, who teaches manners
    to children in workshops all over the country. Also highlights
    her work with corporations, "to impact the social graces to
    bumptious executives."
222 DeShan, E.J., and Strait, Suzanne Hart. "Manners Are From
    the Heart: With Program for Discussion Group." Parents Maga-
    zine, 38:72-3, Nov., 1963.
    Includes program for use in discussion group. The authors'
    philosophy of teaching manners to children is that it is difficult
    to teach children to think about others—before true courtesy
    can be expressed, its techniques must be practiced.
223 Devereux, George. Mohave Etiquette. Los Angeles: South-west
    Museum, 1948.
    Describes "the etiquette of ordinary social relations..." among
    the Mohave, including a description of the general behavior
    of sitting, walking, swimming, dancing, eating, chewing gum,
    tobacco and photography. Under the sub-title, Human Relations,
    the sharing of emotions, intrusion, personal questions, generosity,
    friendship, unsuitable associations, avoidance patterns, praise,
    dispraise, rewards and punishment, and the expectations of
    good manners are discussed. "The essense of Mohave courtesy
    is identical with that of the early Renaissance concept of
    Cortesia—it is the considerateness of kind and fair-minded
    people." Includes bibliography and photos.
    Devine, Elizabeth, joint author See Braganti, Nancy L.
224 DeWitt, Karen. "Etiquette Counts." Black Enterprise, 15:66-7,
    Sept., 1984.
    Describes how manners will help black business people.
225 Diescher, Victor H. The Book of Good Manners; A Guide to
    Polite Usage for All Social Functions. New York: Social Culture,
    1923.
    Book is dedicated to the reader "with the purpose of democratiz-
    ing...the subject of etiquette and making its laws understandable
    and applicable to the daily life of the everyday man and wo-
    man...." Book is divided into five parts: Part I, "Good Manners
    in Daily Life" covers the home and children's manners; Part
    II, "Courtship and Marriage"; Part III, "Christenings and Funer-
    als"; Part IV, "Formal Procedure" which is very detailed instruc-
    tions on topics such as table manners, correspondence, weddings,
    etc.; Part V, "Dress."
226 "Diffusion of Deference." Living Age, 252:633-5, March 9, 1907.
    Laments the loss of deference of youth to age, of ignorance
    to knowledge, and of men to women. "Deference in relinquishing
    her claim to temporal power has increased tenfold the area
    of her spiritual dominion."
227 "Dining Smarts: Table Manners for the Sophisticated (and the
    Self-conscious)." Glamour, 82:45, Feb., 1984.
228 Dixon, C. Madeleine. "Manners for Today." Parents Magazine,
    20:24-5, Jan., 1945.

Encourages parents to teach children that manners can "oil
the gears of living" by showing that learning can be pleasant
as well as practical.
229 Dixon, Jane. "How Uncle Sam Turns Out Gentlemen." American
Magazine, 109:50-3, May, 1930.
Discusses the importance of teaching manners to those boys
attending military academies, since he will spend more time
"representing his country socially than...on the battlefield."
230 Dolan, Rodger. "Strong Advocate of the Money Value of Courtesy." American Magazine, 82:51, Sept., 1916.
Biographical sketch of businessman David Gibson, who taught
railroads and other great corporations the importance of being
courteous to customers.
231 Dolson, Hildegarde. "Ask Mrs. Post." Independent Woman, 20:103-
4, April, 1941.
Biographical sketch of Emily Post includes insights of her
personal life as well as her professional life as social arbiter,
writer, syndicated columnist and radio talk show hostess.
Donald, Elsie Burch See Debrett's Etiquette and Modern Manners.
(1981)
232 "Do's and Don'ts of Christmas Etiquette." Good Housekeeping,
175:184, Dec., 1972.
Advice about Christmas gift giving and cards.
233 Do's and Taboos Around the World. Compiled by the Parker
Pen Co., and Roger E. Axtell, illustrated by Bob Weber and
Howard Munce. Elmsford, N.Y.: Benjamin, 1985.
Addressed to help businessmen in the world market, arranged
alphabetically by country. Included for each country is advice
about protocol, names, greetings, appointments, punctuality,
hospitality, gift-giving, dress and conversation. The use of
"American Jargon and Baffling Idioms" is discussed as well.
Includes index.
234 Doty, Mark A. "The Decline of Civility in America." Christian
Century, 100:1093-4, Nov. 23, 1983.
Contends that the "roots of me-ism...have only sunk deeper
into the soil of American life during the present decade." Suggests that the upswing of thoughtlessness is not confined to
the secular world.
235 Dowdall, Mary Frances Harriet. Manners and Tone of Good
Society. New York: Macmillan, 1926.
Chapters offer advice on dress, "the first desideratum for
anyone about to enter society of any kind is...dress"; table
etiquette, "all eccentric forms of cutlery are out of date...";
guests; popularity; and the management of wealth. There are
chapters called "On the Choice of a Life Partner," "On Respectability and Taking a Nice View of Art," "On Snobbery," "On
the Art of Being a Foreigner" and "The Final Polish." Dowdall
addresses "our novice" throughout, using fictitious situations
and anecdotes for illustration. Includes index.
236 Drew, Elizabeth A. "Behaviourism of Our Grandmother's" Atlantic, 131:530-3, April, 1923.

Reviews correct behavior in the mid–1800's, and focuses on Instructions in Etiquette for the Use of All, written by an instructor at a "considerable school."

237 Drobot, Eve. Class Acts: Etiquette for Today. New York: Van Nostrand Reinhold, 1982.
Arranged by subjects in question/answer format. Addresses some contemporary problems such as birth announcements from unmarried parents and situations with "exes."

238 Drummond, Marshall. "Say It with a Smile." Reader's Digest, 35:72, Nov., 1939.
Contends that tone of voice and a pleasant smile when using the "little everyday courtesies" like "please" or "excuse me" can influence their effectiveness. The effectiveness of the words themselves is dependent upon the sincerity with which they are said.

239 Duke, Angier Biddle. "Functions of Protocol in Today's World." Department State Bulletin, 50:344-7, March 2, 1964.
Address made before the Women's National Democratic Club on February 6, 1964. Outlines his philosophy, as Chief of Protocol, saying that protocol serves two functions, "to be a strong guardian of equality and an agency for the recognition of the superior...however contradictory that may seem."

240 _____. "Protocol and Peacekeeping." Department State Bulletin, 51:736-9, Nov. 23, 1964.
Address made before the Yale Club of Washington, on October 22, 1964. Discusses the role of the United Nations as "the most acceptable channel to conduct America's business overseas." Suggests an international conference to be held to bring about agreement upon the basic ground rules regarding contacts and visits between chiefs-of-state.

241 _____. "Protocol and the Conduct of Foreign Affairs." Department State Bulletin, 49:700-4, Nov. 4, 1963.
Address made before the Publicity Club of Chicago on October 9, 1963. Describes the functions of the Protocol Office and its importance since "the face of the State Department is so often the one presented by the Protocol Office, and that face must be representative."

242 Duncan, William Cary. "Bad Manners Family." Good Housekeeping, 49:32-3, July, 1909.
Poem about the Bad Manners family, who "never were asked, to parties or dinners or teas...," and then giving the many reasons why.

243 Durbin, Karen. "Sexual Courtesy." Mademoiselle, 83:147, March, 1977.
Durbin relates her advice about sexual courtesy in light of the new feminism.

244 Durham, Helen. Correspondence, Invitations and Their Replies. New York: Homemaker's Bureau of People's Home Journal, 1927.
"Correct letter writing is a primary essential of social usage." Describes all aspects of letter writing, including types of paper,

envelopes, salutations and closings. Includes numerous samples
and lists the Do's and Don'ts of letter writing.

245 _____. "How Do You Do? On the Graceful Art of Introducing
People." Woman's Home Companion, 52:52-4, April, 1925.
Introductions of every possible kind are outlined, such as group
introductions and family introductions. Describes "the acid
test of an introduction..." by asking "does it show gracious
consideration of the persons we are introducing?"

246 _____. Manners, American Etiquette. New York: E.P. Dutton,
1928.
Author believes good manners are the "gracious ways of showing
consideration to others." Advice covers manners at home and
abroad, social and business occasions, travel etiquette, correct
behavior at court, or in the nursery. There is a title chart
for addressing dignitaries also.

247 _____. "What to Say When It's Your Cue to Introduce Someone."
Better Homes and Gardens, 9:49, March, 1931.
Outlines proper procedure for introductions in a variety of
situations.

248 Durning, Julia Addis. Book of Modern Etiquette. Foreword by
Mr. Charles Dana Gibson. New York: Black, 1935.
Counsels on all aspects of good manners, giving specific don'ts
as well as conceding "it is done" upon occasion. Topics covered
are good manners of travel, appropriate behavior of hosts
and guests, advice to mothers of young children, divorced
persons, business etiquette, gifts, cards and correspondence.
Also offers advice on dress and etiquette at the White House.

249 _____. Etiquette for Moderns, A Guide for the Executive's
Wife. New York: Walker, 1965.
"Good manners...have become important to one's business
or professional career." Maintains that "the wife is a crucial
factor in the progress of her husband's career." Discusses manners in public, the importance of first impressions, attire,
introductions, conversation, charm, table manners, parties,
host and guest, and social and business correspondence. There
are also chapters on business etiquette, sports, children, travel
etiquette and the United Nations. Concludes with questions
and answers.

249a Eberstadt, Frederick. "Don't Call Me Fred." Vogue, 177:267,
April, 1987.
Praises "old-fashioned good manners..." as the tools of behavior
which draw people closer together. Discusses influence of
informality in present society, maintaining that "informality
is...simply a tiresome affectation."

250 Eberts, Nell M. Social Arts Digest. New York: Suttonhouse,
1938.
Manual provides an outline for teachers and students to use
for teaching etiquette. Topics covered include social conduct,
hospitality, introductions, conversation, table etiquette, dancing,
correspondence, travel, leisure and dress. Chapters include
a basic outline of the topic for discussion, references and a
place for students to write their notes. Includes bibliography.

251 Edgerton, Lillian. "Is Good Behavior On a Vacation, Too?", Delineator, 97:2, July, 1920.
Feels that young men and women are holding themselves superior to manners; "the manner of most up-to-date young people is sheer impertinence." The author is also concerned that "every town...finds a shocking lack of propriety among its 'very best people'."

Eichler, Lilian **See** Watson, Lilian (Eichler)

252 Eisenbrandt, Marie. "Children's Parties, Lessons in Etiquette." American Home, 16:41, July, 1936.
Suggests that children's parties can provide a stage for children to learn social poise and grace, and that children should be included in the planning and execution of simple parties.

253 Eliasberg, Ann P. "What Does the Code Say, Dear?" New York Times Magazine, 87, April 26, 1964.
Describes what different groups of parents have done to establish some "generally accepted standards to regulate their children's active, often frantic, social lives." These "codes" represent an effort by the parents to set guidelines for teen behavior.

254 Eliot, Charles W. "Democracy and Manners: Teaching of Manners in the Public Schools." Century, 83:173-8, Dec., 1911.
Examines the part manners play in the "social education of mankind," and the role the public schools can have in the "diffusion and development of good manners among the people."

255 Elliott, Eleanor. The Glamour Magazine Party Book. New York: Doubleday, 1965.
Guide to all kinds of entertaining, with an emphasis on good manners. Includes menu plans, recipes and has an index.

256 Emerson, Warrington. "Putting Out Fires with Rose-water." Century, 81:797-8, March, 1911.
Suggests courtesy as a solution to the "labor problem." If courtesy were "more generally inculcated in all classes, employers and employed...the chances for a better understanding all round would be greatly improved."

257 "Emily Postism." Musical America, 73:9, Jan. 1, 1953.
Excerpts from an etiquette book called True Politeness, published in 1847, which relates to the "Deportment of the gentle accomplishment of music."

Esquire. Esquire Etiquette. (1987) **See** Waggoner, Glen.

258 Esquire. Esquire's Etiquette; A Guide to Business, Sports and Social Conduct. Philadelphia, J.B. Lippincott, 1953.
Includes for the man "new and current guides on everything from tippling to tipping, from courting to sporting." Divided into three sections: "Business Conduct" describes proper conduct on the job, with the secretary, on the telephone or in conference; "Sports Conduct" covers activities from golf to fishing, including equipment, manners and dress; "Social Conduct" details proper deportment as a guest, host, traveller or date. Indexed.

259 _____. Esquire's Guide to Modern Etiquette. Philadelphia, J.B. Lippincott, 1969.
Addressed to men who want to become knowledgeable about how things are done in "these fast-paced high-pressure days."

The editors have "ruthlessly cast aside all forms of etiquette that no longer make sense or that are uncomfortable and un-natural for a man to follow." Maintains three main divisions found in earlier edition, and differs by the inclusion of theater etiquette, hospital visits, how to communicate via press releases, radio and TV appearances.

260 _____ . New Esquire Etiquette; a Guide to Business, Sports and Social Conduct. Philadelphia: J.B. Lippincott, 1959.
Substantially the same as 1953 edition with some new material on tipping included. The contents have been reorganized for easier reference.

261 "Etiquette." Christian Century, 59:1481, Dec. 2, 1942.
Philosophical discussion of etiquette and courtesy—"in its proper place it simply leaves us free from distractions...."

262 "Etiquette." Living Age, 284:805-8, March 27, 1915.
Examination of the nature of etiquette. Etiquette is "the man-ners of a class and the manners of a time."

263 "Etiquette as a Civilizing Force." World's Work, 27:141-2. Dec., 1913.
Filipino children are taught manners in the schools, as an "at-tempt to use the rules of etiquette as a civilizing force..." by the Bureau of Education at Manila.

264 "Etiquette at Home." Sunset, 55:68-9, Sept., 1925.
Suggests parents begin teaching correct behavior to very young children, in order to assure them of poise throughout their lives. "Those only are thoroughbred who have been reared in honor and unselfishness and have never seen or heard their parents do or say an ignoble thing."

265 Etiquette for Americans. By a woman of fashion. New York: Fox Duffield, 1906.
Detailed manual written to meet "the actual need of an up-to-date manual of American etiquette." Chapter on introductions includes advice on what to do if one fails to hear or remember a name. There is a discussion of etiquette vs. fashion, and chapters on telephoning, smoking, chaperonage and calling are included. Rules for unmarried women are outlined in detail, as are the obligations of bachelors. Interestingly, there is a chapter on the treatment of reporters.

266 "Etiquette for Polar Bears; Socialist Book of Manners." Time, 89:34, March 3, 1967.
Review of How to Behave, the first socialist book of manners, by Milena Majorova, a psychiatrist from Prague. Includes advice such as "It is the height of bad manners to take off your shoes in front of your secretary."

267 "Etiquette for the Wedding." Good Housekeeping, 130:58-9, April, 1950.
A guide to correct etiquette of announcing an engagement, as well as what the bride-to-be must consider in planning the wedding. Lists financial obligations, types of weddings and dress, and describes etiquette of invitations and announcements.

268 "Etiquette for the Wedding Guest." Good Housekeeping, 156: 162, May, 1963.

Brief discussion of wedding etiquette for the guest, which
gives guidelines for gift-giving, ceremonies, receptions, and
dress.

269 "Etiquette of Entertaining." Good Housekeeping, 96:58-9, Jan.;
56-7, March; 54-5, May; 97:56, July; 72, Nov., 1933; 98:72,
March; 75, May, 1934.
Series of articles on entertaining. The first article is called
"Buffet Luncheon" and includes advice on invitations, table
settings and seating arrangements. The second is "The Formal
Dinner" and advises on the order of service, conversation and
table settings. The third article is "Arranging a Smart Wedding"
which details how to organize a wedding. Article four is "Lunch-
ing Out-of-doors Enlivens the Week-end Party" and discusses
informal entertaining. The fifth article is "Smart Appointments
for Appointed Hours" which shows assorted settings for various
meals. "The Engagement Party" is sixth in the series, and makes
suggestions for different types of parties. The last article
is "The Garden Buffet" which describes the buffet as a smart
fashion and a new idea.

270 "Etiquette of Entertaining." Sunset Magazine, 56:72-4, Jan.,
1926.
Outlines the planning of different types of parties, both formal
and informal dinners, as well as luncheons and teas. Suggests
that "informal entertaining is much preferred at present to
the more elaborate form that is apt to result in contraint instead
of gaiety."

271 "Etiquette of Gloves." Good Housekeeping, 152:119, Jan., 1961.
When to wear, take off, wear jewelry with and shake hands
with gloves.

272 "Etiquette Rules of By-gone Days." Hobbies, 45:9-10, June,
1940.
Highlights the etiquette of cycling, including dress and posture,
from days past, with suggestions such as "Don't raise your
hat to ladies either on foot or a-wheel until you have perfect
control of your machine."

273 Etiquette; the Complete Modern Guide for Day-to-day Living
the Correct Way. Edited by Frances Benton, co-edited by General Federation of Women's Clubs, N.Y. New York: Random
House, 1956.
Says that consideration is the essence of good manners, regard-
less of the number of rules of etiquette. Book is a list of 261
rules which cover everything from weddings, dress, table manners, entertaining, cards, correspondence and calling to children.
Illustrated manual has an extensive chart of forms of address,
and an index.

274 Eutychus, IV. "Stop Rapidly, Go Soothingly." Christianity Today,
13;28, March 14, 1969.
Premise is "Discourtesy seems, alas, a necessary adjunct to
a certain sort of evangelical endeavor."

Everett, Marshall, pseudonym See Neil, Henry.

275 Ewertsen, Lillian. "Social Training for Our Boys." National Education Association Journal, 14:116, April, 1925.

Encourages mothers to give their boys "the necessary cultural training for their future success..." and "failing that, to send them to a good school, where the training may be procured."

276 Fadiman, Clifton. "American Manners, New Style." Holiday, 24:8, Nov., 1958.
Fadiman expresses bewilderment at the Casual Era, with its new style of salutations, introduction, and foods such as Dip. He examines the New Behavior as the Cult of Informality, and the domination of the teen-ager in the domain of the American manners.

277 Fairbanks, Douglas. "Who Killed Chivalry?" McCall's, 92:117, Nov., 1964.
Relates what chivalry means to him, and who he considers to exemplify chivalrous manner. Defines men of chivalry as those "with a common belief in behaving decently and in observing the Golden Rule."

278 Fales, D. "How to Make a Proper Pass." Motor Boating and Sailing, 149:104-6, May, 1982.
Tells how to avoid the "acid stomach of confrontation" when two parties are involved in a pass on the water. Suggests larger vessels inform smaller ones of their intentions and that they pass slowly, using the No-rock technique. Gives examples of passes for different types of vessels in different situations.

Faux, Marian, joint author See Stewart, Marjabelle Young.

279 Feifer, George. "Now Moscow Debates Its Manners." New York Times Magazine, 28, Aug. 23, 1964.
Describes Soviet manners with some comparison to those of Americans, particularly forms of address and public manners. Examines the paradox between the Russian's city manners and their warmth and courtesy in personal relationships.

Fenwick, Millicent See Vogue's Book of Etiquette (1948).

280 Ferdon, Constance Etz. "Mind Your Manners; Rules of Etiquette in Ecuador." International American, 5:19-20, July, 1946.
Encourages visitors to Ecuador to pay attention to local customs and manners, and gives rule for visitors to observe.

281 Fermaglich, Mollie. "Minding Your Manners (Some Not So Prim and Proper Advice)." Working Woman, 9:30, Sept., 1984.
Answers questions such as, What is networking? and What is the proper way to fire someone? Defines networking as "the fine art of forming bonds with total strangers, with the express purpose of ultimately abusing that relationship in order to further your career."

282 _____. Mollie's Rules for the Socially Inept: A Guide to Modern Living. New York: Quill, 1984.
Book is "geared to help those of you with questionable table manners, limited social grace, and absolutely no finesse...." Humorous approach to etiquette written in question/answer format covers topics such as taboo table talk, how to complain effectively, decorating the office, asking for a raise, annoying personal habits and conversation. Answers questions such as, How can you avoid contributing to office gifts?, and What precisely does one do with olive and fruit pits?

283 _____. "Tongue-in-cheek Business Rules for 9 to 5." Glamour, 82:118, Feb., 1984.
Question/answer format uses humor to guide people in office etiquette.

284 Fields, Susan. Getting Married Again. New York: Dodd, Mead and Col, 1975.
Discusses the expectations those considering remarrying should have. Chapters include advice on making the decision to remarry, the engagement, how to plan the second wedding and the function of members of the bridal party. The reception, announcements, what to wear and how to handle gifts and flowers are topics addressed. Concludes with a discussion of pitfalls, and advice on telling your ex-. Appended with a checklist.

285 Finch, Lloyd C. Telephone Courtesy and Customer Service. Los Altos, CA: Crisp, 1987.
Designed as a manual to help the reader "become a professional provider of quality customer service." Provides objectives for the reader, defines what makes a quality customer service provider and defines service responsibility. Describes telephone techniques and why they are important to providing service. Explains customer wants and needs and describes the importance of a positive attitude. Teaches the reader how to manage customer perceptions. Includes charts and tests.

286 "Finding $50 Worth of Politeness in Chicago." Literary Digest, 68:43-6, March 5, 1921.
Narrative of a woman's quest for the most polite person in Chicago she encounters in one day, whom she'll reward with fifty dollars.

287 Findlay, Catherine. "What's Your Social I.Q.? How to Be a Genius at Parties." Mademoiselle, 87:111-12, Dec., 1981.
Outlines some smart party strategies such as making an entrance, being confident, mingling and beating a retreat.

288 Fishback, Margaret. Safe Conduct. Illustrated by Helen Hokinson. New York: Harcourt, Brace, 1938.
Advice covers the general scope of most etiquette books, and includes chapters entitled, "On the Wing," "Etiquette in the Office," "Modern Social Menaces," "The Servant Problem," "Other Domestic Crises" and "Civil Virtue." Illustrated and includes index.

289 "$5 for Courteous Drivers." American City, 64:131, Jan., 1949.
Description of a Courtesy Week implemented by various civic organizations in Plymouth, Indiana.

290 Flagg, James Montgomery. "Etiquette of Motoring." American Magazine, 80:96, Dec., 1915.
Humorous article offers advice to the owner, chauffeur and guests of an automobile. To guests he suggests, "If the owner goes over a thank-ye-ma'am, always screech at the top of your lungs."

Flynn, Helen, joint author See Woods, Marjorie (Binford)

291 "Focus on Etiquette." Seventeen, 39:74-5, Oct., 1980.
Pot-pourri discussion includes telephone etiquette, manners practiced in the past, and guest/host manners.

292 Follett, Barbara Lee. Check List for a Perfect Wedding. Garden
    City, N.Y.: Doubleday, 1973.
    Begins by listing those things essential to planning a wedding,
    and discusses all aspects of planning from 4-6 months before
    the wedding up to one week before the wedding. Tells how
    to announce the engagement, and make church arrangements.
    Other topics include types of dress for various participants,
    florists, photographers, music and invitations. Describes the
    duties of the various participants and the nontraditional wedding.
293 _____. Check List for a Perfect Wedding. Garden City, N. Y.:
    Doubleday, 1986.
    Revised and expanded edition designed as much for the mother
    of the bride-to-be as for the bride-to-be. This edition expanded
    to address questions which did not arise when initially published.
    Includes advice on the second wedding as well.
    Fondren, Evelyn Baird, joint author **See** Gross, Mary Preston.
294 Forbes-Lindsay, Charles Harcourt Ainslie. Good Form for Men;
    a Guide to Conduct and Dress On All Occasions. Philadelphia:
    H.T. Coates, 1905.
    "Good Form is addressed exclusively to men, and especially
    to young men.... Its purpose is to help the man...who desires
    to regulate his life after the manner of gentlemen." Begins
    with a discussion of manners in general, and continues to advise
    men on dress and toilet. "The well dressed man is never conspic-
    uous." There is a discourse on public behavior, with advice
    on hat-tipping and bus sitting, i.e., when and to whom you
    offer your seat. Calls and cards, introductions, dinners, balls,
    correspondence, travelling, the club, and smoking are also
    topics covered.
295 Forbes-Lindsay, Margaret Osborne. Good Form for Women:
    a Guide to Conduct and Dress On All Occasions. Philadelphia:
    J.C. Winston, 1907.
    Covers virtually all aspects of etiquette, including table man-
    ners, dress, correspondence, public behavior, and ceremonies
    of life. Aims particularly "to help girls who have not had the
    benefit of proper home training."
296 Ford, Charlotte. Charlotte Ford's Book of Modern Manners.
    New York: Simon and Schuster, 1980.
    Begins with discussion of everyday manners in public places,
    which covers topics ranging from greetings and conversation
    to the disabled, restaurant dining and traditional male courtesies.
    Under this topic, telephone manners, smoking, walking on
    the sidewalk and a conversation with someone older can also
    be found. "Proper Deportment for Entertaining" includes advice
    about guest lists, invitations, and dining. One section is devoted
    to advice about table manners. There are separate chapters
    for weddings, marriage, living together and divorce. Ford's
    intent in writing this book was to "help answer the why's and
    how's of situations for which there are no longer exact standards
    of proper behavior."
297 _____. Etiquette: Charlotte Ford's Guide to Modern Manners.
    New York: Crown, 1988.

Newly formatted, contains additional material and is updated. Includes modern day problems such as coping with visitors who are using drugs, and answering machine etiquette.
298 Ford, Corey. "Speaking Out; Catalogue of Boors." Saturday Evening Post, 235:10, April 7, 1962.
"Boorishness is so widespread...it's time to catalogue and classify the subject," which the author does. For example, he defines the behavior of the Theater Boor, and the Stadium Boor, and others.
299 Ford, James L. "What Is the Best Society?" Munsey, 30:309-13, Nov., 1903.
Uses the party setting, and the different circles found within that setting to define the best society.
300 "Forms and Customs That Govern Everyday Life." Good Housekeeping, 86:47, Feb., 1928.
Highlights points of etiquette such as introductions and table manners with some historical information as to their origin.
301 Fram, Eugene H., and Mossien, Herbert J. "High Scores on the Discourtesy Scale; Thoughtlessness of Business Managers." Harvard Business Review, 54:12, Jan., 1976.
The results of a survey of lower, middle, and upper level managers which focuses on meetings and personal recognition from management are outlined.
302 France, Beulah. "Your Child's Manners." Country Gentleman, 124:69, July, 1954.
Advises how to teach manners to children from early infancy, with specific pointers for parents.
303 Frankel, Tobia. "Etiquette Line for Russians." New York Times Magazine, 90-1, Nov.16, 1958.
Cites writings by N. Giordienko to instruct Soviets on etiquette as the result of an effort to re-emphasize etiquette in the Soviet Union. Topics include "Bourgeois and Social Etiquette," as well as table manners, personal hygiene and public behavior. Consideration is also given to living in a communal apartment.
304 Franklin, Rebecca. "Metropolis of Bad Manners." New York Times Magazine, 24, Aug. 9, 1959.
Describes the well-known, "deplorable state" of the manners of New Yorkers and compares them with other metropolitan areas such as Los Angeles, London and Rome.
305 Frederick, Justus George. Standard Business Etiquette: Personal Codes for Smooth-running Organization Efficiency. New York: Business Bourse, 1937.
Begins by listing 25 rules to follow in order to make a conference run efficiently. Defines business-like behavior. Chapters about telephone use, private secretaries, reception clerks and executives are included. Sets forth standards of courtesy for every phase of the business operation.
306 _____. "Your Secretary Is a Lady: Rules of Working Hours Etiquette." Nation's Business, 29:23-5, April, 1941.
Lists pointers for executives, employers and salesmen on proper deportment in the office.

307 Free, Anne R. Social Usage. New York: Appleton-Century-Crofts, 1960.
"This book is going to describe the mechanical conventions and accepted behavior patterns as they appear in the etiquette of the present time." Advice on appearance, introductions, conversation, public manners, table manners, hospitality, invitations, correspondence, weddings, business manners and travel is offered. Includes numerous lists of do's and don'ts, samples of correspondence, photos, diagrams, a "Tipping Table," and a bibliography.

308 _____. Social Usage. New York: Appleton-Century-Crofts, 1969.
Second edition deletes the chapter on appearance and adds an appendix for correct forms of address.

309 French, M.G. "How To Lose a Man." McCall's, 86:74-5, Nov., 1958.
Pictures illustrate what women sometimes do to men which may cause men to lose interest, such as using affected manners when dining with a date.

310 French, Marilyn. Keys to Etiquette for the Business Girl. Chicago: Dartnell, 1961.
Reminds the reader "to put your knowledge of manners and courtesy to everyday use." Starting with advice for the first day on the job, the author discusses relationships with co-workers as well as the boss. She gives attention to cliques, office wolves and women bosses as well. Includes a list of do's and don'ts for smoking in the office. Uses typical office situations as a means of illustrating good office manners.

311 "French Politeness." Outlook, 97:485, March 4, 1911.
Highlights the controversy in France over the decay of French manners, citing the "haste of modern life, which is destructive of courtesy..." as a possible cause.

312 "French Power Dining." Time, 47, April 28, 1986.
The protocol of seating came under scrutiny at an international banquet attended by Premier Chirac and President Mitterand.

313 Freudenheim, Ellen. The Executive Bride: A Ten-week Wedding Planner. New York: Cloverdale Press, 1985.
Written because marriage is back in style in the 1980's. "But...today's brides are a new, executive breed." Since the bride's time is precious, the book includes special worksheets to help in the decision making, and there are "Advance Planning Tips" in each chapter. There are two main parts; Part I is "Before the Countdown" which is a general discussion of the bride, weddings and the workplace. Part II is "The Countdown" and lists goals for each of the ten weeks before the wedding, starting with the basics, and continuing to invitations, caterers, etc. An epilogue describes "Marriage On the Fast Track—Ultimate Short Cuts."

314 Friedrich, O. "Minding Our Manners Again." Time, 124:62-3, Nov. 5, 1984.
Features the philosophy of arbiter Judith Martin, author of the syndicated newspaper column, "Miss Manners."

315 Froman, Robert. "How's Your Etiquette?" Coronet, 35:131-2, Dec., 1953.
   Excerpts from Thomas E. Hill's Manual of Social and Business Forms, some nostalgic reminders from the days when "our grandparents were young."

316 Fromme, Allan. "What's Happened to Courtesy?" 50 Plus, 19:58, Oct., 1979.
   Fromme contends that the "old order is under attack..." and that social upheaval is the cause for the lack of courtesy shown to the elderly. Offers advice to the elderly on how to cope with the loss.

317 Fury, K. "Do You Have Working Class?" Mademoiselle, 87:230-1, May, 1981.
   Offers solutions to problems encountered in the office, such as what to do when the boss makes a pass, what to call the boss' wife, or when to sit or stand.

318 "Futurist Manners." Atlantic, 112:421-3, Sept., 1913.
   Predicts that manners in the future will become "the new rough-and-tumble ways of our young."
   Gainor, Leo C., joint author See Casey, Thomas Francis.

319 Ganning, London. A Dictionary of Bad Manners. Boston: Houghton Mifflin, 1982.
   "Describes from A to Z the whole range of downright rotten behavior...." Provides names for those bad manners which have previously been unnamed, such as Dastardly Indifference, Fatuitous Dieters, Ghastly Gorger, Hoity-Toity Toe, Loathsome Nickname, Mirror Friends, Pathological Refusal, and Thankless Thanks. Identifies those who commit behavioral atrocities and includes pointers to identify them.

320 Gant, Liz. "For Better...or...for Worse; Wedding Etiquette." Essence, 9:98, June, 1978.
   Tips on how to have a successful wedding.

321 Gardner, Horace J., and Farren, Patricia. Courtesy Book. Foreword by Grace Livingston Hill. Illustrated by Katharine Haviland-Taylor. Philadelphia: J.B. Lippincott, 1937.
   "It is our purpose to...present, in addition to the 'rules of the game', the basic fact that courtesy...is consideration for others...." For use in home and school, topics include a general discussion of courtesy in culture, advice on neatness and clothes, table manners and the art of ocnversation. Etiquette for special events such as birth, christenings, graduation, travel, weddings and funerals is included. Includes bibliography.

322 Garner, Patricia A. The Office Telephone: A User's Guide. Englewood Cliffs, N.J.: Prentice-Hall, 1984.
   "An important goal of this book is to provide information on how to maintain...polite communications in business...." Begins with brief history of communication and a discussion of the importance of the office telephone. Outlines telephone techniques and communication strategies clearly. Concludes with a chapter called "The Future." Appendices include resources available and a glossary. Illustrated with photos, charts and diagrams.

323 Garrigues, C.H. "Most Polite Man; Toll Collector On the San Francisco-Oakland Bay Bridge. Nations Business, 39:72-4, Feb., 1951.
Story about a toll collector who has said thank-you more than 4,000,000 times, with the idea that this courtesy pays off in good public relations.

324 Garrity, Marguerite. "How Good a Host(ess) and Guest Are You?" Better Homes and Gardens, 29:38, Dec., 1951.
Test to score knowledge of entertaining expertise, including that of invitations and introductions.

325 Gary, Romain. "Party of One; Triumph of Rudeness: East or West...." Holiday, 30:8, July, 1961.
Declares rudeness "is perhaps the only true and complete incarnation of fraternity in our time..." between communist Russia and the free West.

326 Gavit, Helen Elizabeth. The Essentials of Polite Correspondence. New York: M. Ward, 1901.
A collection of accepted forms of address and salutations. Gives information on correct usage in social and office correspondence.

327 _____. The Etiquette of Correspondence; Being Illustrations and Suggestions as to the Proper Form in Present Usage of Social, Club, Diplomatic, Military, and Business Letters, with Information on Heraldic Devices, Monograms and Engraved Address. New York: A. Wessels, 1904.
Compendium includes historical correspondence of queens. Comprehensive in scope covers virtually every type of correspondence, with advice on postal regulations, a long list of abbreviations, and a list of foreign words and phrases. Instructions on punctuation and capitalization are also given.

Gelles-Cole, Sandi, editor See Baldrige, Letitia. Letitia Baldrige's Complete Guide to Executive Manners.

General Federation of Women's Clubs, co-editors See Etiquette: The Complete Modern Guide for Day-to-day Living the Correct Way.

328 "Getting Along with Foreigners." Business Weekly, 75-6, June 9, 1956.
Businesses should utilize the expertise offered by anthropologists in order to understand and best relate to foreigners. This expertise could prevent businessmen from pulling "unnecessary boners" which may ruin a foreign venture.

329 Gibson, Janice. "Dining Out with a Toddler." Parents Magazine, 66:108, Jan., 1985.
Tips include making sure the restaurant is comfortable for a toddler, that high chairs are available, that foods are carefully chosen, and that parents are relaxed.

330 _____. "Holiday Meals." Parents Magazine, 59:148, Dec., 1984.
Advises on what to expect from your toddler at special meals, and what to serve.

331 Gillette, Paul. The Single Man's Indispensable Guide and Handbook. New York: Playboy Press Book, 1973.

Book concentrates "on the how rather than the whether of pleasurable living." Offers advice to the single man at home, as a host and as a single man-about-town. Instructs on travel etiquette, with an emphasis on international travel. Careers, on-the-job problems, capital income and investment, and dress are additional topics addressed. Many chapters conclude with "The Playboy Advisor On...."

332 Gillilan, Strickland. "Reformation at One Stroke." Rotarian, 49:5, Nov.,1936.
Suggests the answer "for reforming the world and starting an era of law-abidingness and good manners..." is "Let everybody have his name put on him in large letters so that it can be read 15 feet away."

333 Glover, Ellye Howell. Dame Curtsey's Book of Etiquette. Chicago: A.C. McClurg, 1909.
"Good form is a knowledge of a few universal rules which give one a passport into polite society." Etiquette of cards and calling, ball-room customs, sports, travel, weddings, table manners, introductions and invitations is described. Concludes with general hints such as, "Chewing gum in public is decidedly bad form," and "In dress and hats it is well to choose severely plain styles."

334 Goddard, Gloria. Etiquette for Moderns. Cleveland: World, 1941.
Comprehensive coverage includes advice about what to expect from servants, introductions, table manners, public manners, weddings, business, and etiquette in Washington D.C. There are numerous lists of do's and don'ts. "It is much easier to acquire good manners than it is to acquire a fortune, and the manners are the more valuable asset."

335 Godson, William F.H. "Seven Points of Departure." Atlantic Monthly, 151:766-8, June, 1933.
How to take your leave quickly and effectively: 1. Stand-up; 2. Hold out your hand; 3. Say good-bye; 4. Go to the door; 5. Open the door; 6. Walk out; and 7. Walk away.

336 Good Form. Monroe, Mich.: St. Mary's College, 1915.
Defines good form, which "signifies conformity to the conventionalities and usages of society...." Offers advice on introductions, public behavior, invitations, calling, table manners and other standard etiquette topics. There is a chapter called "Dress—Its Ethics" and on introductions this advice is offered, "Ordinary introductions no longer carry the weight that was formerly attached to them."

337 "Good Form: A Modern Man's Guide to the Social Graces." Esquire, 101:247-8, June, 1984.
Reviews good form when ordering in a restaurant, taking "No" for an answer and complimenting a woman. Describes the new rules of dating and other modern situations which may be encountered by men.

338 "Good Manners." Harper's Weekly, 50:1270, Sept. 8, 1906.
Gives advice on the advantages of practicing good manners, suggesting that by doing so we may "radiate to bring out what is best in all those around us."

339 "Good Way to Develop Leaders: Self-rating Card, Washington School, Fairfield, Iowa." National Education Association Journal. 33:2, Jan., 1944.
Example of a grade card used for children to rate themselves on different points of courtesy as a means of improving their manners during the school year.

340 Goodman, Gary S. Winning by Telephone: Telephone Effectiveness for Business Professionals and Consumers. Englewood Cliffs, N.J.: Prentice-Hall, 1982.
Specific how-to's on tele-time management, including specific phrases to use in order to accomplish specific goals. Tells how to develop the "Telephone Ear" and a power voice. Gives advice on customer relations, the telephone in the professional office and a consumer guide. Uses sample phone conversations to illustrate both the right and wrong way to talk, and tells how to diplomatically screen calls and transfer calls.

341 Goodman, Mary Ellen. "Good Character Is Made, Not Born." Parents Magazine, 39:54-5, Oct., 1964.
The quality of courtesy in children is developed by a day-to-day process of using good manners in the home, exemplified by the parents' behavior.

342 Goodrich, Laurence B. Living with Others, A Book on Social Conduct. New York: American Book, 1939.
"Because of its unique and universal function as an instrument of social adjustment, speech receives conspicuous emphasis throughout the text." Chapters on conversation, the voice, extending and accepting hospitality, at home, office, club and business are included. There is advice on informal correspondence, living with others and relevant readings. Includes index.

343 Gordon, Arthur. "Parent's Thoughts on Good Manners." Better Homes and Gardens, 42:112-3, Nov., 1964.
Outlines ten rules for implanting good manners in youngsters, including advice such as set a good example, respect the child's feelings and don't expect too much too soon. "Good manners are a form of self-discipline, which is a reassuring thing for a child...."

344 Goss, Dinah Braun, and Schwartz, Marla Schram. The Bride's Guide; The Perfect Wedding Planner. New York: Dembner Books, 1983.
Has worksheets to record information, articles to make planning easier, and advice on writing your own ceremony. Includes a countdown calendar, and a service guide which is designed to provide shopping ABC's for wedding expenditures. Advice is divided into two parts—the planning guide and the service guide. Includes many charts, lists, worksheets and illustrations. Indexed.

345 Gould, Kenneth M. "White House P's and Q's." Scholastic, 63:21, Dec. 9, 1953.
Describes a state dinner, and gives the evolution of the "Table of Precedence," which is the guide to rank in official Washington, D.C. The what and the why of the determination of rank is also explained.

346 Gould, Lois. "Good Manners for Liberated Persons." New York
Times Magazine, 24-5, Dec. 16, 1973.
The author feels that it is unfortunate that "etiquette is alive
and well in the age of liberation..." because the traditional
forms of etiquette are politically damaging to women.

347 Gow, Alexander Murdoch. Good Morals and Gentle Manners;
For Schools and Families. Cincinnati: American Book, 1901.
Gow "believes that all schools should be places of true refinement and elegant culture." Divided into three parts. Part I
is concerned with "Moral Law," and discusses, in 15 chapters,
topics such as good society, homicide, covetousness, business
and wisdom. Part II is "Municipal Law" which discusses patriotism, the duties of a citizen, and education. Part III is "Social
Law of Politeness," and has 14 chapters devoted to topics
such as cleanliness, dress, voice, gallantry and "The Educated
Countenance." Includes numerous verses, and anecdotes, and
has questions to be used as lessons at the bottom of each page.

348 "Graces of Yester; Soviet Union." Newsweek, 69:30, Jan. 9,
1967.
Describes current Soviet interest in improving their manners.

349 "Grammar and Courtesy." Outlook, 104:883, Aug. 23, 1913.
"The absence of politeness in directions to the public is still
more noticeable and the absence of the word 'please' is a lack
of courtesy significant of lack of respect for the public." Decries lack of grammar in public directional signs as well as
the lack of courtesy.

350 "Grand Manner." Scribners Magazine, 40:123-4, July, 1906.
Denounces the grand manner as responsible for "tyranny, class
inequality, and oppression..." in America, and contends that
Americans need not regret its disappearance.

351 Graves, Ralph. "Pleasant Friendly Sound of Good Manners ."
Life, 68:2A, June 19, 1970.
Managing editor's notes about the courtesy and goodwill of
people he met while travelling through the Southwest.

352 Gray, Winifred. You and Your Wedding. New York: Bantam,
1965.
Covers bridal procedures and etiquette including all matters
of dress, duties and responsibilities of everyone involved. Outlines different types of weddings, all types of announcements,
rules for divorced parents, parties, gifts and all other traditional
topics associated with weddings. Illustrated, includes sample
invitations, lists to use, and has index.

353 Green, Marylen. "Step Out with Ease." Better Homes and Gardens,
33:171, May, 1955.
Questions and answers about an evening out, wedding receptions,
and the theater.

354 Green, R.L. "New Etiquette; For Single Couples." Harper's Bazaar,
110:119, May, 1977.
Advises on the "new ethic--unmarried: living together..." and
how to deal respectfully with parents, the sexual etiquette
(fidelity), how to make introductions, and entertain. Also touches
upon finances and how to gracefully end a relationship.

355 Green, Walter Cox. The Book of Good Manners; A Guide to Polite Usage for All Social Functions. N.Y.: Social Mentor, 1922.
Dictionary format lists aspects of etiquette "in order to give the reader the desired information as briefly and clearly as possible...." Topics covered include public ball badges, how to address titled persons, cotillions, new acquaintances, patronesses, postal cards, street cars, and street etiquette.

356 Greenbie, Marjorie Barstow. "Why They Shock the World." Parents Magazine, 5:28-30, June, 1930.
Discusses the manners, morals and upbringing of young Americans and the impression they make abroad. Concerned that youth offend their foreign hosts by neglecting formalities, and show a disregard for "what constitutes decorum in older societies."

357 Greenblat, Cathy S., and Cottle, Thomas J. Getting Married. New York: McGraw-Hill, 1980.
Chapters discuss "The Desire to Marry—When Cohabitation Isn't Good Enough," "The Marriage Marketplace," "Designing the Perfect Wedding," and "First Doubts and Second Thoughts." Cites numerous quotations from real-life experiences, to support the stated purpose of "documenting and shedding light upon what people do, think, feel and experience during this important phase of their lives...."

358 Greer, Rebecca. Today's Woman Book for Brides. Greenwich, Conn.: Fawcett, 1965.
Discusses all aspects of weddings, including religious rules and rites, receptions, functions of the members of the wedding party, invitations, and acknowledging gifts. Lists things to do as advance preparation and what to do about flowers, photographs and publicity. Includes numerous photographs, charts, diagrams and lists. Designed to make the wedding day perfect in every way, for no "social custom is as deeply rooted in tradition and bound by convention as a wedding."

359 "Greeter to the World." Time, 64:29-30, Dec. 6, 1954.
Highlights the duties of John Farr Simmons, State Department Protocol Officer.

360 Greeting Card Association. Etiquette of Greeting Cards. New York: Greeting Card Association, 1924.
Gives rules defined by society which govern the use of greeting cards. Begins with a discussion of friendliness and the history of greetings. Tells how to address cards and correct forms of salutations, and lists days to be remembered.

Griggs, Lewis, joint author See Copeland, Lennie.

361 Gross, Amy, and Lovell, Amanda. "New Manners: What's Rude, What's Vulgar, What's Nice." Mademoiselle, 84:132-3, Feb., 1978.
Describes rude behavior such as smoking in the street, snapping gum, "talking dirty" and food-pushing. Also answers questions such as "Should one remove one's shades when being introduced?"

362 Gross, Mary Preston, and Fondren, Evelyn Baird. Mrs. Field Grade: Service Customs and Protocol for a Senior Wife. Chuluota, Fla.: Beau Lac, 1970.

Purpose is to help Mrs. Field Grade "on details concerning military protocol and customs...." Chapters advise on social functions, invitations, coffees, teas, official dinners, receptions, flag courtesy, calls, cards, dress, children and miscellaneous customs. Chapters begin with questions and answers, and continue with advice.

363 Gross, Mary Preston, and Johnson, Joyce. Mrs. NCO. Chuluota, Fla.: Beau Lac, 1969.

"If the wife is well informed as to what is expected of her, the probability is greater that her husband will have an easier and more successful career." Advice on social functions, dress, invitations, teas, receptions, flag courtesy, children, luncheons and dinners and the NCO Wives' Club. Chapters begin in question/answer format and continue with general advice. Includes sample invitations and suggested seating arrangements.

364 _____. The Officer's Family Social Guide. Chuluota, Fla.: Beau Lac, 1985.

"This book was written for people who want simple and direct answers to questions pertaining to military customs and traditions." Discusses traditions, flag courtesy, parades, reviews, invitations, social functions, luncheons and dinners, table manners, receptions, cards, dress and children. In question/answer format, includes samples of invitations, cards and seating arrangements.

365 Groth, Catherine D. "Does It Pay to Be Polite?" Harper's Weekly, 53:29, Dec. 11, 1909.

Laments that the polite person usually finds himself imposed upon. For example, "the disagreeable waiter often gets as big tips as the obliging one...."

366 Gruenberg, Sidonie M. "It Takes Time to Learn Good Manners." Parents Magazine, 35:52-3, Aug., 1960.

Suggests that parents keep their tempers, and mind their manners if they want their children to learn manners.

367 Guerrier, Edith. "Courtesy In Public Libraries." Library Journal, 67:11-3, Jan. 1, 1942.

Using specific instances of courteous behavior, the author supports her premise that courteous treatment of patrons adds to the prestige of the library.

368 "Guider; A. Vanderbilt." Time, 81:67, March 1, 1963.

Biographical sketch of Amy Vanderbilt includes her ideas about manners in an increasingly classless society.

369 Guitar, Mary Anne. "And Now a Word From the Youngsters." New York Times Magazine, 79-80, May 3, 1964.

Gives young people's view on manners, saying that what bothers young people most about adult manners is the implication that children don't count. This attitude is implied by adult behaviors such as yelling and not listening to children.

370 _____. "Can't the Pendulum Swing this Way?" American Home, 68:8, March, 1965.

Guitar wants to return to the days when life was a little less casual, even though formality takes just a little more time and trouble.

371 _____. "What Price, Good Manners?" American Home, 67:30, Sept., 1964.
Encourages parents to treat children with respect, saying that children best learn manners from the example their parents set.

372 Guiterman, Arthur. "Etiquette; Poem." American Magazine, 103:47, April, 1927.
Poem with message: "At home let native custom give the cue, In Rome we'll do as well-bred Romans do."

373 Gunn, Mary Kemper. A Guide to Academic Protocol. New York: Columbia University, 1969.
"Addressed primarily to those people on the newer campuses who are learning to cope with the preparations for public ceremonies." Outlines the protocol for lectures, teas, receptions, dinners, convocations, commencements and inauguration ceremonies. Includes advice on proper dress, and an appendix with a sample budget and check list.

Hackman, Susan D. See Bride's Magazine. New Bride's Book of Etiquette. (1981).

374 Hadida, Sophie C. Manners for Millions; A Correct Code of Pleasing Personal Habits for Everyday Men and Women. Garden City, N.Y.: Doubleday, Doran, 1932.
Comprehensive tome clearly outlines correct bathroom etiquette, use of the hankerchief, making one's toilet in public (with a lengthy discourse on shiny noses), spraying when talking and other topics not formally treated in many etiquette books. Objects to blowing out the candles on the birthday cake; "the germs from all the guests—out traveling on the cake. This act...is a vile one." Also gives comprehensive coverage of the do's and don'ts of correct behavior.

Hahner, Marcella Burns, joint author See Horan, Mrs. Kenneth.

375 Hall, Florence Marion (Howe). A-B-C of Correct Speech and the Art of Conversation. New York: Harper and Brothers, 1916.
Discusses the advantages of the English language, the use of foreign language in conversation, and lists three very serious objections to slang. Also discusses intonation and the incorrect use of words. Outlines the laws of conversation, and the qualities of a good talker, which are the power of thought, brevity and forcible expression. "While some of our modern conditions are unfavorable to the Art of Conversation...others are favorable. Chief among these are the increased intellectual activities and broadened sphere of women."

376 _____. "Are American Women's Manners Deteriorating?" Harper's Bazaar, 40:19-21, Jan., 1906.
Discussion centers on woman's position in society and how it has changed because of prosperity, greater involvement in sports and business, and the changing pace of life. These factors are examined in terms of their influence upon the manners of the American woman.

377 _____. The Correct Thing in Good Society. Boston: D. Estes, 1902.

Advice begins "At the Writing Desk" with a discussion of invitations, calls, conversation, speech and family. Manners at dinner, at the table, dance and afternoon tea are outlined. Consideration is also given to engagements, marriage, dress, travel, public manners, business, shopping, mourning, club, college and the woman's club. Under each topic, on opposing pages, are the headings, "It Is the Correct Thing" and "It Is Not the Correct Thing." "Our increasing familiarity with the customs of the older world, as well as the scientific tendency of the times, makes us more inclined to do all things 'exactly and in order'."

378 _____. "Etiquette for Men." Harper's Bazaar, 41:1095-7, Nov., 1907.
Instructs men on the customs of using cards and calling. Outlines the obligations for the bridegroom, and describes courteous behavior of a gentleman at his country club.

379 _____. "Etiquette of Sport." Harper's Bazaar, 42:1128-30, Nov., 1980.
"They must never forget the courtesy which an American man owes to women. Better lose a game or a set than fail in politeness toward a lady." Advice covers the game of golf, archery, automobiling, and croquet. When automobiling, "a good chauffeur does not constantly toot his horn."

380 _____. "Etiquette of Towns and Villages." Harper's Bazaar, 41:889-91, Sept., 1907.
Describes differences between town and city living, the former "must necessarily be simpler and less formal than that of large cities." Illustrates differences in behavior of dating, use of chaperone, at weddings, in times of grief and in dress.

381 _____. Good Form for All Occasions; A Manual of Manners, Dress and Entertainment for Both Men and Women. New York: Harper and Brothers, 1914.
Begins with advice on visiting a country house. Debutantes, dinners, weddings, balls, the etiquette for the hotel guest, the theater and the opera are all included in this comprehensive volume. Gives explicit details on automobile trips, including what to take, i.e., fur robes and goggles.

382 _____. A Handbook of Hospitality for Town and Country. Boston: D. Estes, 1909.
"The aim of this little book is to show forth...the true spirit of hospitality and to give hints for its exercise in accordance with present day customs." Covers picnics, weddings, visitors, house-parties, teas, luncheons, dinners, dances, musicals and theatricals, card parties and women's clubs. Also includes some "Novel Ideas for Patriotic Entertainments," and "Outgrown Ideals of Hospitality."

383 _____. "Manners in the 20th Century." Independent, 53:2703-6, Nov. 14, 1901.
Addresses the impact of prosperity on republican ideals, particularly attempts to "found an aristocracy in our beloved republic." The author is particularly concerned that this attempt is based upon material possessions rather than upon the virtues of manners and character.

384 _____. Social Customs. Boston: D. Estes, 1911.
There is great interest in social usage now "because the old
order of things is passing away." Gives a history of manners
and a discussion of society. Offers detailed advice on virtually
all aspects of etiquette, from visiting cards to musical parties
and gesture and carriage to country manners. One chapter
is called, "Pride and Parvenus," and another is "Washington
Customs." The author suggests that "as we assimilate the foreigner and make an American citizen of him, so we should
take the rules of behavior of older countries and times, and
shape out from these a code of good manners suited to our
great republic...."

385 _____. Social Usages at Washington. New York: Harper and
Brothers, 1906.
Describes present day usages at the White House, and discusses
the Roosevelt influence on entertaining. Chapters address
the etiquette of entertaining in the White House, precedence,
and military, congressional and presidential official etiquette.
Concludes with a discourse on the distinctive features of Washington society, and the historical contributions to society made
by a number of presidents. "The courtesies which are an indispensable part of civilized life, are of peculiar importance
in a national capital...."

386 Hallock, Virginia Lee, and Ferguson, Susan L. Charm and Charisma. Providence, R.I.: P.A.R., 1974.
Suggests charm and charisma can be acquired by an understanding of courtesy. Tells how to be a successful conversationalist,
and discusses etiquette in terms of male/female interaction,
table manners and the charming hostess. Tells how to succeed
in business by learning etiquette. Fashion etiquette for the
executive is outlined. Illustrated with drawings and photos.

387 Hamel, Marilyn. Sex Etiquette: Should I?, Can I?, May I?, Must
I?: The Modern Woman's Guide to Mating Manners. New York:
Delacorte, 1984.
Compendium of mating manners addresses the New Morality
by providing women with form and "accompanying standards
of conduct." The purpose of this book is to resurrect the virtue
of consideration while offering practical solutions to many
ticklish problems. In question/answer format, chapters cover
all aspects of mating from "Cruising Manners," to "Your Place
or Mine?," to "Transitions: Survival Decorum."

388 Hamman, Mary. The Mademoiselle Handbook; For the Girl With
a Job and a Future. New York: McGraw-Hill, 1946.
Advises a woman on how to decide on a job, or an education.
Tells how to behave at work and around other women and men.
Offers advice on life in the city, personal appearance, marriage
and children, and spending money. Illustrated.

389 Hammarstrom, David. "Coming to Grips." Atlantic, 240:84-5,
Aug., 1977.
Expresses uncertainty about the new handshakes, i.e., when
to use the new "soul shake," "hippie shake" or "what's happ'nin'
shake," and how to teach children which shake to use.

390 Handy, William M. Science of Culture. Garden City, N.Y.: Doubleday, 1923.
Four volume set discusses in great detail the acquisition of
culture, beginning with a definition of culture. The "Bodily
Expression of Culture" is examined in terms of outward appearance, poise, bearing and in meeting with other people. Relates
how people of culture conduct themselves in public, express
their thoughts, and how culture is evidenced in conversation.
Culture is further defined in terms of dining, dancing, entertaining, country life, sports and travel. How culture is expressed
in the home, in business and in personality is also revealed.
Includes illustrations, lists of how to eat certain foods, and
a discussion of the function of the American Society of Culture.
391 Hansl, Eva v B. "Beginning of Manners." Pictoral Review, 37:71,
Sept., 1936.
Defines manners as the combination of outward form and inner
attitudes, and suggests that parents use both firmness and
kindness to promote learning manners in children. Explains
that parents can promote positive inner attitudes by living
by the Golden Rule—the universal standard of good manners.
Harcourt, Charles, pseudonym See Forbes-Lindsay, Charles.
Harcourt, Mrs. Charles, pseudonym See Forbes-Lindsay, Margaret
Osborne.
392 Harding, T. Swann. "Why Don't They Fight Back?" Harper, 164:
633-6, April, 1932.
Tongue-in-cheek discourse about how businesses, sales clerks
and ticket agents won't fight back in response to the author's
provocative letters, which he lavishes with "satire and irony
to excess...," his contention being that "the average customer
likes to be fought with."
393 Hardy, Edward John. How to Be Happy Though Civil. New York:
Scribner, 1909.
Treatise on the true nature of courtesy. Through the use of
anecdotes illustrates true courtesy as sensitivity toward others.
Harland, Marion See Terhune, Mary Virginia (Hawes).
394 Harmon, Jeanette. "How Do You Do at Introducing?" Better
Homes and Gardens, 32:9, April, 1954.
Question/answer format tests knowledge of correct way to
make introductions.
395 Harmon, Nolan Bailey. Ministerial Ethics and Etiquette. Nashville:
Cokesbury, 1928.
"Taking thought for others is the essence of ministerial ethics
and etiquette." Uses the thoughts of many ministers, and "welds
them together in the heat of the Christian consciousness...."
Chapters are organized into discussions of "The Profession,"
"The Man," "The Citizen," "The Brother Minister," "The Pastor,"
"The Church," "Occasional Services," and "Clerical Dress."
Appendix reprints complete codes of behavior for ministers
from many different denominations. Includes bibliography
in introduction.
396 Harragan, Betty Lehan. "Beyond Etiquette." Working Woman,
10:86-8, Jan., 1985.

Advocates the use of rules of protocol to govern business behavior (as opposed to social etiquette) "as bias-free and gender-
neutral, so no better pattern exists for women in the work
world." Cites specific examples such as opening doors, standing,
shaking hands and in elevators in support of the premise.
Harral, Brooks, joint author **See** McCandless, Bruce.

397 Harral, Brooks J., and Swartz, Oretha. Service Etiquette. Annapolis, Md.: United States Naval Institute, 1959.
Addressed to those whose military career is in the Navy. The
instructions in manners are coordinated with the "dictates
of military tradition." Comprehensive in scope covering all
aspects of etiquette. Uniform charts, seating arrangement
diagrams, and diagrams for military weddings and funerals
are included. Do's and don'ts of saluting, forms of address
and flag etiquette are outlined.

398 _____. Service Etiquette. Annapolis, Md.: United States Naval
Institute, 1963.
The second edition is expanded to include all branches of the
military.

399 Harriman, Grace (Carley). Mrs. Oliver Harriman's Book of Etiquette, A Modern Guide to the Best Social Form. New York:
Greenberg, 1942.
Guide has samples of correspondence, and sample menus
for entertaining, with recipes included. Lists requirements
for the well-tended bar, table-setting and the linen closet.
Some of the chapters included are "The Etiquette of Bridge
and Other Games," "Recipes for Social Success," "Army and
Navy Etiquette," "Are Chaperones Dated?," and "State Etiquette." There is a glossary of French terms, and miscellaneous
questions are answered in an appendix. Indexed.

400 Harriman, Margaret Case. "Don't Call Me Lady Chesterfield;
10-minute Biography of Emily Post." Good Housekeeping, 112:34,
June, 1941.
Glimpses of Post's private life and a brief discussion of her
fiction. Gives Post's reaction to being a social arbiter.

401 Harris, Mrs. L.H. "Southern Manners." Independent, 61:321-5,
Aug. 9, 1906.
Contends Southern manners are based on what their heritage
is: "the profounder self-consciousness of what they have been.
This greatly increases their capacity for manners...."

402 Harris, Marlys. "Ms. Money's Guide to Absolutely Correct Financial Manners." Money, 12:205-6, May, 1983.
Ms. Money answers questions such as what to do if you break
a Meissen vase worth $365.00, whether or not you may ask
for someone's broker's name and other sticky money situations.

403 Harrison, Barbara Grizzuti. "This Column Is About Manners.
Please Read It. Thank You Very Much." Mademoiselle, 91:114,
Oct., 1985.
Describes her philosophy of what constitutes good manners,
and cites in a partial listing, that behavior which she cannot
tolerate.

404 Hart, Annetta. "Manners and the Man." Woman's Home Companion,
     72:110-11, Feb., 1945.
     Question/answer format, covers subjects such as introductions,
     dining-out, dancing and walking.
405 "Has the American Bad Manners?" Ladies' Home Journal, 17:19,
     Nov., 1900.
     An American mother focuses on the bad manners of Americans.
     She compares English and American behavior, with the Ameri-
     cans held to be generally less well-behaved than their English
     counterparts.
406 "Haste and Manners." Outlook, 66:390-1, Oct. 13, 1900.
     The fine trait of courtesy that Americans exhibit is being
     lost through haste: "to be in a hurry is to be unable to give
     others that attention which is the soul of good manners." Cites
     the trolley-car as foe to courtesy, contending "there is nothing
     so objectionable as such a crowding of people as puts them
     into uncomfortable physical contact with one another.
407 Hathaway, Charles B. "Good Manners, Extra Dividends." Rotarian,
     54:8-10, May, 1939.
     Suggests that manners can be a profitable asset, supporting
     the premise with examples from the business world and with
     the philosophies of successful business people.
     Hathaway, Helen, pseudonym See Durham, Helen.
408 Hawkes, Evelyn. Social Training as a Curriculum Problem. Phila-
     delphia, 1927.
     Thesis in education "will attempt to discover the extent to
     which individuals acquire the ability to meet social situations
     through the ordinary processes of life." Contents include a
     preliminary study for analysis of social contacts, an analysis
     of general social contacts, formulation of a survey test, deter-
     mination of standards of social conduct, results of the survey
     and a summary of the investigation. Also includes bibliography.
409 Hayes, Mary Jane. "How Launch Drivers See You." Motor Boating
     and Sailing, 151:100, June, 1983.
     Anecdotes from launch drivers from the Northeast Coast which
     illustrates both good and bad behavior.
410 Head, Gay. "Talking It Over with Gay Head; Table Manners."
     Senior Scholastic, 85:34, Nov. 18, 1964.
     An alphabet of table manners, i.e., A is for the American way
     of cutting meat, through Z, for the zeal you display in observing
     good manners.
411 Hearst, Bunky. "On the Water, Discretion Is the Safest Part
     of Valor." Motor Boating and Sailing, 150:80, Sept., 1982.
     Describes how boating courtesy really works, particularly
     in terms of boating safety.
     Heaton, Rose Henniker See Henniker Heaton, Rose.
412 Helgesen, Sally. "The Secret of Good Manners." McCall's, 110:52,
     May, 1983.
     Contrasts the difference between propriety—doing things the
     right way, and real manners—which "are of the spirit." Encour-
     ages readers to have the confidence to set aside the rule book
     and open one's heart and think of other people.

413 Henderson, Ophelia Koontz. Success by Telephone. Fort Scott, Kan.: The Author, 1954.
Book is designed to help people learn how to use the telephone effectively in business and in social life. Discusses the telephone as a communication tool, as a conqueror of distance, a selling tool as a career opportunity. "Telephone Techniques" describes behavior and attitudes a good user should have. Includes bibliographies.

414 Henney, Nella (Braddy). Book of Business Etiquette. Garden City, N.Y.: Nelson Doubleday, 1922.
Discourse on business etiquette, table manners, telephones, writing, morals and manners. The author instructs through the use of anecdotes and by quoting poetry. Gives some very specific instruction to the travelling salesman and to the employer about the treatment of employees. Suggests "good salesmanship relates the product to the customer, and does it in such a way that the customer is hardly aware of how it is done."

415 _____. "What People Want to Know About Etiquette; Interview with Lillian Eichler." American Magazine, 103:46-7, April, 1927.
Lillian Eichler tells about the questions she receives in the hundreds of letters she receives daily asking her advice about etiquette.

416 Henniker Heaton, Rose. The Perfect Hostess. Decorated by Alfred E. Taylor, introduction by Frank Crowinshield. New York: E.P. Dutton, 1931.
Offers humorous advice to the hostess, such as the advisability of having plenty of coat hangers and matches on hand. Includes sample menus for a variety of situations, from serving dinner to the prime minister, to serving tea to the country cousins. Includes ideas for children's parties. Recipes, verses and line drawings included throughout.

417 Henry, Carl F.H. "Evangelical Tongues at 10:50; Church Etiquette." Christianity Today, 21:20-1, June 3, 1977.
Laments the "tornado of chatter" which occurs before church and into the worship service.

418 Henry, Sarepta Myrenda. Good Form and Christian Etiquette. Battle Creek, Mich.: Review and Herald, 1900.
Examines the relationship between social manners and Christianity. Offers advice on how to teach manners to young people, and how to teach children deference to their elders. Manners in public places, gifts, kissing, and conversation are discussed. Concludes with questions and answers about all aspects of good form.

419 Herendeen, Anne. "New Days and Knights." Parents Magazine, 5:24-5, Sept., 1930.
Discusses the practice of modern day chivalry—that which protects and aids women and that which preserves the pleasant social amenities, and the effects of this artificial code upon children's character. For example, the young girl is quick to see she has an advantage "which she did not sustain by her own merits." Suggests that adults "disregard sex chivalry alto-

gether until the natural reticences of approaching puberty
set the child himself hunting for a new code of behavior...."

420 Herrick, Christine Terhune. "Cards and Calling." Woman's Home
Companion, 38:32, Nov., 1911.
Outlines proper procedure when making calls, and tells of
the proper use of cards.

421 _____. "Etiquette of a Formal Dinner." Woman's Home Companion, 38:35, Oct., 1911.
Describes in detail the proper table service and use of each
particular utensil at a formal dinner.

422 _____. "Etiquette of Weddings." Woman's Home Companion,
38:23, June, 1911.
Advises on details of a wedding such as the proper wording
for invitations, the correct dress, music, flowers, refreshments,
the bridegroom's family, church weddings, and home weddings.

423 _____. "Every-day Table Manners." Woman's Home Companion,
38:45, Jan., 1911.
Points out that the "knife is to cut with, the fork is to be used
in eating." Cites the "demon of haste" as a destroyer of table
decorum, and suggests that the same manners used at home
should be company manners as well.

424 _____. "Girls Engagement and Marriage; The Simple Rules
of Etiquette." Woman's Home Companion, 41:25, Nov., 1914.
Outlines what is expected of the bride and her family for a
wedding, with practical advice on the trousseau and furnishing
the new household.

425 _____. "Girl's Good Manners." Woman's Home Companion,
38:31, March, 1911.
Defines acceptable modes of behavior for young girls, emphasizing behavior in public.

426 _____. "Hostess and Her Guests." Woman's Home Companion,
40:45, Dec., 1913.
Suggestions for the hostess on making guests feel comfortable
on social occasions. Advises the guest on responsibility of
consideration.

427 Hick, H.J. "Check Your Etiquette." Ladies' Home Journal, 50:94,
Sept., 1933.
Hints for a variety of situations, i.e., a lady walks on the right
side of her man, and the perennial wedding bouquet snatcher
should let someone else have a turn.

Hickey, Dorothy Coffin, joint author See Wier, Ester.

428 Hicks, J. Allan. "Don't Nag About Manners." Parents Magazine,
6:20-1, Sept., 1931.
Encourages parents not to force adult expectations on their
children simply to avoid their own embarrassment. Suggest
that "continued insistence upon non-essential conventions is
just another source...of conflict and strain between parents
and children." Offers the solution that parents should give
children a good role model instead of insistence on social form.

429 Hidden, Julia A. "Teaching Children Manners." Home Progress,
3:380-2, April, 1914.
Suggests the atmosphere at home can either aid or retard

the growth of courtesy in children. Stories can be a tool in developing thoughtfulness and kindness, and lists specific stories.

430 Higginson, Thomas Wentworth. "Gentlemen by Profession." Independent, 60:850-4, April 12, 1906.
Compares English and American society using the English perception of a gentleman as a basis to do so.

431 Hill, Jeanne. "That Night Jim Stayed to Supper." Reader's Digest, 107:195-6, Nov., 1975.
Story which illustrates the moral: "There ain't nothing more to good manners than making the other person feel at ease."

432 Hill, Margaret. "Is Your Youngster a Welcome Guest?" Nat. Parent Teach., 52:31-2, Dec., 1957.
How the author taught manners to her six year old, with the cooperation of his two older sisters.

433 Hines, Sally. Good Manners in a Nut Shell. Oklahoma City, Okla.: Nut Shell, 1941.
Question/answer format covers customs of men, women and children, introductions, christenings, funerals, telephone correspondence, and White House and official etiquette. Correct behavior for the host, at formal and informal dinners, weddings, on trains, busses and airplanes is included. Club etiquette, and customs of sorority and fraternity houses are included. Occasionally illustrated with photos. Includes chart for tipping, and a chart for "The Correct Way to Write and Speak to Official People of Distinction."

434 Hodge, Harriet Mason. "This Way to Courtesy." Parents Magazine, 15:23, June, 1940.
Suggests parents teach children how to behave in social situations by playing out the situation with them, so that they are able to develop good manners with practice.

435 Hodges, Donald Clark. Ethics and Manners. Ann Arbor, University Microfilms, 1954.
Theory of manners that: "The common essence of manners is the expression of appearance of the ethical." Describes the literature of manners as highly specialized, falling into social, humanistic and technical studies, and that the philosophy of manners serves to integrate these studies.

Hofsess, John, joint author See Crisp, Quentin.

436 Holt, Emily. Encyclopedia of Etiquette; What to Write, What to Do, What to Wear, What to Say. Garden City, N.Y.: Doubleday Page, 1901.
Chapters offer advice on introductions, cards, calling, table manners, balls, dances, luncheons, theater, house parties, receptions and musicales. Describes the etiquette for engagements, weddings, christenings, and funerals. "Bachelor Hospitalities" are discussed, as is proper deportment in public places, when travelling or in the club. Additional topics elucidated are children, servants, and correspondence. Index and illustrations.

437 _____. Encyclopedia of Etiquette; What to Write, What to Do, What to Wear, What to Say. Garden City, N.Y.: Doubleday, Page, 1915.

Second edition revised. "Fundamentally, however, in the laws that regulate manners, little change has taken place." Little change is evident in the second edition.

438 _____. Encyclopedia of Etiquette; What to Write, What to Do, What to Wear, What to Say. Garden City, N.Y.: Doubleday, Page, 1923.
Third edition carefully updated "in order to record the variations in the customs of society and respond to the ever-increasing demands for a responsible guide in the graceful practice of the social amenities." Examines change in dress, balls, dances and other changes which "prosperity and the automobile have wrought...."

439 "Home Front Memo; True Anecdotes of Courteous Service in Wartime." Rotarian, 66:15, April; 31, May; 21, June; 67:19, July; 21, Aug.; 27, Sept., 1947.
Series of true stories of courteous behavior encountered by people all over the country.

440 "Home Truths from Abroad." Collier's, 114:90, Dec. 16, 1944.
Examines the American perception that "politeness demeans a free-born American..." and suggests this notion may "bring their practitioners much needless grief...."

441 Hopkins, Mary Alden. Profits from Courtesy; Handbook of Business Etiquette. New York: Doubleday, Doran, 1937.
Begins with a general discussion of the advantages courtesy brings to business, and methods of training employees. Specific advice is tailored to specific professions such as office workers, delivery service, gasoline station attendants, beauty-parlours, retail selling, hotels and restaurants and theater employees. Also advises on employees' uniforms, techniques complaint clerks and managers can utilize in dealing with people, and on training the public in manners. Illustrated. "Large concerns have discovered that courtesy takes less time in the long run than discourtesy."

442 _____. "Youth Shapes Its Social Code." Parents Magazine, 9:20-1, Aug., 1934.
Maintains that the social code of the young must necessarily be dissimilar to earlier codes, partly because of technology and changing social structures, i.e., the decrease of servants and the necessity of nearly all girls going to work. Describes courses in manners added to high school curriculum and what young people want to learn from these courses.

443 Horan, Mrs. Kenneth, and Hahner, Marcella Burns. 100 Points in Etiquette and 101 Don'ts. New York: Grosset and Dunlap, 1929.
List of do's covers traditional topics found in most etiquette, i.e., introductions, invitations, luncheons, weddings and table manners. Don'ts are generally focused on deportment in public. There is an appendix of don'ts for bridge and golf. Includes index.

444 Horosko, Marian. "Open Letter; About Autograph Hounds." Dance Magazine, 32:29, Dec., 1958.

Discusses the autograph seeker "from the other side of the footlights..." and makes suggestions to them, requesting basic consideration for the performer, i.e., don't push and shove, always have pen and paper, etc.

445 Horwill, Herbert W. "Revolution in City Manners." Harper's Weekly, 47:2056, Dec. 19, 1903.
Discusses impact of modern conditions in urban living upon the manners of city dwellers.

446 Hosmer, Frank Alvan. Manners Maketh Man: An Address by F.A. Hosmer, Delivered Before the Students of Oahu College, June 20, 1900. Honolulu, Hawaiian Gazette, 1900.
College president calls upon students to "let the moral tone of the school be against rudeness." Gives historical concept of Noblesse Oblige, and cites Japanese politeness as exemplary.

447 "How Custom Governs the Use of Visiting Cards and Calls." Good Housekeeping, 86:61, April, 1928.
Historical perspective of cards and callings as well as advice on the various uses of cards and how they should be printed.

448 "How I Trained My Boys to Be Gentlemen." As told by their mother. Ladies' Home Journal, 26:28, March, 1909.
Believing that "breeding in courtesy should be started early..." outlines the first act of courtesy this mother taught her sons.

449 "How Shall Letters to People of Standing Be Addressed?" Harpers, 116:148-51, Dec., 1907.
Discussion of correct address to use to those in a greater station in life, as well as to each other.

449a "How to Butter an Ear of Corn and Other Dining Dilemmas." Glamour, 85:290-1, Aug., 1987.
Illustrated article tells how to cope with problems which may arise when eating, such as what to do to stop a beer from overflowing, or how to eat a taco without making a mess.

450 "How to Eat Hard-to-handle Food." Good Housekeeping, 170:174, May, 1970.
How to eat shrimp cocktail, lobster, artichokes, whole fish, steamed clams and other difficult foods.

451 "How to Handle Anything on the Menu. Better Homes and Gardens, 49:107, April, 1971.
How to eat lobster and crab, clams and oysters, escargot, fried chicken, and more.

452 "How to Sponsor a New Ship: Etiquette Hints for Christening." Life, 11:79-82, Nov. 17, 1941.
Pictures illustrate correct attire, stance, grasp of bottle and general deportment for those who plan to sponsor a new ship.

453 "How to Succeed in Business by Polishing Your Manners." US News and World Report, 45, Oct. 28, 1985.
Interview with Letitia Baldrige, etiquette authority, focusing on office manners.

454 Howard, Clifford. "How Some Familiar Things Came to Be." Ladies' Home Journal, 17:2, June, 1900.
Traces the origins of a pot-pourri of customs, sayings and everyday items, such as Christmas customs, marriage customs and shaking hands.

455 Howard, Lois. "How Do You Do, Junior?" Woman's Home Companion, 72:114-5, Nov., 1945.
   Lists do's and don'ts for grown-ups when interacting with children. "Grown-ups who consider a youngster's feelings will find that children reflect their courtesy."

456 Howe, Maud. "Importance of Good Manners." Harper's Bazaar, 41:1233-5, Dec., 1907.
   Illustrates the need for good manners using several anecdotes. Encourages Americans to adopt the French motto, Noblesse Oblige.

457 _____. "Visits and Visiting." Harper's Bazaar, 42:1241-3, Dec., 1908.
   "Busy people have a most fatal attraction for the idle." Fewer women are able to give the time to punctilious visiting their mothers gave. Society generously concedes the working woman and does not demand 'quid pro quo' of calling and card leaving.

458 _____. "What Is a Lady?" Harper's Bazaar, 43:179-82, Feb., 1909.
   "It is not much easier to truly be a lady than it is to be truly a Christian." Lists tips on how to be a lady, including a few don'ts.

459 Howells, W.D. "Politeness to Servants." Harpers, 116:309-12, Jan., 1908.
   Discussions around motives of employers who expect "respect as well as love, the sort of thing that money used to buy..." and their attitude toward servants.

460 Howitt, Florence. "How to Behave in Public Without an Escort." Good Housekeeping, 117:40, Sept., 1943.
   Gives few fundamentals on going out without an escort, such as don't overdress, don't drink, and don't flirt with stag parties.

461 _____. "Place for the Extra Women." Good Housekeeping, 120:29, April, 1945.
   Tips for the woman who finds herself the third wheel, including don't feel sorry for yourself, and don't hurl yourself at a man who casually joins the party.

462 "How's Your Etiquette?" Changing Times, 12:46, Jan., 1958.
   22 true/false questions to test etiquette knowledge.

463 How's Your Telephone Personality?" Better Homes and Gardens, 32:136, May, 1954.
   28 questions/answers illustrate good telephone manners.

464 Hoyt, Mrs. Lydig. "How to Avoid Social Blunders." American Magazine, 93:34-5, Jan., 1922.
   Detailed instructions for making introductions, walking, smoking, cards and calling, invitations and other points of etiquette.

465 Hulbert, Ann. "Why Manners Matter." New Republic, 187:24-7, Dec. 6, 1982.
   Discussion of manners centers on a comparison of Miss Manners' Guide to Excruciatingly Correct Behavior by Judith Martin and The History of Manners and Power and Civility, both by Norbert Elias, and refers to other arbiters as well.

466 Hunt, Effie Harder. How to Have a Perfect Wedding. New York: Frederick Fell, 1969.

How to announce engagements, plan a wedding calendar, choose a trousseau and the duties of the wedding parties are given. Also tells what the monetary obligations of both parties are, and discusses different kinds of weddings. Illustrated.

467 Hunter, Lucretia P. "Laboratory Method for Social Guidance." Educational Review, 75:30-4, Jan., 1928.
Describes technique employed to teach manners in the classroom, and the evolution of informal chats with students into an organization designed solely for teaching social skills.

468 Hutten, Joanna. "How Good Are Your Manners?" Better Homes and Gardens, 25:94, Oct., 1946.
20 questions test basic knowledge of good manners.

469 Huttenlocker, Fae. "How to Set a Company Table; With Answers to Most-Asked Questions on Serving." Better Homes and Gardens, 26:46-7, March, 1948.
Illustrated with photos, author suggests planning a company dinner with guest's convenience in mind.

470 _____. "Let's Have a Cup of Coffee." Better Homes and Gardens, 26:48-9, Jan., 1948.
In question/answer format, tells how to serve coffee in formal and informal settings.

471 Ide, Emily Katherine. Etiquette and Ceremonies of the Stars and Stripes; National and Personal Salute Required by United States Army Regulations. Boston, nd, 1915.
Etiquette of raising and lowering the flag, the hand flag salute, oral flag salute and how to portray, display and use the flag on different occasions is given. Also includes a general discussion of flags and a biography of Francis Scott Key.

472 "Importance of Good Manners." Literary Digest, 116:20, Dec. 2, 1933.
Discussion of the lack of good manners among American youth. Included is a discussion of a questionnaire sent to youth about table manners by Dr. Ruth Strang, Assistant Professor of Education at Teacher's College, Columbia University.

473 "Improvement in Box Office Manners Would Help to Revitalize Playgoing." Saturday Evening Post, 225:12, Jan. 31, 1953.
Asserts that in order to improve attendance at theaters, it would behoove management to examine the manners of the box office salesmen.

474 "Improving One's Neighbors." Independent, 61:165-6, July 12, 1906.
Encourages Americans to accept the instructions of the British on matters such as "the ways of good society..." because "England is socially older than America."

475 "Indirect Etiquette." Scribners Magazine, 38:634-5, Nov., 1905.
Protests novelists presumption in instructing the reader in etiquette, disguising the instruction within the context of the literary work.

476 "Informal Tuition in Courtesy." School Review, 42:164, March, 1934.
Outlines campaign developed at Central High School in Minneapolis for teaching manners.

Innis, Pauline, joint author **See** McCaffree, Mary.

477 "Interracial Etiquette." America, 112:796, May 29, 1965.
Proposes five basic rules of communications etiquette by Fr. Albert S. Foley of Springhill College for use in mediating interracial relations.

478 Irwin, John Webb. Manners and Personality in School and Business; A Brief Handbook for Students in High Schools and Business Colleges. Delaware, Ohio: School and College Service, 1938.
Designed to offer sane guidance based on "very definite realities in life." For use as text in business colleges, each chapter ends with questions and topics for use in discussion. Covers manners and personality, conduct at school, social customs, table manners, dress and appearance, business etiquette, tact, and conversation. Includes bibliography.

479 Irwin, T.D. "Doctor of Courtesy." Woman's Journal, ns, 15:46, Dec., 1930.
Introduces Joan Wing, originator of a courtesy system which upbuilds good will among business. Tells how Wing's success grew, citing her contention that "courtesy is the cheapest commodity on the market...."

480 "Is Chivalry Dead?" Outlook, 126:611-3, Dec. 1, 1920.
Defends males as courteous, and declares there is no deterioration in manners because of men, and if there has been it is because "so many women show not the slightest appreciation of the courtesy."

480a Ishige, Naomichi. "(Table) Manners Makyth Man." Courier, 40:18-21, May, 1987.
Offers an anthropological perspective on the importance of mealtime in the development of man, and suggests that the rules each society has which govern eating behavior may be "the outward sign of the power of either the head of the family or of religion." Suggests that table manners were established as a means of keeping order. Concludes by saying that even in our technologically advanced society, the preservation of the common, i.e., family, meal is important, since it still offers "the opportunity to confirm membership of the group."

481 Jacobs, Jay. Winning the Restaurant Game. Drawings by Ronald Searle. New York: McGraw-Hill, 1980.
After defining the game of dining out, Jacobs instructs those who want to win the game with assurance and panache. Likens winning the game to winning at any other sport, and tells how to gain the home-field advantage. Gives advice on ordering from French and Italian menus, includes a "Pronouncing Glossary of Essential World Menu Lingo," and a chapter on wines. Much detail is given to definitions of menu items. Describes the five stimuli which impel people to restaurants as pleasure, prestige, profit, obligation and seduction.

482 Jaine, Barbara. The Wedding Book; A Dream Come True; A Wedding Guide for the Ecstatic Bride to Be. Beaverton, Ore.: Wedding Belles, 1983.
Discusses all aspects of weddings, from the engagement, deciding on a style of wedding, a date, to the reception. Advice ranges

from planning the ceremony to how to deal with step-parents and special people. Details the dress for the bride, groom and attendants. Examines professional services such as the florist, caterer, musicians and photographer. Appendix describes financial responsibilities and has a planning calendar schedule. Illustrated.

483 _____. The Wedding Planner: A Dream Come True; A Wedding Planner for the Ecstatic Bride to Be. Beaverton, Ore.: Wedding Belles, 1983.
Chiefly a book of forms to be used in order to insure a smoothly run wedding. There are forms for finances, flowers, music, wedding cake, stationery, trousseau, guest list and honeymoon plans, and more.

484 James, Barry. A Man's Guide to Business and Social Success. Bronx, N.Y.: Milady, 1966.
"Even the most considerate person needs to learn the rules of society." Contends appearance is the key to acceptance and devotes units to the topics of grooming, wardrobe and physical fitness. Business etiquette and the social graces are units which address the "techniques of social custom." Includes advice on telephone manners, oral communication, the psychology of success, salesmanship, public relations and relaxation. Has check-lists, illustrations, charts, quizzes and an index.

485 James, Henry. "The Manners of American Women." Harper's Bazaar, 41:355-9, April; 537-41, May; 646-51, June, 1907.
Lengthy discourse on the state of manners among American women cites innumerable examples, so that "one's speculation" will not "lose itself in any whole view of the state, of the visible cultivation or the visible neglect, of the amenities."

486 Jankowic, Elena, and Bernstein, Sandra. Behave Yourself; The Working Guide to Business Etiquette. Englewood Cliffs, N.J.: Prentice-Hall, 1986.
First chapter describes five myths about business etiquette and tells how to stand out in a corporate crowd (adverse behavior). The "Rules of the Game" are outlined, and the corporate network of top management, peer relationships and subordinates, clients, suppliers and families is examined. Effective communication is defined in terms of introductions, visitors, meetings and other situations. Table manners, restaurant savoir-faire, women in business, and corporate travel etiquette are additional topics covered. Offers advice on international protocol for a number of countries, and concludes with questions/answers on a miscellany of topics. Indexed.

487 Jerome, Sally (Hunter), and Shea, Nancy Brinton. Marine Corps Wife. New York: Harper, 1955.
Explicit instructions to the bride of a Marine including the military custom of paying calls. Advice covers giving parties, joining clubs, budgeting, training children in manners and travelling. Includes brief history of the Marine Corps and an explanation of the importance of tradition in the military. Includes lists and diagrams as needed.

488 Jeune, Mary. "Decay of the Chaperone." <u>Living Age</u>, 227:372-9, Nov. 10, 1900.
Predicts young generation will play an increasingly prominent part in the intellectual and social life of the twentieth century. Calls the "new independence of women..." the cause for all the social changes at present and says, "Let us cherish our belief...that the dethronement of the chaperone is only temporary and not a visible and outward sign of her decay."

489 Johnson, Chet. "Victim Looks at Huckleby Fever; Bungling of Introductions." <u>Rotarian</u>, 52:26-8, March, 1938.
Huckleby Fever is defined by example, having to do with screwy behavior.

490 Johnson, Dorothea. <u>Entertaining and Etiquette for Today</u>. Washington, D.C.: Acropolis, 1979.
Aimed at today's casual lifestyle. Topics include introductions, handshaking, invitations, correspondence, table manners, pet etiquette, children, telephones, anniversaries, weddings, dress, guests and living abroad. There is a section called "Easy Entertaining" which gives directions for buffet suppers in great detail. An appendix called "A Party Record" has forms for organizing a party. Includes illustrations and an index.

Johnson, Joyce, joint author **See** Gross, Mary Preston.

Johnstone, Elizabeth, joint author **See** Ritter, T.M.

491 Jonathan, Norton Hughes. <u>Guide Book for the Young Man About Town</u>. New York: Winston, 1948.
Author's intent is to give the young man self-confidence in any social situation. Advises on what to do and say on innumerable social occasions, including making dates, conversing with girls, giving parties, sending flowers and driving automobiles.

492 Jones, Elmer C. "Train Leaders and Courses in Etiquette Conversation and Discussion." <u>School Life</u>,16:197, June, 1931.
Reviews teacher training courses which are focusing on etiquette at Long Beach, California adult education classes.

493 Jones, Pamela. "Et-i-quette: The Happy Way of Doing Things." <u>American Home</u>, 68:33, March, 1965.
Discusses the casual way of modern living and the current mood of rush and pressure, and these influences upon manners.

Judge, Lucille, joint author **See** Bennett, Marilyn.

494 "Just a Minute, Please!" <u>System</u>, 35:836-7, May, 1919.
Wonders how often the distance separating people on the telephone accomodates itself to discourtesy, and cites examples of business lost because of bad telephone manners.

495 Kandaouroff, Beris. <u>Art of Living; Etiquette for the Permissive Age</u>. Secaucus, N.J.: Citadel, 1972.
Addressed primarily to women with the contention that courtesy can be a powerful weapon in a woman's arsenal. Advises on points of etiquette in interpersonal relations as a means to self-improvement. A chapter called "Love, Men and Marriage" describes how women should relate to men, including how to be unfaithful and what to do if you want a gigolo. Families, entertaining, household management, travel, money, business, and pastimes are additional topics covered.

496 Kansas. State College of Agriculture and Applied Science. De-
      partment of Food Economics and Nutrition. Practical Cookery
      and the Etiquette and Service of the Table. Manhattan, Kan.:
      The Department, 1941.
      Second half of book discusses table etiquette, beginning with
      advice about invitations. Continues with description of seating
      arrangements, general deportment at the table, and the use
      of the napkin, knife, fork, and spoon. Also tells how to arrange
      the table, and describes serving and the duties of the waitress.
      Family dinners, buffets, receptions and community meals are
      discussed. Indexed and illustrated with photos and diagrams.
497 Karma, Inez. "Cocktail Party Namesmanship; Embarrassment
      of Forgotten Names." New York Times Magazine, 78, March
      18, 1956.
      Humorous article, in which the author relates how to avoid
      the embarrassment of forgotten names by using "Eleven Methods
      of Introduction" which includes techniques such as mumble-clar-
      ity, sneaky-avoid, or the outer-space ruse.
498 Katz, Lilian G. "Manners 1A." Parents Magazine, 59:114, Aug.,
      1984.
      Advice on teaching basic manners to children, and how to
      handle the occasional slip-up.
499 _____. "Social Graces for Beginners." Parents Magazine,
      56:92, April, 1981.
      How to teach social graces to young children and when to
      and when not to scold or correct behavior.
500 _____. "Well, Excuse Me!" Parents Magazine, 61:248, Nov.,
      1986.
      Offers practical advice on how to teach manners to 3 and
      4 year olds, such as well-mannered parents provide the best
      teaching method, and don't try to extort manners from your
      child.
501 Kelly, Fred C. "Courtesy in Business." American Magazine,
      81:11-13, May, 1916.
      Relates stories about sales clerks and railroad employees which
      illustrate the advantage to business of having considerate,
      courteous employees.
502 Kelly, Rene. "Commerce and Courtesy." Harper's Weekly, 62:308,
      March 25, 1916.
      Suggests that Americans are setting a higher value upon courtesy,
      and that value should be regarded as a cash asset as well as
      a social lubricant.
503 Kerr, Sophie. "It's Not in the Etiquette Books, But—." Woman's
      Home Companion, 55:9, Jan., 1928.
      Elaborates on the rudeness of talking shop to professionals
      at social gatherings. Laments the telephone as a tool for solicit-
      ing charitable contributions, and for issuing invitations.
504 Keun, Odette. "Sorry, Madam, Thank You Madam; Perennial
      Politeness of the English People." Reader's Digest, 29:85-6,
      Sept., 1926.
      Reflections on the politeness of the English people, based
      upon the author's experiences.

505 Keyes, Mary Willard. "Teaching Good Manners to Children."
Home Progress, 1:9-13, June, 1912.
Outlines specific program for parents to use in teaching the
qualities of kindness, thoughtfulness and sincerity to children.
506 King, Henry Churchill. "What Are Good Manners?" Delineator,
88:8, June, 1916.
Author's thoughts on "the science and philosophy of good manners...," which include a definition of a gentleman, the value
of positive ideals, and the golden rule of unselfishness.
507 King, Mrs. John Alexander. "America Changes Her Table Manners; The Vogue of Eating in the European Way." Delineator,
109:24, Nov., 1926.
Instructions on eating the European way. "The chief changes
from the old and more provincial ways of eating introduce
ease by decreasing numerous fussy movements and emphasize
daintiness by increasing the number of utensils used."
508 _____. "Good Manners and the Fork." Delineator, 110:50,
April, 1927.
Illustrated, greatly detailed discussion of forks, with suggestions
for use of the fish fork, fruit fork, tea fork, ramekin fork.
509 King, Steve. "It Pays to Be Polite; Cross-country Tourist in
the Make-yourself-at-home Towns." American Magazine, 130:39,
Nov., 1940.
Suggests that courteous behavior to town visitors has a pay-off
in monetary advantages.
510 Kingsland, Florence. The Book of Good Manners; Etiquette
for All Occasions. New York: Doubleday, Page, 1901.
Comprehensive volume covers etiquette from introductions
to afternoon teas. Tells how to introduce a debutante, and
use a chaperone. Gives proper procedure for weddings and
engagements. Tells how to behave at the opera and theater.
Other topics include entertaining, guests, dress and deportment,
table manners, conversation, manners in public, sporting etiquette, children, funerals, and christenings, servants, and "Hints
of Foreign Etiquette." Includes index.
511 _____. The Book of Weddings; A Complete Manual of Good
Form in All Matters Connected with the Marriage Ceremony.
New York: Doubleday, Page, 1902.
Illustrated volume describes etiquette for weddings in great
detail. Begins with "A Forward to the Bride" and "A Word
to the Bridegroom." Advice covers naming the wedding day,
preparations and expenses, the gown and accessories, the trousseau and proper forms for invitations and announcements. Dress
and duties of the attendants is outlined. Rehearsal, music
decorations, receptions, types of weddings, second marriages,
wedding guests and a description of how other people marry
are additional topics included.
512 _____. "Prevailing Etiquette for Young Men." Ladies' Home
Journal, 17:22, Oct., 1900.
Directs young men in the choice of proper clothing, in deportment in public places and in society's expectations.

513 Klein, Elinor. "Welcome but Warning." Harper's Bazaar, 103:84-5, Aug., 1970.
Suggests that, apart from traditional visiting etiquette, her guests are welcome to offer a helping hand, and addresses guest issues such as dieting, bad weather and invitations.

513a Klinkenborg, Verlyn. "Bug Slaying and Other Minor Chivalries for the Man of the Eighties." Glamour, 85:390, Sept., 1987.
Examines bug killing as a minor chivalry, outlining one principle rule of chivalry as that which "states that a man must accept whatever interpretation the woman he's about to assist places upon the event." Outlines a code for bug killing, and suggests that men who are squeamish about bug killing try other minor chivalries like "The Midnight Glass of Water" or "Opening Jars."

514 Knight, George W. The Second Marriage Guidebook: Dealing with the Unique Factors of the Second Wedding. Brentwood, Tenn.: J.M. Publications, 1984.
Developed to address the trend in remarriages toward more elaborate ceremonies. The book underscores the differences between second and first-time "trips to the matrimonial altar." Examines all the possibilities for the type of ceremony, including examples from actual weddings. Also tells how to merge two households as well as how to cope with remarriage adjustments such as money and step-children. Concludes with questions/answers on a variety of topics. Has a checklist for getting ready for the wedding.

515 "Know Your Crowd Courtesy?" Today's Health, 44:12, May, 1966.
True/false questions designed to test knowledge of crowd courtesy, i.e., in the theater it is always proper to stand when someone passes through your row.

516 "Kodak Manners." Ladies' Home Journal, 17:16, Feb., 1900.
Urges "the code of good breeding..." to be used by the "Kodaker" in his pursuit of pictures. Suggests the photographer not use the camera "in violation of private rights."

517 Laimbeer, Nathalie Schenck. "Good Manners in the Home." Ladies' Home Journal, 39:181-2, March, 1922.
"Courtesy...transforms the shabbiest home into a place of beauty." Urges the use of good table manners and the niceties of speech to enhance home life.

518 Lancaster, Mrs. Leicester. "Social Affairs; Calling, the Bride in a New Community." Good Housekeeping, 99:72-3, Oct., 1934.
Describes the social obligations of the bride in a new community and what she can expect. Describes the cards and other stationery the bride may use.

519 Landreth, Catherine. "Table Etiquette for the Very Young." Woman's Home Companion, 60:35, April, 1933.
Practical advice on how to teach very young people table manners, such as coping with accidents and techniques on how to eat.

520 Lane, Annie E. "Afternoon Calls." Fortune, 85:696-706, April, 1906.
  Tongue-in-cheek narrative of one afternoon of calling on an assortment of acquaintances by the author, the author being "deeply engaged studying the philosophy of calls."
521 _____. "Minor Crimes." Fortune, 85:1143-52, June, 1906.
  Declares umbrellas and canes dangerous weapons, and considers fruit peels, pianos in hotel parlours, amateur music critics and children as instruments for the perpetration of the crimes.
522 Langewiesche, Priscilla. "Who's Afraid of Children?" House Beautiful, 100:112-13, June, 1958.
  Describes with humor how teaching manners to children was introduced into their household, and outlines the advantages of having children who can behave themselves. Lists points of attack such as restaurants, parties, cars and visiting, and how to teach children to behave at each point.
523 Langway, Lynn. "Minding Manners Again." Newsweek, 102:58-9, Aug. 29, 1983.
  Looks at the "White Gloves and Party Manners" schools of Marjabelle Stewart, and other places where formalities proliferate. Examines why there is a growing interest in etiquette.
524 Lareau, William. Conduct Expected; The Unwritten Rules for a Successful Business Career. Piscataway, N.J.: New Century, 1985.
  "This book's presentation throws out the theoretical nonsense and gets to the heart of the matter: how organizations and the people in them behave." Discusses rules of behavior to utilize in trying to be a success in business. There is "Hard Talk About Some Hard Facts," and "The Rules" for understanding an organization. Also advises on managing peer relationships at work, managing your bosses, and supervising employees. Includes charts and appendices.
525 Laselle, Mary Augusta. Young Woman Worker. New York: Pilgrim, 1914.
  Advises girls who earn their own living on matters of manners, health, dress, friends, habits and aims. Includes illustrations.
526 Laskin, David. "Party Manners." Esquire, 102:C44-C45, Nov., 1984.
  Discusses guest manners, invitations, gifts, arriving and leaving a party, and thank-you's.
527 Laster, Thomas G. How to Profit Through Politeness, or, Good Manners Can't Be All Bad! Palo Alto, Calif.: R&E Research Associates, 1982.
  Says that looking well mannered is important, and discusses aspects of etiquette such as seating a lady, approaching people, shaking hands, smoking, being on time and the telephone. Illustrates the need for departing at the proper time, and the importance of language and laughter. Suggests table manners are important to those representing a corporation. Lists "Pet Peeves" such as chewing gum, picking teeth, and food spots on clothing. Addressed to businessmen, executives and salespeople.

528 Latner, Helen. The Book of Modern Jewish Etiquette; A Guide for All Occasions. New York: Schocken Books, 1981.
The introduction relates Jewish thought to etiquette saying—there is "an entire minor tractate of the Talmud (Derekh Eretz, or Proper Conduct) dealing with good manners and rules of etiquette." Advice includes everyday good manners, covering family life, personal and social interaction, dress, table manners and Jewish practices such as Kosher or Kashrut table ceremonies. Also advises on the Hebrew calendar and festivals, and living in a pluralistic world, or how to cope with Christmas, weddings, and "Happy Occasions and Difficult Times."

529 _____. Your Jewish Wedding; A Complete Guide to Arranging a Wedding, Large or Small, in the Unique Jewish Tradition. Garden City, N.Y.: Doubleday, 1985.
Describes those aspects which make a wedding Jewish, and lists guidelines for pre-wedding festivities. Includes Jewish wedding traditions, the events in a traditional ceremony and appropriate music for a Jewish wedding. Tells when weddings are permitted, where to hold the wedding, and what to do if there is a difference of religion. Other information includes costs, invitations, groom's responsibilities, wedding gifts, announcements and receptions. Appendix includes expense record and calendar.

530 Laughlin, Clara E. "Bad Manners to the Poor." Ladies' Home Journal, 36:118, June, 1919.
Author proposes that "poverty intensifies but does not alter human nature" and that "bad manners are deplorable at any time...in no case let us display those bad manners to the poor."
Lawrence, Richard L., joint author See Becker, Esther R.

531 "Leagues for Courtesy." Outlook, 77:14-6, May 7, 1904.
Editor proposes to "the teachers of the country that they shall organize everywhere in the schools' leagues for courtesy...for the purpose of advancing the standards of manners and of developing those instincts of courtesy...which are characteristic of the American...."

532 Learned, Ellin Craven. The Etiquette of New York To-day. New York: F.A. Stokes, 1906.
Etiquette of invitations, formal and informal dinners, parties, teas, luncheons, dances, table service and cards and calling is covered. Also includes advice for those moving to a small town. A chapter called "Talk and Talkes" includes hints on how to make small talk.

533 _____. Everybody's Complete Etiquette. N.Y.: F.A. Stokes, 1923.
Comprehensive coverage ranging from salutations, cards and visits to teas and garden parties. Manners and appointments at the table, dances and balls, debutantes, weddings, hospitality, dress and club etiquette are among additional topics covered. There are chapters for those in a small town and those who are shy. A special section called "Good Manners for Boys and Girls" instructs on early training in manners, with the essentials such as personal appearance and behavior in public highlighted. Includes index.

534 Lee, Nata. The Complete Book of Entertaining; A Guide for Every Hostess with Plans, Charts and Etiquette Tips for Parties from Two to Two Hundred. With an introduction by Alice Wilson Richardson. Illustrated by Mircea Vasiliu. New York: Hawthorn, 1961.

How to plan and execute all kinds of parties, from wedding receptions to business parties. Focuses on the mechanics of food service and planning, emphasizing the proper way to serve food.

535 _____. The Complete Book of Entertaining; Nata Lee's Guide for Every Hostess with Plans, Charts and Etiquette Tips for Parties from Two to Two Hundred. New York: Hawthorn, 1968.

Revised second edition includes expanded recipe section.

536 Legg, C.D. "Does an Artichoke Scare You?" Farm Journal, 79:90-1, Jan., 1955.

How to prepare and eat an artichoke properly.

537 Leppert, Paul A. How to Do Business with Chinese; a Taiwan Handbook for Executives. San Diego, Calif.: Patton Pacific, 1984.

Includes cultural background "before you begin your business dealing with Chinese you will want to learn everything you can about them as individuals." Discusses Taiwan business and economy, including "The Etiquette of Bargaining" and advice on "The Personal Experience." Includes bibliography.

538 "Let Them Eat Cake—But Not at Their Desks." Newsweek, 97:40, Feb. 9, 1981.

Describes the "return to punctilio" in the Reagan White House.

539 Levine, Bob. Panache and the Art of Faking It. Illustrated by Peter Steiner. New York: Tribeca Communications, 1982.

Supplies the reader with the knowledge necessary to develop the "art of faking it in conjection with panache to succeed in today's 'Age of Unenlightenment'." Begins with knowing the right booze to order and continues with how to finesse your way into the right restaurants. A chapter called "Aural Gratification" provides flat statements to make about music which imply great knowledge, and there is advice on how to talk "Hollywood" and "Books." Chapters are devoted to competition and adult toys and give advice on how to adapt to different professional worlds, i.e., High Finance.

539a Levine, Judith. "Say Thank-you When You Take My Heart: A Good-manners Guide for Lovers." Mademoiselle, 92:184-5, Nov., 1986.

Contends that familiarity should not justify slacking off on observing good manners with one's lover. Advises on courteous behavior while on each other's turf, giving each other space, respecting privacy and being aware of the flexible nature of courtesy, "the subtle differences...if your notions of politeness and your lover's don't dovetail."

540 Levitt, Mortimer. Class, What It Is and How to Acquire It. New York: Atheneum, 1984.

Divides class into four basic components: 1. "What you say," 2. "How you say what you say," 3. "How you look," and 4. "What

you do." Gives different V.I.P.'s definitions of class. Numerous
lists include grammatical errors to avoid, what to wear, and
do's and don'ts for parties. The author believes that class is
equated with integrity.
541 Levy, Robert. "Vanity in the Executive Suite." Dunn's Business
Monthly, 72, Sept., 1985.
Discusses male executives seeking cosmetic surgery, and "the
growing interest of gauche businessmen in being schooled in
the social graces...," because of fears they may have about
their careers.
542 Listowel, Judith (Marffy-Mantuano) Hare. Manual of Modern
Manners, A Practical Up-to-Date Guide for All Occasions.
Illustrated by Jill Francksen. Hollywood-by-the-Sea, Fla.:
Transatlantic, 1960.
Discusses home and personal conduct, including family relationships, house guests, conversation and meeting new people.
Describes the etiquette of life's milestones, such as christenings,
coming of age, engagements, weddings, and funerals. Invitations,
formal occasions, parties, dances, business conduct and precedence and forms of address are covered as well. Advises on
tipping practices, public speaking, correspondence and club
life also. Lists foreign phrases in common use. Illustrated.
543 Loeb, Robert H. Manners at Work; How They Help You Toward
Career Success. Illustrated by John Voulgaris. New York: Association, 1967.
Lists the "Ten Strictly Personnel Commandments" for work,
i.e., "Thou Shalt Not Be Late;" "Thou Shalt Not Feign Illness."
One chapter is called "Being a Symbiote Does Not Mean Being
an Idiot in Business," and advises one not to bite the hand that
feeds you. Tells "How to Be Bossed and Not Get Lost," and
discusses "Very Civil Rights."
544 _____. Manners to Love By; For Young Couples. Preface
by James A. Peterson. New York: Association, 1971.
Advice written to address "problems facing today's young couples
in their marital adjustments." Subjects touched upon include
money matters, relationships with inlaws, communication
in marriage, and sex.
545 Loomis, Bettina. "Engagement Etiquette." Good Housekeeping,
140:22, April; 22, May; 22, June; 141:22, July; 22, Aug.; 34,
Sept., 1955.
Series of articles tell how to get the engagement off to a good
start, how to solve the engagement ring question, announce
the good news, have an announcement party, share the limelight
with fiancee, and enjoy the showers.
546 Lorimer, Sarah. "Our Family Doesn't Do That." Ladies' Home
Journal, 53:42-3, Sept., 1936.
"I believe the first law of every family should be consideration,
based on...kindness." The author reflects on her own childhood
when rearing her children.
547 Loughbridge, Nancy. Dictionary of Etiquette. New York: Philosophical Library, 1955.

Dictionary ranges in subject from Accessories and Afternoon
Tea to Sea Travel and Secretary. Cross-referenced, includes
a list of French phrases and French culinary terms. Scattered
throughout are bits of quotations about etiquette from a number
of 19th century sources.

548 Louie, Elaine. "Entertaining Solutions: New Manners for New—and
Old—Dilemmas." House and Garden, 153:24, April, 1981.
Advice for the single woman going to a black-tie party; what
to do when you like only one of a couple and want to invite
them to a party; and how to entertain with take-out food.

Lovell, Amanda, joint author See Gross, Amy.

549 Lucas, M.R. "Boy's Grandfather and Lamb's Essay on Modern
Gallantry." Outlook, 92:901-2, Aug. 14, 1909.
Letter to a boy from his father discusses the merits of the
works of Charles Lamb, in particular the essay "Modern Gallantry," as a "never out-of-fashion message from life."

550 Lutes, Della Thompson. Gracious Hostess; A Book of Etiquette.
Indianapolis, Bobbs-Merrill, 1923.
Counsels that true refinement comes from within, and that
in order to be a gracious hostess one must be gracious as a
guest, and indeed in all aspects of life. Book encompasses
etiquette for all occasions. The author believes in changing
to less formality in entertaining. Describes business etiquette
as well. Lists examples of awful characters, some drawn from
her own experience.

551 Lyle, Robey. Mademoiselle's Handbook for Bridal Consultants.
New York: Mademoiselle, Street and Smith, 1946.
"The considered purpose of this book is to place in the hands
of Bridal Consultants and their assistants a workable manual
and guide...." Scope is broad, encompassing virtually all aspects
of pre-wedding and wedding planning. Describes different
types of weddings, including Catholic, Jewish, military, garden
double, club and hotel weddings. There are "200 Spot Questions
Asked and Answered." Legal information about licenses is
given for each state. There are charts for daytime and evening
wedding dress, processional and recessional flow chart, and
seating of guests at the bride's table.

552 Lynes, Russell. "On Good Behavior." Architectural Digest, 50,
May, 1986.
Illustrated article with general observations on manners (sub-
stance) and etiquette (form).

553 _____. "Speaking Out; How America Invented Manners."
Saturday Evening Post, 235:10, Dec. 22, 1962.
Traces the evolution of American manners from aristocratic
manners to democratic manners, the latter "based on the individual's belief in his own dignity."

554 _____. "We Are Fashioning a New Formality." House and
Garden, 111:56, March, 1957.
Suggests the "age of informality" is ready to be re-examined,
not so much as to recapture the old formality of thirty years
ago as to tidy up the casual life of today. Suggests that the
idea of informality has become tiresome.

555 _____. "Why Do Women Have to Be So Rude?" McCall's, 91:71, Aug., 1964.

Observes that women are rude to each other, in department stores, or on subways, and examines the reasons why. Theorizes that this may be because "the measure of a man's success was how useless and pampered his wife could be...." Lynes categorizes the types of rudeness as "careless rudeness," "calculated rudeness," and "up-from-nowhere rudeness!"

555a Lyon, David. "Hey You! Make Way for My Technology." Technology Review, 90:28-9, Aug.-Sept., 1987.

Suggests that civilized behavior is based on man interacting with man, rather than man interacting with "a mechanical or electronic extension of another person." Examines the automobile, answering machine, personal computer, telephoto lens and walkman radio as "pervasive instrument(s) of uncivil behavior." Considers consumer technology responsible for the "decline of civilization as we have known it...."

556 Lyon, Jean. Manners of the Moment. N.Y.: Thomas Crowell, 1938.

Volume illustrated by the author, with humorous advice on table manners, male/female relationships, weddings, home life, guests, "dropping in," tea, personal appearance, shopping, office manners, travel, and "Other People's Children."

557 Lyons, Lucie. "It's Good Manners When You Telephone." McCall's, 80:24, March, 1953.

Pointers on polite usage of the telephone include writing down messages, considering the hour before phoning, and keeping your curiosity under control.

558 MacGibbon, Elizabeth Gregg. "Etiquette for Office Hours." Independent Woman, 13:43, Feb., 1934.

Defines a need for a code of behavior for men and women in the office setting. Maintains that social etiquette is not necessarily applicable in an office setting. Divides business etiquette into ethics and behavior, and answers many questions about business etiquette, including those about smoking in the office, make-up, dress and introductions.

559 _____. Manners in Business. New York: Macmillan, 1936.

"This book is the result of a widespread demand for a codification of the prevailing rules of business etiquette..." and as a result of the author's own business experience, where she has "observed the difficulties girls have in adjusting themselves to such ill-defined rules as exist in most offices." Topics covered include the job hunt, appearance, attitude, getting along with others, correspondence and office introductions. There are chapters on sex in a business setting, and the office party.

560 _____. Manners in Business. New York: Macmillan, 1954.

Revised and enlarged edition, in which the author contrasts the difference in women in the office in 1936, during the Depression, when she tried to discourage young women from going into office work, with 1954, when a large number of women are working. Deleted two chapters—"Business Looks at Weddings" and "After Office Hours" because they are no longer relevant.

561 Mackenzie, Catherine. "Overtraining for Politeness." New York
    Times Magazine, 34, March 31, 1946.
    Focuses upon Nina Ridenour, PhD, and her philosophy of teaching
    manners to children. Dr. Ridenour believes in general that
    parents should try to steer between extremes of overemphasis
    and conformity when teaching children, and they should avoid
    the "bland ignoring of rudeness...."
562 MacKnight, Leleths. Instant Etiquette for Businessmen. Illustrated
    by M.E. Palm. New York: Arc Books, 1966.
    Lists illustrated examples of the right and wrong way to make
    introductions, use the telephone, make an official call, smoke,
    have a business lunch and more. Very brief, and very illustrated.
563 MacNachtan, Ethel R. "High School Course in Social Training."
    Journal of Home Economics, 20:473-6, July, 1928.
    Describes a course at Julia Richman High School, Manhattan,
    New York, which was designed to "do what the home was not
    doing in training girls for social contacts."
564 Madarassy, Elizabeth. "Court Ceremony Cullings." Literary
    Digest, 124:27, Oct. 16, 1937.
    Sketches of old court customs in France, Hungary, Spain and
    Vienna.
564a Mahon, Gigi. "Manners for the Eighties: How to Master the
    Daily Dance of Life in New York." New York, 20:46-54, Dec.
    14, 1987.
    Observes that to those who don't understand the New York
    lifestyle, New Yorkers may seem rude. Arranged in question/an-
    swer format to answer an "eclectic collection of etiquette
    questions...." Among the topics covered are hailing cabs, drop-
    ping names, tipping and smoking.
565 "Manila Takes a Lesson in Courtesy." Rotarian, 74:15, June,
    1949.
    Outlines seven points of courtesy for employees in the Philip-
    pines, which are the products of a courtesy school sponsored
    by the Rotary Club.
566 "Manner Is a Great Matter." Century, 83:310-2, Dec., 1911.
    Calls for a cooperative effort of women in the revival of man-
    ners, a function which is "obviously...the duty of women...,"
    and therefore a suitable topic for consideration among the
    Federation of Women's Clubs, so that they may "arouse us
    to the fundamental importance of good manners."
567 "Manners." Harper's Weekly, 55:6, Sept. 9, 1911.
    Considers what constitutes good and bad manners, bad manners
    caused by "lack of heart and of interpenetrative imagination..."
    and good manners requiring "living for the moment in the experi-
    ence of another."
568 "Manners." Living Age, 278:637-9, Sept. 6, 1913.
    Discusses the historical literary allusion to good manners as
    a disguise to the black heart, and compares this with the popular
    view "that as we have sloughed off manner we have taken on
    honesty." Asks, "Where is the consolation in a man being natural
    if he is naturally offensive?"

569 "Manners." Nation, 133:352, Oct. 7, 1931.
   Discourse on the nature of manners, both good and bad.
570 "Manners and Business." Outlook, 79:165-6, Jan. 21, 1905.
   Advises young American men "to understand that lack of manners, instead of indicating strength of character, is an expression of ignorance, and that it stands in the way of success...."
571 "Manners and Menus." Coronet, 31:16, Feb., 1952.
   Six pictures illustrate don'ts when ordering in a restaurant, such as check-haggling, combing hair and berating the waiter.
572 Manners and Rules of Good Society, or Solecisms to Be Avoided.
   By a member of the aristocracy. New York: Frederick Warne, 1926.
   Etiquette "embraces the whole gamut of good manners, good breeding, and true politeness." Includes chapters on both leaving cards and paying calls. ("Ladies stand upon strict and ceremonious etiquette with each other as regards both paying and receiving calls.") Includes rules on weddings, luncheons, bowing and shaking hands. Although published in America, directed toward English society.
573 "Manners and the Puritan." Atlantic Monthly, 110:137-40, July, 1912.
   Discusses the impact of the Puritan tradition on American manners.
574 "Manners Are Back in Style." House and Garden, 122:146-7, Sept., 1962.
   Indications are that parents **are** teaching their children manners, a premise supported by anecdotes from children.
575 "Manners as a Fine Art." Craftsman, 11:481-5, Jan., 1907.
   Comparison of American, British and Oriental manners. Suggests the teaching of manners to children should be carried out with caution—referring to natural courtesy rather than to conventional regulations. Maintains that manners "rest on the two fundamentals of human intercourse—truth and sympathy..." and discusses manners as one of the means of the deliverance of one's own character.
576 "Manners for Men." Living Age, 263:689-91, Dec. 11, 1909.
   Examination of the relationship between men and women socially in America, contending men need not be made to defer to women socially when women demand all the rights of equality. "If there is no stronger sex and no weaker, a generous forebearance seems out of place on either side."
577 "Manners in a Democracy." Outlook, 113:1027-9, Aug. 30, 1916.
   Declares as wholly false the idea of democracy which "breeds suspicion of manners and identifies independence with rudeness and crudity." Concedes that the typical American has the root of good manners but lacks the finer qualities. Good manners are more essential in a democracy because they are an expression of respect for the dignity and integrity of others.
578 "Manners in America." Harpers, 102:316-8, Jan., 1901.
   Discussion centers on the relationship between American manners and American morals, and the transitional state of American manners. "We have no manners because we are waiting

to get the best; and there is a play of rudeness in our life which is no real reflection of our character."

579 "Manners, Mind and Money." Century, 71:653-4, Feb., 1906.
Asks, "Has our conception of society kept pace with our opportunities?" Correlates manners with the opportunities available to Americans in terms of financial advancement not previously available to so many.

580 "Manners, Mr. Harper." Harpers, 214:77-8, June, 1957.
Suggests that perhaps the reason there is a growing concern about manners in America is that people are living in closer quarters than in the past, and that "manners of crowded countries are...more formal than those of open countries...."

581 "Manners of Speaking." Money, 13:142, April, 1984.
This "guide to terribly proper answering-machine etiquette" refers to Judith Martin's and Letitia Baldrige's advice on answering machine manners.

582 "Manners Still Matter." America, 104:112, Oct. 22, 1960.
Refers to William Caxton's Conversation Book, published in 1482, to reflect upon the career of Emily Post, who died September 26, 1960.

583 Mannes, Marya. "What Do You Get for What You Pay?" McCall's, 92:14, July, 1965.
Civility and service are not offered by most people paid to serve the public, even though citizens "pay more and more for the privilege of getting less and less..." according to the author.

584 Manning, Doug. Don't Take My Grief Away from Me; What to Do When You Lose a Loved One. San Francisco: Harper and Row, 1984.
Handbook addresses the number of decisions to be made after a death, and is intended "to help the bereaved cope with the emotions...." Section I guides one through the funeral, what to do. Section II helps in trying to understand death. Section III discusses the stages of grief. Section IV describes the search for appropriate behavior. Section V offers advice on how to say good-bye, and how to rebuild life while taking to heart the lessons death and mourning impart.

585 Marbury, Elisabeth. "Where Are Our Manners?" Collier's, 75:25, May 9, 1925.
Marbury believes "that classes in common sense could be opened in every school throughout the country, because I believe that these would go far to drive out common manners."

586 March-Phillipps, Evelyn. "In Pursuit of Courtesy." Living Age, 282:136-47, July 18, 1914.
Traces original home of manners to ancient Babylon and the development of good manners or ceremonial observances throughout the world to the Middle Ages. "Good manners are to particular societies what good morals are to society in general--their cement and security."

587 Marden, Orison Swett. Good Manners; A Passport to Success. New York: T.Y. Crowell, 1900.
Primarily general discussion of the nature of good manners,

covering home training, self-respect, self-control, tact, business manners, public manners and kindness. Has many anecdotes about famous people and nobility, and includes their portraits.

588 Marion, J.H. "Courtesy Across the Color Line." Christian Century, 57:638-9, May 15, 1940.
Discusses racial discourtesy in the South, particularly in forms of address, which is "unworthy of the best in southern people."

589 Markel, Helen. "If You Make a Date, Keep It." Reader's Digest, 73:100-2, Nov., 1958.
Tells why people break dates (according to psychiatrists) and lists five ground rules for people who want to kick the date-breaking habit, i.e., don't take advantage of those who love you.

590 "Marketing Manners." Coronet, 33:8, March, 1953.
Six pictures illustrate courteous behavior for salespeople and shoppers.

591 Martens, Frederick H. Book of Good Manners; A Guide to Polite Usage for All Social Functions. New York: Social Culture, 1923.
Defines etiquette as the great body of rules to which good society conforms. Good manners are based on the kindness of heart and courtesy of mind in which they originate, and are a fundamental of civilized life. Good manners are chronicled through life starting with the birth announcement, child-rearing, young people in society, weddings, the matron in society and funerals. Includes numerous lists, such as foreign words and phrases apt to occur in conversation, a menu guide, and what the courteous card player does.

592 Martin, Dorothy McKay. Christian Etiquette for Everyday Living. Chicago: Moody Bible Institute of Chicago, 1969.
Begins with personal appearance, including cleanliness, contemporary styles and community standards. Outlines correct church behavior, and covers table manners, introductions, conversation, correspondence, dating, engagements, weddings and funerals. Advises on business courtesy, parliamentary etiquette and travel etiquette. Includes index and cites numerous Biblical verses as a means of illustration.

593 Martin, Frederick Townsend. "Have Americans Any Manners?" Harper's Bazaar, 46:544, Nov., 1912.
Discusses reasons why American manners are good: because they lack inherited snobbery and because of an informality which leads to "a certain dignity."

594 Martin, I.T. "Hats Off in Oklahoma." Harper's Weekly, 55:24, Jan. 14, 1911.
Suggests that there is "more courtesy shown to women...in the far West," and tells of experiences in Oklahoma which give credence to this suggestion.

595 Martin, Judith. Common Courtesy; In Which Miss Manners Solves the Problem That Baffled Mr. Jefferson. New York: Atheneum, 1985.
Examines how to adapt European systems of etiquette and protocol (The Problem) in order that they work in a democracy.

Martin deviates from the traditional approach to etiquette to make a distinction between morals and manners, unlike "my colleague Cotton Mather and his friend God, to blur the distinction in order to be able to call out the moral militia for transgressions of manners." Martin advocates the basic technique of those who "mercy teaches manners, which is nagging."

596 _____. Miss Manners' Guide to Excruciatingly Correct Behavior. Illustrated by Gloria Kamen. New York: Atheneum, 1982.
Covers standard fare of etiquette books, with some material drawn from letters written in her syndicated newspaper column. Martin clearly explains in her introduction that "'Assertiveness', 'Looking Out for Number One', and other systems for the dissemination of rudeness are abhorrent to Miss Manners." Begins with "Some Thoughts on the Impulse Rude," and chapters cover birth, "Basic Civilization" (advises silence can be a social skill), "Messy Emotions and Minor Emotional Distress," "Disgusting Habits and Politics" and a number of other social difficulties. Concludes with "Death" and "Answers to Questions Nobody Asked." Illustrated, with index.

597 _____. Miss Manners' Guide to Rearing Perfect Children; A Primer for Everyone Worried About the Future of Civilization. Illustrated by Gloria Kamen. New York: Atheneum, 1984.
Declares the chief tools of child-rearing "are example and nagging." Chapter 1, "Theory and Skills," outlines Martin's philosophy of child-rearing, and the format follows the childhood years by school categories, i.e., pre-kindergarten through postgraduate, utilizing the Miss Manners' Gentle Reader throughout. Advice covers a diversity of topics with wit and humor, everything from christenings to car pooling, and from empty nesting to respecting adults. Illustrated, with index. "Manners are the basis of civilized society, and passing on the civilization to the young, so that they...can live easily...within the accumulated traditions and standards of society is what child-rearing is all about."

598 _____. "The Pursuit of Politeness." New Republic, 191:29-34, Aug. 6, 1984.
Martin's contention is that the "failure to distinguish between manners and morals suggests, erroneously, that acceptable social behavior follows effortlessly from personal virtue." She examines the "Jeffersonian system of non-hierarchical etiquette."

599 _____. "Why Manners Matter." Harpers, 36, Aug., 1984.
Suggests that standardized manners are necessary to an orderly civilization, and that in order to prevent social chaos everyone should adhere to the same system of etiquette.

600 Marty, Martin E. "Ecclesiastical Etiquette." Christian Century, 97:503, April 30, 1980.
Satirical list of questions on problems of etiquette which arise in the "Religious Situation 1980."

600a _____. "Mister Marty's Manners." Christian Century, 104:1103, Dec. 2, 1987.

Responds to "one of several people who sent...clippings of an item from Judith Martin's 'Miss Manners' etiquette column..." which likened the author to a man described in the column.

601 "Marx and Manners; Russia's Standards of Diplomatic Deportment." Time, 110:37, July 11, 1977.
Review of Diplomatic Protocol and Practice by F.F. Molochkov, indicating that "Soviet officialdom" is showing increasing interest in manners.

602 "Maryland Coeds Demonstrate Do's and Don'ts of Campus Etiquette." Life, 10:38, Feb. 17, 1941.
Pictures illustrate do's and don'ts of campus life, including table manners and dance etiquette.

603 Matthews, Elizabeth. "Are Your Table Manners Showing in the Kitchen?" Woman's Home Companion, 80:54-5, July, 1953.
Advice on how to arrange and eat in the kitchen without sacrificing good manners.

604 Maule, Frances. She Strives to Conquer; Business Behavior, Opportunities and Job Requirements for Women. New York: Funk and Wagnalls, 1934.
Divided into two parts, the first illustrates proper business behavior for women, including a discussion of attitudes toward work, co-workers as well as dress and personal grooming. The second part describes job opportunities for women and what a woman needs to do to get a job.

605 Maxon, Monica J. "Caring as a Calling." Christian Century, 101:93, Jan. 25, 1984.
Advice on how to be compassionate at times when fear of saying or doing the wrong thing inhibits people. "We can't assume that people are aware of how much we feel without our showing them."

606 Maxtone-Graham, J. "Who Taught You to Eat That Way; Origin of American Table Manners." Holiday, 53:30-2, Jan., 1972.
Englishman discusses the American habit of shifting the fork from hand to hand, traces the history of the fork in America and advises on the English style of fork use.

607 Maxwell, Elsa. Etiquette Book. New York: Bartholomew House, 1951.
Discusses the advantage of having good manners, topics include introductions, names and how to use them, use of foreign words, slang, conversation, "Manners in Public Places," cards and their uses, invitations, engagements, weddings, birth, table and telephone manners and more.

608 Mazzei, George. The New Office Etiquette; A Guide to Getting Along in the Corporate Age. New York: Poseidon Press, 1983.
Encompasses the many facets of contemporary business etiquette, from awkward office situations, gifts, the business lunch, travel, dress and covering for the boss to the office affair. Advises the "Women at Work" about the problems contemporary men and women encounter which may not have established guidelines. Illustrates advice with anecdotes from own working experience.

609 McAlister, James. "Are You Hurting Your Company's Bottom Line?" Machine Design, 105, Sept. 11, 1986.
Addressed to engineers, discusses rude behavior such as posing as a pompous expert, concealing a crisis, hiding behind habits, taking a myopic view, denying errors, and ignoring costs, with suggestions on how this negative behavior can undermine business.

610 McAndrew, William. "America's Bad Manners." Delineator, 87:1, Sept., 1915.
Declares Americans need to learn refinement in their manners and that the greatest need in American schools is a text-book on good manners.

611 McBride, Angela Barron. "In Search of a New Etiquette." Ms, 8:104, Jan., 1980.
Relates technique for entertaining, and expresses concern that although there is equality of labor in preparation the guests see only the more traditional roles. Includes concrete tips for the new order as well, i.e., hostess gifts are passe, and the focus is on having manners (being considerate) rather than being mannered (full of affectation).

McBride, Mary Frances, joint author See Alsop, Gulielma Fell.

612 McCaffree, Mary Jane, and Innis, Pauline B. Protocol; The Complete Handbook of Diplomatic, Official and Social Usage. Englewood Cliffs, N.J.: Prentice-Hall, 1977.
Addressed to the newcomer to official life, offers guidance on the local, state, national and international levels of protocol. Defines protocol as the set of rules prescribing good manners in official life. Beginning with the Order of Precedence, there is a greatly detailed discussion, with charts, of the forms of address and titles. The formality of calling and calling cards is examined. One chapter is devoted to places to entertain in Washington, and one covers White House entertaining. The appendix addresses some minor points such as coping with the press, dress, and a list of United States Chiefs of Protocol.

613 McCall, Anne. "Happy Way of Doing Things." Woman's Home Companion, 50:38, Dec., 1923.
General discussion of manners with special reference to Ralph Waldo Emerson's essays on manners, from which the popular saying (the happy way...) hails.

McCall's Magazine, joint author See Bevans, Margaret (VanDoren).

614 McCandless, Bruce; Harral, Brooks J.; and Swartz, Oretha D. Service Etiquette; Correct Social Usage for Service Men on Official and Unofficial Occasion. Annapolis, Md.: Naval Institute, 1959.
Written specifically for the young officer; "the aim of this book is to reach all officers at all bases and stations." Sections cover everyday manners, social life, table manners, entertaining, correspondence and invitations, conversation, good sportsmanship, service etiquette and personal matters in everyday life, i.e., proper military weddings. Includes bibliography and index.

615 McCarthy, Abigail. "Infectious Incivilities." Commonwealth, 113:200-1, April 11, 1986.

"Incivility is...the accepted mark of supposedly rational discussion on national issues." Maintains that the incivility we confront daily leads to violence and disorder.

616 McCracken, Elizabeth. "How to Teach Courtesy to Children." Home Progress, 5:177-82, Dec., 1915.
Courtesy is the lesson of kindness and self-control. Suggests reading the old hero tales, i.e., tales of the Round Table, and connecting the lesson learned with the child's daily life. Cites specific passages from the stories which can be used in specific instances.

617 _____. "Teaching Children Manners." Home Progress, 6:369-71, April, 1917.
Suggests different books and stories which can be used in teaching manners to children. Encourages parents to develop a sense of humor in children in order to develop "the best general solvent of problems of courtesy and manners that there is...."

618 McCrady, Marjorie Ellis (Ferguson), and Wheeler, Blanche. Manners for Moderns. New York: E.P. Dutton, 1942.
The authors intend to "lift the old taboos,...scrap obsolete rules and give you in their places easily followed manners for moderns." Gives attention to letters, weddings, invitations, travel, tipping and military manners. There is a chapter on office behavior, which includes a list of twenty office commandments, i.e., Be Cheerful, Be Tolerant, etc. There is a chapter on entertaining, and the final chapter is "Miscellaneous Chit Chat," with advice on manners for men, and rules for being popular.

619 McDonald, Susan S. "Crime and Etiquette." National Review, 28:734-5, July 9, 1976.
Discusses the relationship between criminal behavior and public behavior. "The very rules of public etiquette that protect us from intrusion under conventional circumstances endanger us when we are victims of criminal intent."

620 McElligott, Raymond Thomas. Service Etiquette and Courtesy, Some Hints on Procedure for Cadets of the U.S. Coast Guard Academy. New London, Conn.: The Academy, 1942.
The book's purpose "is to assist cadets and young officers in their official and social duties. It is elementary in scope and covers only the more common amenities and conventions." Examines the merits of the relationship between leadership and discipline, and carries it into a discussion of official courtesy. Emphasis is on military custom, and covers advice on social functions, introductions, military weddings, calls, dress, table manners, correspondence and dress. Includes diagrams, samples of correspondence and words to official songs of the Coast Guard.

621 McEvoy, Peggy. "Long Gray Line of Gentlemen; Good Manners as Taught at West Point." Ladies' Home Journal, 73:59, Aug., 1956.
Describes the course on social conduct and military courtesy taught to freshmen at West Point, including interviews with teachers and subjects covered.

622 McGivern, Maureen (Daly). Perfect Hostess; Complete Etiquette
    and Entertainment for the Home. New York: Dodd, Mead,
    1950.
    "By being 'hospitality-minded' you are...teaching the art of
    sharing and gracious living." Encompasses all aspects of enter-
    taining, from giving dinners, luncheons, and teas to being an
    unharried hostess. Special days such as New Year's Eve and
    Easter, special parties for children, showers and party games
    are covered. Also gives suggestions for entertaining for fund
    raising and outdoor entertaining. Includes recipes.
623 McGrath, Charles, and Menaker, Daniel. "Together Dude; A
    Guide to the New Etiquette." New Yorker, 52:34-5, May 17,
    1976.
    Humorously addresses situations one may find oneself in because
    of the rapidly changing social life in America, including the
    "etiquette of grass."
624 McKee, Mabel F. "Experiment in Guidance." Social Review,
    54:39-42, Jan., 1946.
    Outlines program which aims to make "every individual conscious
    that there is an acceptable behavior..." at Amos Hiatt Junior
    High School, Des Moines, Iowa.
625 McLean, Beth Bailey. Meal Planning and Table Service; For
    the American Home without Servants. Peoria, Ill.:Manual Arts
    Press, 1924.
    Analyzes table service and gives basic rules. Suggests in maidless
    homes a boy or girl of twelve can be trained to wait on and
    set the table properly. Says the aim of table service is to place
    food in perfect condition before diners, and to do so without
    disturbance so the guest is never conscious of the performance
    of the service. Covers virtually all aspects of table service
    from gracious dining, meal preparation through the clean-up.
    Includes photos.
626 _____. Meal Planning and Table Service; For the American
    Home without Servants. Peoria, Ill.: Manual Arts Press, 1936.
    New edition includes a re-written chapter on meal planning.
    Added new chapter for dinner parties, and suggestions for
    teaching meal planning. Updated photos.
627 _____. Meal Planning and Table Service; For the American
    Home without Servants. Peoria, Ill.: Manual Arts Press, 1949.
    Revised and reset edition addresses the simpler style of living,
    which comes with foods requiring less preparation, new equip-
    ment and new table accessories. Cites trends towards fewer
    courses, less foods, better cooking methods and greater freedom
    in expression as factors simplifying food service in the home.
628 _____. Table Etiquette; Nine Enlarged Illustrations from
    Meal Planning and Table Service. Peoria, Ill.: Manual Arts
    Press, 1937.
    Portfolio of 12"x16" photos illustrate correct utensil usage.
629 _____. The Table Graces; Setting, Service and Manners. Peoria,
    Ill.: Manual Arts Press, 1941.
    Offers advice on selecting table equipment, rules for setting
    the table, types of service, i.e., English or Russian, meal service

for special occasions, table graces such as the art of conversation, and numerous do's and don'ts of table etiquette. Illustrated with photos.

630 McLeod, Edyth Thornton. The Bride's Book. Be the Bride of Your Dreams! Modern Etiquette, New Wedding Dresses, the 1950 Trousseau, Today's Wedding Budget. New York: Archway, 1950.

Illustrated with numerous photos, describes all types of weddings. Advice offers engagement and trousseau tips, second wedding etiquette, bride's and groom's financial responsibilities and the etiquette of showers, bachelor parties, decorations, music, dress and the honeymoon.

631 McManus, Patrick F. "Well, Excuuuuuuse Me!" Field and Stream, 86:118, Oct., 1981.

Tongue-in-cheek review of fishing etiquette.

632 McNaught, Margaret Schallenberger. Training in Courtesy; Suggestions for Teaching Good Manners in Elementary Schools. Washington: U.S. Government Printing Office, 1918.

As title implies, advises teachers on programs for teaching children in schools manners—everything from table manners to propriety in public. Includes a play teachers can use. "The importance of education in manners is due to the fact that a knowledge of social customs and social usages is almost as necessary to civilized man as a knowledge of how to earn a living."

633 McVey, William Estus. Minimum Essentials in Manners and Right Conduct for Schools. Columbus, Ohio: The School Speciality Press, 1929.

"Instruction in correct social practice...deserves a definite place in every curriculum...." Provides instructions for manners at school, home and in public. Also includes flag etiquette and a copy of the High School Morality Code, by Vernon P. Squires.

634 Mead, Elsie C., and Abel, Theodora Mead. Good Manners for Children. New York: Dodd, Mead, 1926.

Gives practical advice for mothers in teaching manners of sports, social occasion, and at the table. Suggests that each "don't" be accompanied by a "because," so the child will understand the consequences of the lack of good form. Also discusses problems peculiar to the shy, spoiled, only or nervous child. Includes bibliography.

635 _____. "Growing Up Politely." Delineator, 107:20, Sept., 1925.

Advises parents on the manners children should know growing up, such as rising to greet visitors, correct way to make introductions, and telephone manners.

636 _____. "Traveling." Delineator, 103:49, July 23, 1925.

How to behave traveling on a train includes advice on proper etiquette of the dining car or sleeping car, and in the use of the wash-room. "A good traveler should be quiet, neat, calm, thoughtful of others and patient with unavoidable annoyances."

637 Meade, Marianne. Charm and Personality; A Modern Guide
to Good Form. Cleveland, Ohio: World Syndicate, 1938.
"Good manners add to your enjoyment of social contacts and
give you the poise and assurance which you must have for
charm and a pleasing personality." Describes appropriate attire
for all occasions, how to make introductions, proper public
conduct, table manners, formal and informal entertaining
and etiquette for young people. Meeting callers, using the
telephone and personal relations are elements of business etiquette which are outlined. Includes index.

638 _____. How to Write Good Social Letters; A Modern Guide
to Good Form. Cleveland, Ohio: World Syndicate, 1938.
Covers formal and informal social correspondence thoroughly.
Describes different parts of a letter. Discusses the best English
for social usage, gives details on punctuation and capitalization,
and looks at different kinds of stationery. Includes samples
of telegrams, radio and cable messages, and letters written
by famous people. The correct form for invitations, acceptances,
formal letters and thank-you notes is illustrated. Indexed.

639 Measures, Howard. Styles of Address; A Manual of Usage in
Writing and in Speech. New York: St. Martins, 1969.
"This book is designed to show...the form of address and title,
the salutation and...the complimentary close." Salutations
are arranged alphabetically by title, and subarranged by degree
of formality. Includes political and religious as well as royal
titles, everything from Bahadur to Baron to Sheikh.
Menaker, Daniel, joint author See McGrath, Charles.

640 Mercer, Marilyn. "Art of Defensive Party Going." Working Woman,
3:48-51, Dec., 1978.
Advice on how to manage time when attending numerous
holiday parties, i.e., how to look like you stayed for an evening
when in fact you stayed only a half an hour.

641 Merser, Cheryl. Honorable Intentions; The Manners of Courtship
in the '80's. New York: Atheneum, 1983.
Suggests the old rules of etiquette and chivalry may no longer
apply to the rules of etiquette today which apply to love. Addresses issues such as the etiquette of a "sleep-over date,"
exchanging house keys, introducing new lovers to old friends,
and children. Chapters include "Courtship: Revisionist Thinking,"
"Measuring Love," "The Players, and the Games," "Relationship
Blues," "The Negotiating Table" and more. Includes bibliography
and index.

642 Meyers, John A. "Modern Manners." Time, 4, Nov. 5, 1984.
Author discusses what he calls the modern dilemma of manners,
with examples of courtesy from contemporary arbiters.

643 Michaels, L. "Checklist; Business Etiquette." Working Woman,
4:14, May, 1979.
Encourages women not to set themselves apart from the team
by blowing up gestures of old school ways in manners. Lists
specific suggestions for the woman to help her get along in
the business world.

644 Miles, Mary. "Business Etiquette Abroad." <u>Computer Decisions</u>, 166, Jan. 15, 1985.
In the global market it is essential to acquaint oneself with cultural differences, and by doing so one can gain distinct business advantages. Cites authoritative business people and their advice in order to support this premise.

645 Miller, Alice Duer. "I Like American Manners." <u>Saturday Evening Post</u>, 205:5, Aug. 13, 1932.
Suggests that to be civil in America it is necessary to convey equality, and compares American and European manners using personal anecdotes.

646 Miller, Llewellyn. <u>The Encyclopedia of Etiquette; A Guide to Good Manners in Today's World</u>. With an introduction by Cleveland Amory. New York: Crown, 1967.
Encyclopedia covers topics ranging from Apologies and Excuses (with subtopics) to Whiskey and Other Spirits. Covers some less traditional topics such as Escalators, Security Clearances, Moving and Party Crashing. Illustrations and diagrams supplement topics such as Table Setting and Weddings. Extensively cross-referenced, with index.

647 Miller, Marion M. "Good Manners Every Day." <u>Delineator</u>, 121:12, Sept., 1932.
Discusses the advantages well-mannered children have, saying that "manners have their roots in the attitudes of people towards one another..." and that the "primary essential, therefore, is a home life...where each human being is of real worth."

648 Miller, Robin. "When Royalty Comes to Call." <u>Coronet</u>, 48:25-30, Aug., 1960.
Member of the Grenadier Guards tells of humorous experiences he had when the protocol for royal visits wasn't observed.

Millet, Ruth L., joint author See Stephenson, Margaret Bennett.

649 Million, Helen Lovell. "Is Chivalry Dead?" <u>Outlook</u>, 126:344, Oct. 20, 1920.
Relates experiences of the author when men failed to give up their seats to her while riding public transportation.

650 "Mind Your Make-up Manners." <u>Good Housekeeping</u>, 111:76-7, Sept., 1940.
What to do and what not to do when making-up in public.

651 "Minding America's Manners; Views of Letitia Baldrige." <u>Reader's Digest</u>, 114:155-8, March, 1979.
Baldrige says that today Americans are tired of so much aggressiveness, and addresses the "conundruns that have arisen in the turmoil of morals, sexual roles and obsessive candor of the past decade."

652 "Minding Our Manners." <u>Newsweek</u>, 59:90-1, Aug. 11, 1958.
Biographical comparison of Amy Vanderbilt and Emily Post, examines what some of the differences in advice they offer are, and their different styles as social arbiters.

653 "Minding Our Manners." <u>Scribners Magazine</u>, 56:120-30, July, 1914.
In response to the criticism that the younger set is less polite than previous generations, the suggestion is made that "each

generation is governed by different conditions, and the outward demonstrations of youth are different...," but not necessarily less polite.

654 Moats, Alice-Leone. "Do It Your Own Way." Woman's Home Companion, 67:66, Jan., 1940.
Advises that the casual approach to etiquette is best, and that life should be approached with a sense of humor.

655 _____. "I Hated to Shoot a Lady." Saturday Evening Post, 207:23, April 20, 1935.
Title refers to the statement made by the sheriff who shot Bonnie Parker, "I hated to shoot a lady, 'specially when she was settin' down." The author sees this statement as an example of chivalry, "a fairly typical example of the slightly muddled reasoning displayed by the logical male in his dealing with the intuitive sex."

656 _____. No Nice Girl Swears. New York: St. Martin's Marek, 1933.
Advice reflects the contemporary social scene, and includes advice such as the girl may smoke and drink only after she has been out with a boy for two years, that nice girls write bread and butter letters, and how nice girls can be popular. There are also chapters on coming out, getting married and keeping young men at bay.

657 Modern Bride Guide to Your Wedding and Marriage. With Stephanie H. Dahl, foreword by Cele Goldsmith Lilli, illustrations by JoAnn Wanamaker. New York: Ballantine Books, 1984.
Divided into three parts: Your Engagement, Your Wedding, and Your Marriage. "New research, interviews with clergy, professional marriage counselors, and couples...brings you a compendium of experience and information...." Chapters include "Lifestyle Preparations," "Wedding Diplomacy," "Love and the Laundry" and "Epilogue: Your Challenge for the Future" among others. Also gives all the detailed advice found in most wedding etiquette books. Includes a bibliography, and is illustrated, with sample invitations and charts.

658 Moffat, Donald. "Savoir-vivre." New Yorker, 26:77-8, Dec. 9, 1950.
Discusses aspects of a French etiquette book, Usages du Monde, by Baronne Staffe, as they pertain to the author's experience as a visitor to France. Concludes that the French still have manners and that their tradition is in good order and good taste.

659 Moffett, M'Ledge. When We Meet Socially; A Guide-book to Good Form in Social Conventions. New York: Prentice-Hall, 1939.
Arranged in outline form, with "Problems" at the end of each chapter, and a "Summary Test of Your Ability to Adapt Various Phases of Good Form to Some Common Experiences." Topics covered include introductions, conversation, formal calls, daily living, friendships, social correspondence, parties, dances, receptions, table manners, travel, salutations, clubs and committees.

Moloney, Kathleen, joint author **See** Waggoner, Glen.

660 Moltke, Mab Wilson. <u>What to Do When</u>. New York: Harper, 1953.
Tells what to do when you want to get rid of people, with difficult people and what to do about gossip. New situations such
as when you're new in town or new on the job are also covered.
Advice covers what to do as a hostess, at home, abroad, when
writing a letter or getting a divorce. The ultimate what-to-do
considers appropriate actions for those in a state of embarrassment.

661 Monroe, Anne Shannon. "Happy Ways." <u>Good Housekeeping</u>,
73:25, July, 1921.
Author believes manners "will carry you through life on such
well-oiled wheels..." and expresses concern about American
manners "we have a people much cruder in manner than in
sentiment...."

662 Morgan, Len. "A Gentleman's Profession." <u>Flying</u>, 112:10, July,
1985.
When flying, consideration means "preserving the other fellow's
neck as well as your own." Outlines the necessity of good manners as essential to the safety of flying.

663 Morris, Allen Covington. <u>Practical Protocol for Floridians</u>.
Tallahassee: Florida House of Representatives, Office of the
Clerk, 1984.
Florida precedence and receiving lines for different governmen-
tal functions are described. Seating arrangements for head
tables, forms of address, official travel, inaugural ceremony
schedules and the investiture of a justice of the Supreme Court
are among topics included. Also covers flag etiquette, how
to greet foreign dignitaries, business customs of the Orient
and the definition of a consul. Includes diagrams, samples
of correspondence and an index.

664 Morris, Charles. <u>The Standard Book of Etiquette</u>. Philadelphia,
1901.
Discusses what the general principles of good manners are.
The art of conversation, ladies and gentlemen, dress, introductions, balls, meal times, courtship, funerals, the club and travel
are among the subjects examined. Illustrated.

665 Morris, Charles Edward. "From the Cradle of True Politeness."
<u>St. Nicholas</u>, 45:1030-1, Sept., 1918.
Tells the story of a young Japanese boy from the "Cradle of
True Politeness" and the cruel manner in which an American
treated him. Primary message: "Then they were all happy,
just as all people who think of others' comfort before their
own always are."

666 Morton, Agnes H. <u>Etiquette, Good Manners for All People, Especially Those Who Dwell Within the Broad Zone of the Average</u>.
Philadelphia: Penn, 1915.
"I have endeavored to suggest some of the fundamental laws
of good behavior in every day life." Discussion begins with
an examination of the "Ethics of Etiquette," and includes those
topics such as cards, weddings, entertaining, table manners,
personal appearance and conversation which dwell within the
broad zone of the average etiquette book. Also includes a

discussion of the American chaperone—"a perplexing problem," and a chapter called "Gallantry and Coquetry" wherein the author contends "flirting is a plebian diversion."

Mossien, Herbert J., joint author **See** Fram, Eugene H.

667 Mothershead, Alice Bonzi. Dining Customs Around the World; with Occasional Recipes. Illustrations by Marilena Perrone. Garrett Park, Md.: Garrett Park Press, 1982.

Dining customs for fifty-three countries are given, contents arranged alphabetically by country, with a brief description of the country, a map and advice on what to expect as a guest in the home. Includes the native words for thank-you, and how the guest should express his gratitude.

668 _____, and Crawford, Miriam. Manners and Social Customs in the United States; Guide for the Foreign Student. Illustrated by Maria Mothershead. Pasadena, Calif.: Mials Press, 1957.

"Handbook is designed to help you, the foreign student or visitor, understand differences in manners and customs between the United States and other countries...." Includes advice on seeking employment, being a house guest, table manners, automobiles and travel, and general etiquette advice on introductions, correspondence, dancing and manners in public. Includes miscellaneous information, such as where to go for help or information, barber and beauty shops, sports, religion and speech-making. Illustrated.

669 Mulher, Alice. "Ladies." Commonwealth, 14:402-3, Aug. 26, 1931.

Reminiscence of manners at tea time used by ladies.

670 Muller, Gladys Blanchard, and Bennett, Dorothy Blanchard. I Seen Him When He Done It; A Handbook on Christian Etiquette. Wheaton, Ill.: Kampen, 1951.

Book "written in a humorous style to stimulate thinking..." on "bad habits practiced in Christian circles...." Laments congregational offenses such as rushing in church, sitting in the front, the Sunday manicure and gum chewing. The choir, ushers, Sunday school and organizational behavior in church are topics for a chapter. "The Rev. and His Mrs." tells how ministers should dress, speak, make friends with members in the congregation and avoid reputational hazards and gossip. Outlines proper table manners, and examines tract distribution of the Word. The final chapter "Flotsam" gives definitions for bits of miscellany. Contains some poems.

671 Mullett, Mary B. "Men, Women, and Their Manners on an Ocean Steamship." American Magazine, 92:24-5, July, 1921.

Elucidates the customs and manners on a steamship, from the duties of the chief steward, to the promenade around the deck, and the styles of dress.

672 Munson, Mary Lou. Practical Etiquette for the Modern Man; Your Questions Answered. New York: Taplinger, 1964.

Organized in question/answer format by subject. Advises on manners in public, such as introductions, conversation and dining out and on manners in the business world, such as the job, the new employee, telephone etiquette and the business

lunch. Sports, traditional ceremonies, travel, parties, entertaining, table manners and dress are subjects receiving attention
also. Author contends, "men are responsible for the carrying
out of good manners in most social situations."
673 Murphy, Ann Pleshette. "Awkward Edibles; An Update on Dining
Finesse." Harper's Bazaar, 117:102, April, 1984.
How to eat escargot, soft-shell crab, clams, asparagus (the
finger debate is touched upon), and artichokes.
674 Murphy, Edward F. "Be Nice!" New York Times Magazine, 42,
March 5, 1967.
Compilation of quotations from a variety of people pertaining
to courteous treatment of one another.
675 Murphy, John Allen. "Business Hangs Out the Welcome Sign."
Reader's Digest, 40:81-3, Feb., 1942.
"More and more companies are finding it pays to greet callers
with friendly courtesy." Tells of different ways business visitors
are greeted by companies around the country, emphasizing
the notion that it pays to be cordial.
676 Murray, Kathryn. "Be Hep, Keep in Step; Dancing Manners."
Dance Magazine, 31:64, July, 1957.
Emcee of NBC-TV "Arthur Murray Party" gives advice on
dance manners, i.e., accepting invitations, or the cut-in system.
677 Myers, Elizabeth. The Social Letter. New York: Brentano's,
1918.
Endeavors to "place a few stepping-stones in the rushing river
of social obligations...." Defines the function of the social
letter, forms, stationery etiquette, and gets as specific as
telling how to date the letter. The proper use of invitations,
thank-you letters, and letters of congratulation, condolence,
and club correspondence are all determined. Includes numerous
examples and concludes with a chart of address for "Titular
persons."
678 "Mysterious East; Advice to Businessmen." Time, 82:73, Aug.
16, 1963.
Advice on manners for the businessman bound for Southeast
Asia.
Nadeau, Gisele, joint author See Ardman, Harvey.
679 Naifeh, Steven W., and Smith, Gregory White. Moving Up in
Style; The Successful Man's Guide to Impeccable Taste. New
York: St. Martin's, 1980.
Advises on the rules of style, with suggestions to avoid artificial
things, avoid excessive materialism and that the notion of
style is that less is more. How to dress in style, design your
home in style, buy art and learn the style-is-success philosophy
as elucidated. Also directs on how to present yourself with
style, i.e., preparing a resume, and on good manners in the
office. Filling the leisure hours with style concludes the advice
by suggesting how to eat out, travel and acquire hobbies. Includes references and illustrations.
680 Nathan, George Jean. "Table Manners." American Mercury,
16:497-9, April, 1929.
After examining the history of American table manners, Nathan

concludes that "the national table manners have so improved that today they are at least the equal, in gentility and bienseance, of those of the average New York Alsation waiter."

681 "Nature's Ladies." Atlantic, 98:574-5, Oct., 1906.
Attempts to determine whether the characteristics which define a lady are in-born or acquired.

681a Neff, David. "Down Side of Civility." Christianity Today, 31:13, Feb. 6, 1987.
Looks at a study of evangelical college and seminary students conducted by James Davison Hunter, sociologist from the University of Virginia. The study suggests that evangelical courtesy has "enfeebled the doctrine of salvation through faith in Christ alone..." and that the tolerance for others has lead to "evangelical ineffectiveness on the political front." The author concludes, "we must guard against civility breeding timidity and cancelling the compelling message of salvation through the one and only Way, Truth and Life."

682 Neil, Henry. The Etiquette of Today; A Complete Guide to Correct Manners and Social Customs in Use Among Educated and Refined People of America. Henry Weil, 1902.
Emcompasses virtually all aspects of etiquette, including office and street etiquette, street-car civilities, marriage, language, table manners, visiting and house parties, correspondence, bachelor hospitalities, servants, horseback riding and much more. Contains many pictures of women prominent in society, as well as the interiors of homes. "The simple and most direct route to culture is contained observation...."

683 Nelson, John Howard. The Handy Etiquette Manual; For Office, School, and Home. Boston: Bruce Humphries, 1957.
Concise manual offers guidance on all matters of etiquette, such as introductions, invitations, correspondence, entertaining, table manners, travel, club etiquette, and school manners. Also includes tips to smokers, and hints on menu reading.

684 "New Etiquette; Symposium." Esquire, 88:129-36, Dec., 1977.
Symposium uses humor to examine the new etiquette, and includes a list of people to look up to, a list of boors, a list of prominent people's "rudest thing," and advice on table manners.

685 "New Gauge for Good Manners." Vogue, 134:120-1, Oct. 15, 1959.
Etiquette in the past twenty years has become less arbitrary and more democratic. "Good behaviour is everybody's business, and good taste can be everyone's goal."

New York Society of Self-Culture See Correct Social Usage.

686 Nicholls, Charles Wilber de Lyon. The 469 Ultra-fashionable of America, A Social Guide Book and Register to Date. New York: Broadway, 1912.
While not specifically an etiquette book, this is referred to frequently enough in the literature to merit inclusion. Begins with advice on how to become ultra-fashionable, contending that "since the death of Mrs. Astor...the power of money has asserted

itself as never before in society's somewhat checkered history."
Declares that those in the White House "stand in no integral
relation to national society." Much of the book is dedicated
to listing names and relationships of the ultra-fashionable
and the characteristic manners of Washington, Philadelphia,
Boston, Providence, San Francisco, Chicago and Newport. The
300 of New York and Newport society are worthy of their
own chapter. Concludes with "The Misadventures of Mrs. Detri-
mental—A Social Career."

687 _____. The Ultra-fashionable Peerage of America; An Official
List of Those People Who Can Properly Be Called Ultra-fashionable in the United States. New York: G. Harjes, 1904.
Predecessor to the "469," the author contends that, aside from
wealth, "one's manners must also be 'comme il faut'..." if one
hopes to enter "into the composition of this big social trust
whose subjective aim is pleasure...." Defines smartness and
tells how the ultra-smart man dresses, what the style of living
is and how the ultra-fashionable entertain.

688 Nickerson, Hoffman. "Gentlemen Wanted." American Review,
7:422-41, Sept., 1936.
The stated purpose of the article is to "see what the term
gentleman once meant, to consider how the gentry..have
been...terminated, and to note how their disappearance has
aggravated the troubles of the modern world."

689 Norman, Dawn Crowell. "Everyone Can Have Beauty in Manners."
Ladies' Home Journal, 75:57, Sept., 1958.
Questions for readers to ascertain how good their own manners
are, and examples of how mothers teach their children manners
by using a positive approach and setting an example.

690 Norwood, Hayden. Common Sense Etiquette Dictionary. Emaus,
Pa.: Rodale, 1937.
Introduction discusses the changing of manners through time.
Dictionary is cross-referenced, and advises on subjects ranging
from Comb to Swearing (it is always considered bad form).
Advice is administered in concise language, i.e., "Cup-Finger
Quirking—Do not quirk the little finger while holding a cup
to your lips." Also touches upon topics traditionally found
in etiquette books such as table manners, gift-giving, weddings,
funerals, public transport and invitations.

691 "Now Maybe We'll Get Courtesy." Saturday Evening Post, 218:124,
Feb. 9, 1946.
Anecdotes about returning servicemen who offer courteous
service to a traveler.

692 "Obligation of Courtesy." Century, 89:317-20, Dec., 1914.
Address delivered by President Arthur Twining Hadley of Yale
University on Oct. 4, 1914, a day of prayer for peace, in which
he calls for the use of courtesy in daily life which will broaden
to influence world politics.

693 Oettinger, Elizabeth. "Emily Post." American Heritage, 28:38-9,
April, 1977.
Biographical sketch of Emily Post looks at her private life
as well as her role as social arbiter and author.

694 Olander, Oscar G. "Courtesy." American Magazine, 126:59,
Aug., 1938.
Examines the use of courtesy in business. "He who regards
the respect which is due others cannot fail to inspire in them
respect for himself."
695 "On Your Feet, Man!" America, 105:145, April 15, 1961.
Acclaims a campaign in the New York City Subway System
which encourages men to offer their seats to women, suggesting
this courtesy as a simple beginning towards a remedy in a
"world falling apart at the seams."
696 Ordway, Edith Bertha. Etiquette of To-day. New York: George
Sully, 1913.
Examines the relationship between personality and the rules
of etiquette. Details manners at home, such as table etiquette,
friends, illness and courtesy to servants. Also defines the duties
of various servants, and describes tasteful furnishings for the
home. Proper deportment for guests, hosts public behavior,
and the duties of the chaperone are elucidated. Other topics
covered include weddings, mourning, and etiquette for children.
Includes samples of correspondence and an index.
697 _____. Etiquette of To-day. New York: George Sully, 1931.
Expanded and revised edition expresses "the peculiar quality
of that courtesy which is characteristic of the present day."
698 O'Rourke, P.J. Modern Manners. Illustrated by Robert Neubecker.
New York: Dell, 1983.
Satire which details "all the most up-to-date forms of vulgarity,
churlishness and presumption." Discusses material usually
found in etiquette books, for example, chapter called "The
Horrible Wedding," "The Hip Funeral," and "Guests, Including
Pets and Old Friends from College" are included. "The latest
fashions in discourtesy and barbarous display are catalogued,
and particulars of effrontery are given for every occasion."
Illustrated, with index.
699 O'Shaugnessy, Marjorie. Etiquette for Everybody; Including
the Bride's Book. Edited by Miriam B. Reichl. New York: Homemaker's Encyclopedia, 1952.
Encompasses everyday manners, conversation, correspondence,
forms of address, travel, business etiquette, christenings, and
funerals. Includes extensive coverage of wedding etiquette.
There are numerous photos, samples of invitations and correspondence, and illustrations.
700 Ostrander, Sheila. Etiquette for Today. New York: Barnes and
Noble, 1967.
Brief yet comprehensive coverage of those topics such as table
manners, weddings, correspondence and special occasions. Advice on manners in the dormitory, apartment or house is given.
"Good manners can make communal living more tolerable."
There is a list of pointers to help one avoid getting into awkward
situations, as well as the etiquette of hands, chairs, coats,
hats, applause, the theater and cigaretiquette. The appendix
includes lists of menu terms in seven languages, a list and
description of wines and a list of proper forms of address.

701 "Oteliaquette at Chapel Hill." Time, 82:45-6, July 19, 1963.
   Profiles Otelia Connor, who became an unofficial campus
   institution as a social arbiter for the students at Durham, N.C.

702 "Other View of Manners." Scribners Magazine, 34:251-2, Aug.,
   1903.
   Discusses the digression from the point of view of Emerson
   that "manners are the happy ways of doing things..." to the
   view that "manners...become distrusted as the badge of an
   unadmitted superiority, or suspected as the mask of insincerity."

703 Otsubo, Mayumi. "A Guide to Japanese Business Practices."
   California Management Review, 28, Spring, 1986.
   Focusing upon Japanese business etiquette, details use of the
   business card, bow, the guest room, and the gift-giving custom.
   Corporate titles and organization, with a detailed accounting
   of rank and importance is included. Also examines Japanese
   decision making.

704 Page, Thomas Nelson. "Decay of Manners." Century, 81:881-7,
   April, 1911.
   Lengthy discourse which considers the subject of manners
   "with a view to determining whether our manners are worse
   or better than those of our fathers...."

705 Palmer, T.M. "North Bay Attracts Added Tourist Dollars Through
   Police Tourist Courtesy School." American City, 67:157-8,
   April, 1952.
   Describes the school, which teaches the value of courtesy
   as an asset to the tourist trade.

706 Parent, Gail. "The New Etiquette; How to Survive a Second
   Marriage." Harper's Bazaar, 117:112, Oct., 1984.
   Tips for the second time around includes advice on how to
   handle yours, theirs and ours (children), that divorce and remarriage is expensive, and that it is ill advised to get too friendly
   with your ex- and his new wife.

707 Parker, George Lawrence. "Taking Off One's Hat." Atlantic,
   108:135-8, July, 1911.
   Correlates the seven stages of removing the hat with the seven
   stages of man, the growth from infant to old man.

708 Parker, Judith. "Manners in a Man's World." Rotarian, 69:26-8,
   Oct., 1946.
   Looks at the manners of clubmen, utilizing Mr. Howe Brashley
   Grating and Mr. Noble Mannerly. Gives advice on the smoothly
   run meeting and the treatment of guests at the club also.
   Parker Pen Company, joint author See Do's and Taboos Around
   the World (1985).

709 Parker Publishing Company. Business Etiquette Handbook. West
   Nyack, N.Y.: The Company, 1965.
   "Your business career can suffer unless you master the art
   of courtesy." Comprehensive volume discusses all aspects
   of business etiquette, beginning with the office and covering
   working with others, introductions, office parties, business
   cards and office memorandum. Tells how to welcome guests,
   use the telephone, and be courteous sales and service personnel.
   Business travel, entertaining, meetings and conventions and

White House etiquette are additional topics examined. Includes
a guide to parliamentary procedure, flag etiquette and correct
forms of address.

710 Parrott, Lora Lee (Montgomery). <u>Christian Etiquette</u>. Grand
Rapids, Mich.: Zondervan, 1953.
Encompasses all aspects of etiquette, saying, "the goal of
Christian etiquette is poise." Lists graciousness, common sense
and propriety as the spirit of Christian etiquette. In addition
to the usual topics in an etiquette book, discusses church etiquette, the church choir, Sunday as a family day, and church
socials. Advises upon the etiquette at camp, of conventions
and conferences as well.

711 "Party Disasters." <u>Glamour</u>, 77:172-5, Dec., 1979.
Picture of a party on a two-page spread illustrates different
behaviors and lays a foundation for advice to party-goers about
everything from bad breath to a firm handshake.

712 "The Passing of Good Manners." <u>Harper's Bazaar</u>, 42:408, Jan.,
1908.
Finds the decline of manners in America to be "sadly evident
in our trolley cars or on our public streets."

713 Pastor, Maud. "Victorian Etiquette Book." <u>Hobbies</u>, 57:63, Aug.,
1952.
Highlights amusing and different advice culled from a number
of different Victorian etiquette books, "these books represent
a true and amusing record of the modes and manners of those
brought up in strict observance of early Victorian proprieties
in America."

714 Paul, D.L. "On Approaching Holy Men." <u>American Mercury</u>,
10:183-92, Feb., 1927.
Confronts the issue of precedence, where to seat clergy, how
to address them and how to introduce them, contending "it
is strange...that in all the current handbooks of etiquette eccle-
siastics should receive less attention...."

Pawlas, George **See** Bennett, Marilyn.

715 Payne, Mildred M. <u>What Do I Do Now? A Guide to Conduct
and Dress for Business People</u>. New York: Gregg, 1940.
Begins with a discussion on the relationship between manners
and personality. Includes advice on establishing a broad background and one's personal appearance, in order to be more
employable. Instruction on the correct behavior of travel,
correspondence, dinner and conversation is included.

716 Peale, Norman Vincent. "Courtesy; Key to a Happier World."
<u>Saturday Evening Post</u>, 247:37, May, 1975.
Offers advice on how to improve manners and says that "it
all comes down to how you regard people.... The only constant,
daily, effective solution is politeness."

717 _____. "Manners Make a Difference." <u>Reader's Digest</u>, 104:99-
101, March, 1974.
Suggests life's difficulties could be overcome, if not avoided,
if people treated each other with courtesy. Lists specific things
anyone wanting to improve their manners can do, i.e., practice
courtesy, think courteously, and accept courtesy.

718 Pegler, Westbrook. "Table Manners a la Francaise." Reader's
   Digest, 30:18, Jan., 1937.
   Comparison of French, American and English table manners.
   "The Frenchman's enjoyment and simple skill at table are admir-
   able...."

719 Pennell, Elizabeth Robins. "Our Democracy of Bad Manners."
   Forum, 73:504-12, April, 1925.
   Decrying the lack of courtesy in America, the author says,
   "one advantage of living in a land where all men are equal
   is that you can be rude to everybody."

720 "Perhaps We Need an Etiquette Book on Good Manners While
   Motoring." Saturday Evening Post, 226:12, May 1, 1954.
   Discusses Missouri State Highway Commission's request that
   those who use the state highways as a trash can also throw
   out a nickel to help defray clean-up expense. Suggests the
   litter bug problem has something to do with the disappearance
   of good manners "the moment the American gets into an automobile."

721 Perry, Josephine. How and Why of Home Etiquette. Seattle:
   Lowman and Hanford, 1934.
   Based on a course offered to maids at the Seattle YMCA. Describes the correct procedure for setting and waiting the table,
   receiving guests, and other functions to do with the household.

722 Peterson, Barbara. "Etiquette for You and the Bride." Better
   Homes and Gardens, 31:191, June, 1953.
   Question/answer format answers questions about bridal showers
   and wedding gifts.

723 _____. "When You're Eating Out, Here's How." Better Homes
   and Gardens, 31:246-8, May, 1953.
   Question/answer format addresses restaurant etiquette such
   as when to be seated, how long to wait to be served, etc.

724 _____. "Which to Use: Knife, Fork, Fingers?" Better Homes
   and Gardens, 31:217-9, Sept., 1953.
   Question/answer format tells how to eat different fruits.

725 "Petty Selfishness." Living Age, 246:244-7, July 22, 1905.
   Cites examples of selfishness such as hoarding newspapers
   in the club, holding up lines with unintelligent inquiries, smoking
   on the omnibus, tying shoe laces in the middle of the sidewalk,
   and selfishness in domestic life exhibited by both men and
   women.

726 Phelps, William Lyon. "Men, Women and Manners." Delineator,
   118:17, Feb., 1931.
   Examines the decline of formality in American manners. In
   trying to determine if there is a real decline in manners as
   perceived by the older generation toward the younger, Phelps
   contends, "we must be careful not to confuse the absence of
   elaborate formalities with bad manners." Suggests a lack of
   time experienced by people as a possible factor in the decrease
   of formality.

727 Phillips, Eleanor H. "Theater Manners." Ladies' Home Journal,
   31:66, Oct., 1914.
   Lists annoying mannerisms by people which can spoil an evening's

entertainment. Concludes with a brief synopsis of "little matters based on unselfishness...which make for good manners at the theater."

728 Phillips, H.I. "Are You the Master of Your Forks, the Captain of Your Spoons?" American Magazine, 100:60-1, Sept., 1925.
Relates childhood memories of reading an etiquette book called, Hill's Manual of Social and Business Forms, by Thomas Edie Hill, and in this light discusses modern manners with humor, particularly table etiquette. Phillips contends that "etiquette is used too little for comfort and too much for display." Also suggests there are too many rules for the table and not enough rules where they are really needed.

729 Phillips, R. le Clerc. "Etiquette Old and New." Bookman, 62:259-66, Nov., 1925.
Says that the precepts in mediaeval etiquette books are essentially the same as now, and includes highlights from some very old etiquette books, such as Boke of Nurture by John Russell and William Caxton's Book of Curtesye.

730 Piccione, Nancy. Your Wedding; A Complete Guide to Planning and Enjoying it. Englewood Cliffs, N.J.: Prentice-Hall, 1982.
"The format of the book is dedicated to the proposition that a wedding...should be a celebration...." Contents are arranged alphabetically beginning with Announcements, to Bridal Wear and ending with Zoom Lens. Duties, expenses, kinds of weddings, showers, second marriages and unusual circumstances appear also. Lists what the duties of the different attendants are, what papers you may need to sign, and sample wording of invitations. Gives the history of certain wedding traditions. Includes index.

Piers, Maria W., joint author See Smallenburg, Carol.

731 Pierson, Irene Dorothy. Campus Cues. New York: Interstate, 1956.
Arranged in question/answer format, responds to more than 500 questions typically asked by college students. Introduction lists four reasons why good manners are important. Introductions, appearance, conversation, dating, theater manners, dining etiquette, travel etiquette, smoking and drinking, hopitality, gifts, telephone, correspondence, and wedding and business etiquette are topics covered. Illustrated, with index.

732 Pileggi, Nicholas. "Quality of Rudeness." Esquire, 61:98, Jan., 1964.
Discusses rudeness displayed by men at the top, which "seems quite in order today as long as this can be justified by success...," and examines some reasons for this attitude.

733 Pinchot, Ann. "Good Manners Mean Good Times." Woman's Home Companion, 77:66-7, Jan., 1950.
Describes the Good Manners Program at the Madison School in Phoenix, Arizona, a plan implemented in the cafeteria to teach students good table manners.

734 Platt, Joseph B. "Etiquette of the Entrance Hall." Delineator, 125:22-3, Oct., 1934.
"The ideal entrance hall is one we love to go into and hate

to leave." Detailed advice on how to decorate the entrance hall, and appropriate etiquette, i.e., never hand your card to the hostess.

735 "Pocket Guide to North Africa; Abridged." Life, 14:59-60, Jan. 11, 1943.
Discusses this guide, prepared by the War Department for soldiers so that there won't be "mistakes in your dealing with the people of North Africa so that we may have their friendship and cooperation." Highlights Moslem women, food, customs at mealtime and shops.

736 "Pocket Handkerchief." Independent, 63:1386-8, Dec. 5, 1907.
Traces the origins of the handkerchief, from a gentleman's article of dress to carrying the handkerchief in the hip pocket as a "perpetration of the uncouth habits of the kerchief class...," and on to a discussion of spitting with the final words, "do not spit at all, but if you must, then use your handkerchief."

737 "Politeness in War-time." Literary Digest, 55:24-5, Sept. 15, 1917.
Suggests that there is a need for courtesy from railroad employees, and that this need applies equally well to everyone.

738 Pollock, Channing. "After the War, the Worm May Turn! Lack of Manners in Wartime." Rotarian, 66:14-5, Feb., 1945.
Using innumerable examples gleaned from the author's own experience, and those of friends, the author contends that "the fact that we are at war has become the blanket alibi for every variety of bad service and bad faith."

739 _____. "Art of Being Kind." Rotarian, 47:11-3, Dec., 1935.
Discusses the rewards of "affability and considerateness" and encourages people to like one another. "I think life would be easier if more of us liked people."

740 Pomeranz, Virginia E., and Schultz, Dodi. "Propriety in Public Places." Parents Magazine, 57:76, July, 1982.
Encourages parents to assume responsibility for containing and restraining youngsters in public places, and offers practical advice on containment strategies.

741 Pope, E. "Posture, Poise and Polish; Physical Fitness Institute, White Plains, N.Y." McCall's, 83:18-20, Sept., 1956.
Highlights program at this institute which features instruction in walking downstairs, juggling teacups, etc., in an effort to teach poise.

742 Post, Elizabeth L. "All About Weddings." Good Housekeeping, 182:92, June, 1976.
Question/answer format covers advice about weddings such as inviting people from the office, clergy, receiving lines and more.

743 _____. Emily Post on Entertaining; Answers to the Most Often Asked Questions about Entertaining at Home and in Business. New York: Harper & Row, 1987.
Question/answer format with chapters covering these topics: party planning, invitations, dinner parties, table setting, dinner service, buffets, cocktail parties, obligations of guests and hosts, and entertaining for business.

744 _____. Emily Post's Complete Book of Wedding Etiquette.
Illustrations by Nomi Raia Friedman. New York: Harper &
Row, 1982.
Includes specific how-to's for pre-engagement behavior, through
the engagement party and to the wedding. Obligations on both
sides of the wedding party are outlined, and samples of all
the necessary correspondence is included. Book concludes
with a chapter of the answers to sixty frequently asked questions.

745 _____. Emily Post's Etiquette. New York: Harper & Row,
1984.
Fourteenth edition of Etiquette; In Society, in Business, in
Politics, and at Home, by Emily Post. Cites two changes which
have "profoundly affected modern society and our manners..."
and they are the number of women in the work place, and
changes in the way single people are viewed by society. In
order to address these changes, two new sections—"Your Personal Life" and "Your Professional Life" have been added to
this edition. The scope remains comprehensive, even though
the information has been reorganized.

746 _____. Emily Post's Wedding Planner. New York: Harper
& Row, 1982.
Designed to help organize preparations for the wedding, the
planner includes pages to list names and addresses of guests
and relatives, special pages for listing the caterer, florist,
photographer and other services. There is a bride's check-list
with timetables, charts to help decide what type of wedding
and reception to have, and lists for bride's and groom's expenses.

747 _____. "Etiquette for the Holidays." Good Housekeeping,
181:60, Dec., 1975.
Question/answer format covers topics such as Christmas card
protocol, unexpected gifts, thank-you notes and holiday tipping.

748 _____. The New Emily Post's Etiquette. New York: Funk
& Wagnalls, 1975.
Thirteenth edition of Etiquette; In Society, in Business, in
Politics, and at Home, by Emily Post. Divided into parts which
cover the art of conversation, correspondence, official protocol,
public manners, travel, parties, entertaining, special occasions,
weddings, dress, home life and the family. Throughout the
book are excerpts from the original edition which serve to
illustrate changes in manners through the years.

749 _____. Please, Say Please. A Common Sense Guide to Bringing
Up Your Child. Boston: Little, Brown and Co., 1972.
Suggests to parents it is their job to sort out and pass on the
best rules of etiquette. Opening chapter suggests outlining
a plan for child-rearing and lists some qualities needed for
good parenting. Asks questions to help parents determine what
kind of relationship they want with their child, and discusses
courtesy as a pleasure and a privilege for parents to teach.

750 _____. "What's Your Etiquette I.Q.?" Ladies' Home Journal,
101:36, Nov., 1984.
Seventeen question true/false quiz about table manners.

751 Post, Emily (Price). "Any Fork Will Do." Collier's, 83:21, April
20, 1929.
Advises to do what is natural and not to worry about etiquette,
"providing that your natural impulses are not likely to affront
the ordinary requirements of civilized behavior."

752 _____. "Check Up Your Manners; Test Your Etiquette Picture."
American Magazine, 131:20-1, March, 1941.
Picture of a party in which people are depicted breeching
the rules of good etiquette, reader is instructed to look for
14 errors, and turn to page 81 for the answers.

Post, Emily (Price) See Post, Elizabeth. Emily Post of Entertaining (1987).

Post, Emily (Price) See Post, Elizabeth. Emily Post's Complete
Book of Wedding Etiquette (1982).

754 _____. Emily Post's Etiquette; The Blue Book of Social Usage.
Revised by Elizabeth L. Post. New York: Funk & Wagnalls,
1956.
Modernized to reflect "the less formal life that most of us
lead today." Eleventh edition of Etiquette, remains comprehensive in scope, with some condensing of information, i.e., that
on conversation, and the language has been modernized. "How
to Address Important Personages" changed to "Addressing
Important Persons."

755 _____. Emily Post's Etiquette. Revised by Elizabeth L. Post.
New York: Funk & Wagnalls, 1969.
Twelfth edition of Etiquette, includes some up-dating of content.
Two new pages of material on Bar Mitzvah have been added,
and six pages of new information on celebrating anniversaries
is included. Also allows for changes on wedding invitations
(names of both divorced parents) and includes a new chapter
of gifts, as well as advice to women on wearing slacks.

Post, Emily (Price) See Post, Elizabeth Emily Post's Etiquette
(1984).

Post, Emily (Price) See Post, Elizabeth. Emily Post's Wedding
Planner (1982).

756 _____. Etiquette; In Society, in Business, in Politics, and
at Home. New York: Funk & Wagnalls, 1922.
Instructions embrace introductions, conversations, cards and
calling, formal and informal dining, including teas and luncheons,
balls, engagements and weddings. Proper conduct in public
is outlined. Covers virtually all aspects of etiquette, from
cradle to grave. Uses characters, i.e., Mrs. Toplofty, as a means
of illustration. More notable chapters include "The Well Appointed House," "Country House Hospitality," "House Party
in Camp," "Clubs and Club Etiquette," "In Business and Politics"
and "Etiquette for Children."

757 _____. Etiquette; The Blue Book of Social Usage. New York:
Funk & Wagnalls, 1927.
New and enlarged edition, introduction contains letter explaining
what "Best Society" is. Note title change also.

758 _____. Etiquette; The Blue Book of Social Usage. New York:
Funk & Wagnalls, 1931.

This edition illustrated with private photos and facsimiles of social forms. Includes 48 pages of answers to readers' questions.

759 _____. Etiquette; The Blue Book of Social Usage. New York: Funk & Wagnalls, 1937.
New changes include chapters called "Modern Man and Girl," "Modern Exactions of Courtesy," "Etiquette in Washington and State Capitals," "American Neighborhood Customs," and "The Vanished Chaperone and Other Lost Conventions."

760 _____. Etiquette; The Blue Book of Social Usage. New York: Funk & Wagnalls, 1942.
New edition contains war time supplement, with few other significant differences.

761 _____. Etiquette; The Blue Book of Social Usage. New York: Funk & Wagnalls, 1945.
Includes new chapter "Concerning Military and Post-War Etiquette."

762 _____. Etiquette; The Blue Book of Social Usage. New York: Funk & Wagnalls, 1950.
Includes new chapter "Preparation for Their Future Home as the Wedding Day Approaches." "Telephone Courtesy" and "Smoking Etiquette" expanded to become separate chapters. Dropped chapter "Concerning Military and Post-War Etiquette."

763 _____. Etiquette; The Blue Book of Social Usage. New York: Funk & Wagnalls, 1955.
"The emphasis has shifted in time to the problems of living gracefully in a small and simple household." Ninth edition, somewhat different format.

764 _____. Etiquette; The Blue Book of Social Usage. New York: Funk & Wagnalls, 1960.
Tenth edition substantially the same as the ninth.

765 _____. "Etiquette of Smoking." Good Housekeeping, 111:37, Sept., 1940.
The where's and how-to's of smoking etiquette for host and guest.

766 _____. "How I Came to Write About Etiquette." Pictorial Review, 38:4, Oct., 1936.
Recalls writing the first edition of Etiquette, with discussion of personal philosophy of etiquette. Also describes some of the questions she receives in her mail, and from whom.

767 _____. "It's All in the Day's Mail." Collier's, 83:16, June 29, 1929.
Post describes how many letters she receives, where they come from and what sort of questions are put to her. The greatest number of letters received ask routine questions, "but very few people think enough about it to realize that the subject of etiquette is practically unlimited;...it is the foundation upon which every business as well as social structure is built."

Post, Emily (Price) See Post, Elizabeth. The New Emily Post's Etiquette (1975).

Poston, Gretchen, joint author See Boggs, Barbara.

768 Powell, Marcia, and Graeme, Lynn. The Honeymoon Handbook; A Guide to Life's Most Romantic Adventure. New York: Macmillan, 1980.

Advice covers travel etiquette, dining out, social skills and conversational arts. Describes the etiquette for a variety of public places also. Grooming and dress, a travel directory with travel tips, writing effective business letters, and a guide to tipping are among the subjects included. There is a "Directory of Romantic Travel Possibilities" and a list of books for additional reading, includes index.

769 Poynter, Josephine. "Teaching Please Takes Patience." Better Homes and Gardens, 25:56, Jan., 1947.

How to teach your child manners by example.

770 "Profiles; A.B. Duke." New Yorker, 40:34-6, Aug. 15, 1964.

Defines the responsibilities and duties of the Chief of Protocol, Angier Biddle Duke, (under the Kennedy administration) with examples of the role in the administration played by the Chief of Protocol.

771 "Progress of Manners." Independent, 52:1747-9, July 19, 1900.

Describes the well-bred person in America, and bemoans the "average incivility of the average throng..." in New York City. Emphasizes the moral obligations of executives to enforce good manners among employees.

772 "Proper Way to Make Introductions." Good Housekeeping, 166:190, March, 1968.

Concise instructions include how to introduce family members, and people at a large gathering, as well as providing general guidelines.

Proxmire, Ellen, joint author See Boggs, Barbara.

773 "Public Manners." Scribners Magazine, 54:787, Dec., 1913.

Contends that Americans are universally friendly and correlates the equality in America with "the particular brand of good manners that flourishes in this country."

774 Puner, Helen. "Habit of Courtesy." Parents Magazine, 32:30-1, Jan., 1957.

Relates discovery that not all habits of courtesy come from within naturally in children, and that the lack of attention to manners resulted in her own children's behavior being "downright rude," and the realization on her part that this was an injustice to the children.

775 Purnell, Max, and Witting, Clifford. "This First-name Business; Debate." Rotarian, 89:9, July, 1956.

Purnell argues for the use of first names at Rotary Club, saying the intimacy which comes with the use of first names is heartwarming. Witting says the formality has merit.

Putnam, James W., editor See Witan. University of Kansas.

776 Pye, Anne Etheldra Briscoe, and Shea, Nancy Brinton. Navy Wife. New York: Harper, 1942.

Begins with a description of appropriate behavior as a guest at Annapolis, i.e., what to wear, dances and graduation. For the wives of Navy pilots there is a list of terms used in Naval Aviation, and one for the Undersea Navy as well. Includes a chapter about Navy personnel, the Marine Corps, and the Coast Guard as well. The etiquette of engagements, weddings, entertaining and children is described. "Navel Customs and Traditions" and the "Business of the Naval Household" are also discussed. "Navy Life in Washington," and "Etiquette for Civilians Visiting a Navy Yard" are additional chapters. Includes a glossary of Navy terms, and an index.

777 Rachlin, Seth, and Van Hoomissen, George. Where the Girls Are Today; The College Man's Roadtripper Guide to All Women's Colleges. New York: Crown, 1984.
Describes the art of roadtripping—men searching for women's colleges. Tells how to find the college, and how to behave once it's found.

778 Radlovic, I. Monte. Etiquette and Protocol; A Handbook of Conduct in American and International Circles. Preface by John F. Simmons. New York: Harcourt, 1956.
Includes, in considerable detail, official etiquette for Americans at home and abroad. Protocol in Washington, the diplomatic corps, the armed forces and in the United Nations is outlined. Includes ecclesiastical forms of address and protocol pertaining to European royalty also. Standard forms of invitation and regret are covered, along with a glossary of diplomatic terms and titles, seating arrangements for official dinner parties, and an annotated bibliography.

779 Radziwill, Lee. "Conversation on Manners." Ladies' Home Journal, 79:50-1, Feb., 1962.
Informal conversation includes author's thoughts on meeting people, conversation, guests, parties, note-writing and teaching children manners.

780 Raemers, Sidney Albert. Catholic Gentleman; A Manual of Christian Practice and Etiquette for the Use of Catholic Secondary Schools. New York: W.H. Sadlier, 1938.
Divided into two parts, "The Christian Gentleman" and "The Catholic Gentleman." The first part aims to formulate the rules which every gentleman should know, and the second "gives the forms for correct conduct which are of particular application to the Catholic...." Subject matter encompasses table manners, travel, work, guest, reading, and writing, as well as a chapter called "The Gospel and Christian Etiquette." Advice is also addressed to the penitent Catholic, the sick Catholic and the Perfect Catholic Gentleman. Includes index.

781 "Railroad Rights and Wrongs." Coronet, 34:18, June, 1953.
Six pictures illustrate courteous behavior on the train.

782 "Raising the Perfect Child; Miss Manners Tells How." U.S. News and World Report. 98:60-1, Jan. 14, 1985.
Questions about children and manners and Martin's responses are included, in which she refers to such time-honored phrases as "Because it's good for you" and "You'll freeze that way."

783 Random House Book of Etiquette. New York: Random House, 1967.
Comprehensive volume covers the etiquette of everyday behavior such as table manners or telephone manners. Also describes

public manners, travel etiquette, communication etiquette, ceremonies of life, table service, business etiquette, and etiquette for salespeople, and more. Includes illustrations, samples of correspondence, and index.

784 Raphael, Bette-Jane. Can This Be Love? New York: Arbor House, 1985.
Much of the material in this book was published in the monthly column by the same name in Glamour magazine. Discusses the relationship between couples, starting with the decision of "live-in love." Advises on how to choose the right partner, how to break up, how to survive the holidays and how to maintain privacy. Some chapters are called "Differences, Incompatibilities and Other Natural Phenomena" and "The Fight as a Learning Experience," as well as "Fanning the Flames of Romance." Written with humor.

785 _____. "Etiquette? Is That a New Perfume?" Glamour, 83:217, Aug., 1985.
Tongue-in-cheek pointers on situations "designed to prove that the rules of proper etiquette serve your relationship better than do those of your State Boxing Association."

786 Raymond, Louise. Good Housekeeping's Book of Today's Etiquette. New York: Harper & Row, 1965.
Includes advice on charm, dress, children's manners, guests, entertaining, correspondence and how to plan a gracious home. Includes information on "Occasions of Ceremony," such as engagements, weddings, Bar Mitzvahs, confirmations and funerals. Includes index and illustrations.

787 "Real, Inside Top Secret." Collier's, 135:86, Jan. 21, 1955.
Discussion links the global and national political atmosphere to a "spree of bad manners..." and suggests that there is nothing wrong in America "that a return to good manners...wouldn't cure."

788 Reardon, Maureen Elena. The New Etiquette. Kansas City, Mo.: Sheed, Andrews and McMeel, 1976.
Begins by defining the new etiquette. Divided into five parts which cover general manners, dealing with others, in your home, while you're out and for weddings. Includes standard features such as table manners, children's manners and business etiquette. There are topics such as awkward moments, and treating the elderly as people, wines and cheese, and surviving the slumber party. Includes some comparison of the new etiquette with the traditional.

789 "Red Skelton's Impressions of a TV Pest; Photographs." McCall's, 80:4, Feb., 1953.
Photos depict rude behavior exhibited by viewers such as the "dial twister" and the "view blocker."

Reichl, Miriam B., editor See O'Shaughnessy, Marjorie.

790 Reid, Lillian N. Personality and Etiquette. Illustrated by Mary McMahon. Boston: D.C. Heath, 1950.
Introductions, host and hostess, guests, public behavior, dress, travel, teas, table manners, conversation, letters and chapters concerned with personality traits such as tact and humor are

all addressed in the text. References are included at the end
of each chapter, as well as a review of the chapter and written
exercises. Indexed, with illustrations.

791 "Respecting People and Titles." Christian Century, 81:229,
Feb. 19, 1964.
Maintains that whites should use customary titles of respect
when addressing Negroes. "In racial encounters politeness
is both inexpensive and precious."

792 Richards, James Albert. The Book of Culture. New York: J.A.
Richards, 1924.
Compilation of different essays includes: "The Book of Good
Manners," by F.H. Martens, "Essays of Culture," by Harriet
Lane, "Physical Beauty," by Florence Courtenay, "Color Harmony
and Design," by Millicent Melrose, "Sex," by Henry Stanton,
and "Chesterfield's Letters."

793 _____. Things We Don't Talk About. New York: True Story,
1934.
Chapter One discusses "The Niceties of Social Intercourse
in Public," including the bow of acknowledgment and hat tipping.
"The Proprieties of Speech and Conversation" are detailed,
including the Ten Commandments of Well-bred Conversation.
Discusses calls, cards, visits, and correct manners in the hotel.
In the chapter on dancing, the "Feminine Prerogatives" are
outined! Ponders the question "What is Physical Beauty?" and
tells "How to Make and Keep the Figure Beautiful." There
is a chapter on "Sex." Color in dress is detailed and dress is
discussed.

794 Richardson, Anna Steese Sausser. The Bride's Book of Etiquette.
New York: Harper and Brothers, 1930.
Introduction states that "among the factors which have influenced wedding customs may be mentioned the World War;...the
economic independence of women...the shrinking family background...and the craze for dieting." Describes the preparation
necessary for a wedding, invitations, the bridal party, the
trousseau, receptions, breakfasts, entertaining for the bridal
party and gifts. Book is primarily in question/answer format
and includes samples of invitations, as well as illustrations.
"What is dignified is right. Simplicity is always safer than
ostentation."

795 _____. "Does it Pay to Be Polite?" Woman's Home Companion,
65:17, July, 1938.
Says courtesy is never out of style, and gives anecdotes of
young people getting ahead because of their courteous behavior.

796 _____. Etiquette at a Glance. New York: D. Appleton, 1927.
Fundamentals of good form are set forth in alphabetical order,
and discussion encompasses bridge, business, cards, club customs,
dancing, dining, dress, letters, luncheons, manners in public,
official etiquette, table manners, teas and more.

797 _____. "Etiquette at a Glance." Woman's Home Companion,
53:30, Aug.; 31, Sept.; 42, Oct.; 36, Nov., 1926. 54:34, Jan.;
46, March; 36, April; 36, May; 40, July, 1927.
Series of articles cover "Manners and Graces in Public Places,"

i.e., who goes first, "When You Dance," "A Chart of Table Manners," "Your Manners When You Travel," "Some Vacation Pointers," "Giving a Dinner," "Teas," "Weddings," and "The Wedding Day."

798 _____. "Politeness—A Business Asset." Woman's Home Companion, 37:63, Sept., 1910.

Courtesy is the key to self-respect, and self-respect represents "contentment which salary cannot buy." Explores examples in which politeness is a business asset, and where rudeness has had an adverse effect upon one's job.

799 _____. Standard Etiquette. New York: Harper, 1925.

"In no country is this knowledge of etiquette so useful and important as in America, where, all men being equal, there is no limit to the progress they can make...if they have brains, ability, persistency and good manners." Comprehensive in scope, covers same topics as those in Etiquette at a Glance. Format includes advice and then questions and answers. Illustrated with sample cards and invitations. Indexed.

800 _____. "Telephone Courtesy." Woman's Home Companion, 40:43, March, 1913.

Outlines proper telephone manners, listing specific responses to give and detailed how-to's.

801 Richardson, Robert Charlwood. Official Courtesy and Customs of the Service. New York: New York University, 1936.

"Prepared to assist West Point cadets in both their official and social duties." Describes the value of discipline to an organization and discusses relationship between an officer and his men. Official courtesy such as saluting, courtesy calls and different situations is described. Describes the role of custom in determining appropriate conduct, and highlights some social customs such as table manners, introductions, cards and calling.

802 Rickary, J. "Civism, Civility and Urbanity." American Catholic Quarterly, 37:692-7, Oct., 1912.

Establishes the view of early Greeks that "individualities anarchically triumph over civic harmony..." and relates this notion to "human respect for the agreed upon code..." and "politeness of mere convention."

803 Ridgely, Benjamin H. "Questions of Local Color." Atlantic. 95:708-11, May, 1905.

Contends the world is growing commonplace, and draws from his travel experiences to illustrate that the "couleur locale" of Europe is becoming Anglicized.

804 Riggs, H.K. "Right Way." Yachting, 13:104, Jan., 1972.

Reviews certain nautical etiquette because of the "distressing lack of manners being demonstrated afloat today...." Highlights the etiquette of flags and signals.

805 "Right Way to Do 73 Different Things." Mademoiselle, 84:188-93, Nov., 1978.

Answers some of the most popular questions about etiquette, tells the right way to do everything from accept a compliment, end a meal, eat by yourself, eat ice cream, apply make up in public, to ending a conversation.

806 Riley, Kay. "Charmed--But Not Very." Drawings by Gracie
P. Smith. Good Housekeeping, 107:8, Oct., 1938.
Verses of reminders on proper introductions with accompanying
illustrations.

807 Riley, Marie Acomb. Handbook of Christian Etiquette. Saint
Paul, Minn.: Bruce, 1945.
The fundamentals of etiquette begin the discussion, and lead
into a discussion of the forms of manners such as introductions.
Manners on the street and in public are outlined, as are those
for the table, cards, conversation, personality, friendship and
dating. Gives detailed advice on what is good taste in weddings,
and the final chapter explores marriage. Includes many Biblical
references.

808 Ringold, Evelyn S. "Whatever Happened to Please?" New York
Times Magazine, 49-51, Dec. 15, 1963.
Says that adults have the distinct impression that "manners
among the young have suffered an undeniable decline...." Cites
behaviors lacking among teens to support the contention, and
gives possible reasons why. For example, the casual society,
lack of parental involvement in teaching manners, or the idea
that today's kids should be thinking about more important
things.

809 Rinzler, Carol E. "Talking with...Judith Martin." Redbook, 161:62,
July, 1983.
Interview with Judith Martin, emphasizing her views on child-
rearing.

810 Ripperger, Henrietta. "Woman of the Whirl." Good Housekeeping,
113:10, Dec., 1941.
Comparison of successful and unsuccessful guests at a party,
emphasizing manners as an enhancement to socializing.

811 Ritter, T.M., and Johnstone, Elizabeth. Mother's Remedies;
Over One Thousand Tried and Tested Remedies from Mothers
of the United States and Canada. Detroit, Mich.: G.H. Foote,
1916.
Manners and social customs are a major part of this compendium.
The official title is "Manners and Social Customs for Our Great
Middle Class as Well as Our Best Society." Advises upon correspondence, cards and introductions, dress, weddings, christenings,
funerals, social functions, dinners, gifts, showers and calls.
Includes sample invitations, a discussion of table etiquette,
hospitality in the home, visiting etiquette for girls, the debutante, manners for men, and duties and dress of servants. Concludes with a long list of "Remembers," and has index.

812 Rives, H.E. Modern and Complete Book of Etiquette. New York:
Winston, 1939.
Describes how to lay the foundations of good manners for
children and teen-agers. Examines the usefulness of the chaperone. Includes a chapter on office etiquette, one for the
bachelor, and much advice about engagements and weddings.
Table manners, servants, introductions, cards and letter writing
are included. Outlines the "Code of the Highway," advises
the "Clubman and Clubwoman," and looks at "Official Society

at Home and Abroad." Other chapters are "Business Woman
as an Executive," "When and Where Ladies Smoke," "Motoring
Parties," "Life in a Hotel," and "Maid Service for the Business
Couple." Includes photos and index.

813 Roberts, Helen Lefferts. The Cyclopedia of Social Usage, Manners
and Customs of the Twentieth Century. New York: G.P. Putnam's
Sons, 1927.
Describes in detail the changes in the etiquette of calls, and
the different types and formats of cards. Covers topics such
as weddings, dinners, table manners, balls, luncheons, public
entertainments, house parties, and proper deportment for
servants. The etiquette of sports and games, in the street,
shopping, at church, receptions and for travel by land and
water is outlined. Includes index.

814 Roberts, Kenneth L. "Circumspect Seventies." Saturday Evening
Post, 197:17, Jan. 24, 1925.
Tongue-in-cheek review of Decorum, 1877 makes comparisons
to contemporary youth.

815 Roberts, Patricia Easterbrook. Table Settings, Entertaining,
and Etiquette; A History and Guide. New York: Viking Press,
1967.
Covers all aspects of dining from table settings, linen, glass-
wares, decorations, entertaining, parties and tea. Includes
a pictorial history of the habits and customs of table settings.
Contains numerous photos throughout. Has bibliography, and
appendix of miscellaneous information.

816 Robinson, Elizabeth C. "Your Manners Are Showing." American
Home, 70:60, March, 1967.
Suggests making introductions simple by remembering three
things: age, sex, and social or business position.

817 Robinson, Henry Morton. "Speak Up for Courtesy." Review
of Reviews, 93:44-5, Jan., 1936.
Gives examples of several encounters with public servants
who display a lack of courtesy, contending the best way to
rectify this discourtesy is to "boldly speak up for good manners
and let our voices be heard in every boorish corner of our world."

818 Robinson, Jill. "Manners." House and Garden, 150:184-5, Nov.,
1978.
Particular examples of the "just plain rudeness..." going around
are given. "In every area of social interaction there are formal
rules, and they can always be broken—with charm. But not
with hostility or defiance."

Rogers, Lois V., joint author See Willson, Nina Cotton.

819 Rogers, Will. "Etiquette, As Lassoed by Will Rogers." Literary
Digest, 79:46-50, Oct. 6, 1923.
Will Rogers' review of Emily Post's Etiquette in terms of his
own social experiences, marvelling that he should "be so dumb
as to not have at least one of these forms of Etiquette right."

820 Rook, Clarence. "American Manners." Living Age, 249:86-90,
April 14, 1906.
As an Englishman travelling in America, Rook suggests differ-
ences in social language as an explanation why New Yorkers

are considered rude by visitors. He appreciates the "frank inquisitiveness of Americans," saying each nation develops manners which suit its particular lifestyle.

821 Rooney, Richard L. Courtesy in Christ. St. Louis, Mo.: The Queen's Work, 1941.
Defines courtesy and courtesy in Christ and lists points for discussion. Chapters include "Courtesy in Christ—A Challenge to Self-Conquest," "Courtesy in Christ Begins at Home" and "Courtesy in Christ Entertains Guests." Other topics include courtesy in travel, in public and in business. Discusses Christian manners at social gatherings and with public servants. Includes lists of do's and don'ts, and a list of pleasant attributes to strive towards.

822 Roosevelt, Eleanor. Book of Common Sense Etiquette. New York: Macmillan, 1962.
"The basis of all good human behavior is kindness." Begins by looking at the family at home, tells how to behave with servants in the home, and when the family entertains. Discusses the family in the community, with advice on getting acquainted, calling, invitations and table manners. Tells how to be a good neighbor in the apartment, and how to behave on the street, when driving or travelling. Covers special occasions such as birth, engagements, anniversaries, surprise parties, weddings and funerals. Office etiquette is outlined in detail, and a chapter called "V.I.P.'s" lists "special marks of respect to certain people...." Includes a chapter for teens, the handicapped, telephones and conversation, and one called "Patriotism, the Flag, and the National Anthem." Includes bibliography and index.

823 _____. "Good Manners." Ladies' Home Journal, 56:21, June, 1939.
Roosevelt's views based on the philosophy to act "with fundamental courtesy and consideration." Includes her experiences in different parts of the world and from her childhood. "Cultivate the kindly heart which flowers in good manners."

824 _____. "Modern Children and Old-fashioned Manners." Redbook, 119:47, Oct., 1962.
Basic premise is that if you act with kindness toward others, you will never go very far wrong, and that children will absorb this premise from parents by example, thereby laying the foundation for teaching manners to children.

825 Rose, Kathryn. "Etiquette for the Wedding Guest." Harper's Bazaar, 108:87, June, 1975.
How to behave at a morning wedding.

826 Rosemond, John K. "Kids and Manners; A Fresh Approach." Better Homes and Gardens, 63:68, Nov., 1985.
Ideas for teaching kids manners listing practical suggestions such as work on one thing at a time, be tolerant of mistakes, reward the child for being good, prompt with questions and set a good example.

827 Rosenberg, Henrietta. The Dollar Book of Etiquette. New York: Plaza, 1953.
"Manners are the restraints and obligations required by your

participation in society." Highlights table manners, introductions, visiting, entertaining, dating, dress, and rules of sportsmanship. Also touches briefly upon proper etiquette at weddings and funerals, bread and butter letters, travelling, tipping, manners for motorists, and business etiquette.

828 Rosenfield, Loyd. "Down With the Little Things." Collier's, 124:36, Nov. 19, 1949.

Humorous look at the "little things society has come to accept as common courtesy," including those little things women expect from men, with the result that "women achieve much of their ever-ascending dominance by making men look silly."

829 _____. "Introductions." Atlantic, 204:87, July, 1959.

Relates humorous situations encountered during introductions.

830 Rosenhouse, Annette. "Our Eat-and-Learn Program Works." Practical Home Economics, 3:23, Nov., 1957.

Discussion of program used to teach children manners using the school cafeteria as a teaching forum.

831 Rosiere, Gabrielle. "Announcing the Engagement of Mary Louise." Delineator, 84:17, March, 1914.

Different forms to use for announcing an engagement are illustrated, since "it is not good form for the fiancee to make the verbal announcement herself."

832 _____. "E.T. Quette Family and Cousin Marye of Quetteville." Delineator, 83:17, Oct., 1913.

Using the adventures of the Quette family, illustrates correct use of cards and calling, down to the type of print to use.

833 _____. "E.T. Quette Wedding." Delineator, 84:10, April, 1914.

Examples of correct forms of wedding invitations, includes size and type of engraving as well as announcements to be sent after the ceremony and to whom they should be sent.

834 _____. "E.T. Quettes at Home." Delineator, 83:10, Nov., 1913.

Gives the correct form for invitations at home, and dinner, and of acceptances and regrets, in great detail.

835 _____. "E.T. Quettes Give a Bridge-Luncheon and Auction-Tea." Delineator, 84:17, Feb., 1914.

How to write invitations for these occasions, as well as how to set the table and what to serve.

836 _____. "Fifty Do's and Don'ts." Woman's Home Companion, 42:31, Nov., 1915.

Do's and don'ts "in the world of courtesy and good form..." covers cards and calling, weddings and invitations.

837 _____. "Miss E.T. Quette's Bridal Perplexities." Delineator, 84:51, June, 1914.

Advice on the etiquette of proper use of married names, who calls on whom, and the use of a husband's cards.

838 _____. "New Year's Dance at the E.T. Quette's." Delineator, 84:42, Jan., 1914.

Illustrates the correct form of invitation, how, what and when to serve the New Year's supper, and dancing etiquette.

839 _____. Japanese Business Etiquette; A Practical Guide to Success with the Japanese. New York: Warner, 1985.
Illustrates how Westerners can adapt to rigid rules of conduct in Japan, including the etiquette of drinking, dining, gift giving and socializing in Japanese baths, spas, and bars. Describes the Japanese style in making presentations, and how to criticize and compromise. Appendices include where to print Japanese business cards, so called survival numbers, organizations, and recommended reading. Has glossary, and an index.

840 Ruark, Robert C. "Old Man and the Boy." Field and Stream, 59:10-11, Nov., 1954.
Tells the likes and dislikes of the old man which are rules of etiquette, actually. For example, the old man "couldn't abide a loud talker...," and "he said that 'sir' and 'please' and 'thank-you, ma'am' were as cheap as dirt...." The old man's views on hunting etiquette are set forth as well.

841 _____. "The Unspeakables; Trespassers Exercise the Right to Maim and Destroy." Field and Stream, 66:16, Nov., 1961.
Bemoans lack of courtesy exhibited by campers who trespass on his property, litter the environment, show no boating courtesy saying "courtesy and consideration...were solid components of outdoor courtesy...."

842 "Rudeness; An Epidemic in the Land; With an Interview with J. Freedman." U.S. News and World Report, 86:41-2, June 25, 1979.
Consultations with sociological experts examine the reasons for rudeness, including an interview with Jonathan Freedman, Professor of Psychology at Columbia University.

843 Rudolph, Marguerita. "They Have Such Awful Manners." Woman's Home Companion, 79:60-1, March, 1952.
Advises parents to create a home environment of friendliness in order to teach children respect for others, and that good manners develop naturally if those around them have good manners.

844 Rugh, C.E. "Social Standards." School and Society, 20:351-61, Sept. 20, 1924.
Suggests that the embarrassment to college deans caused by breaches of etiquette by students can be overcome. "If deans are living embodiments of sweetness and light, the higher democratic social standards can and will be secured and maintained."

845 Rush, Sheila, and Clark, Chris. How to Get Along with Black People; A Handbook for White Folks and Some Black Folks Too. New York: Third Press, 1971.
Written because "whites need to know the numerous little faux pas that can cause discomfort and worse—and the ways in which they can be relieved." Discourse on inter-racial social intercourse has advice which includes, "What to Call Them," "Racial Refrains" and how to "Avoid White Liberalisms." Gives suggestions on jokes and small talk, shopping, dining out, domestics, schools and civic contacts. Also suggests cliches to refrain from using, and the last chapter considers "What Next?"

846 Rutherford, Beatrice. <u>Good Manners and How Life May Be Made</u>
<u>More Pleasant</u>. New York: Bahtavi-Rothberg, 1940.
Opening chapter discusses the lack of the educational system
in teaching manners, and is followed by a chapter describing
good manners as quietness, cleanliness, and being considerate
of others. Tells how to run a well-mannered home, including
advice on furnishing and cleaning. Covers table manners, public
deportment, children, introductions, guests, personal appearance,
speech, weddings and leisure time. Includes photos and sample
menus.
Rutherford, Nancy Gill, joint author **See** Saputo, Helen Norman.

847 Sallis, James. "Civility." <u>America</u>, 150:152-3, March 3, 1984.
"Poor manners may indeed become a way of self-assertion.
Discourtesy results from the ever-increasing frustration and
powerlessness...we feel daily."

848 Salmon, Lucy Maynard. <u>Domestic Service</u>. New York: Macmillan,
1901.
Considers the historical aspects of domestic employment,
including service during the colonial period, and since. Examines
difficulties in domestic service from employer's standpoint,
such as having to assimilate a person into its domestic life
and the spirit of restlessness, as well as the industrial and
social disadvantages of domestic service. Discusses the improvement of social condition for the domestic servant as
a means of improving degradation experienced by those in
the occupation. Concludes that personnel in domestic service
has been transformed through industrial, political and social
revolutions; that it has been influenced by the commercial
and educational development of the country. Includes bibliography and index.

849 Sangster, Margaret Elizabeth Munson. <u>Good Manners for All</u>
<u>Occasions, Including Etiquette of Cards, Wedding Announcements</u>
<u>and Invitations</u>. New York: Cupples and Leon, 1921.
The etiquette of entertainment, of social-intercourse, correspondence, and happy living is outlined. Chapters cover table manners, children, travel, correspondence, introductions, marriage,
entertaining, visiting, mourning and in church. Includes correct
manners for men, in business relations, and a description of
suitable dress for all occasions and ages. Tells women how
to open a bank account and write checks, and how to add to
"their stock of pin money...." Quotes extensively from other
social arbiters, i.e., Sherwood and Hall. Includes photos and
numerous poems.

850 Saputo, Helen Norman, and Rutherford, Nancy Gill. <u>Secretary's</u>
<u>New Guide to Dealing with People</u>. Englewood Cliffs, N.J.:
Prentice-Hall, 1986.
Preview lists twenty ways this book will help the secretary,
including how to get along with executives, be a diplomat,
balance social and office life, and be an effective supervisor.
Chapter One considers the effect the secretary has on others,
and the subsequent chapter tells how to expand skills to meet
the demand of the changing office. Other topics include tech-

niques for greeting callers, telephone communication, and greeting the public. Tells how to participate successfully in the office social life, and strategies for handling difficult situations. Also includes advice on how to be more attractive and create a pleasant atmosphere. Indexed.

851 Sara, Dorothy. Bride's Encyclopedia. New York: Crown, 1951. Compilation of advice from leading authorities includes advice on etiquette for the newly married, entertaining, parties and games, budgeting, interior decorating, housekeeping, food, flowers, sewing, and beauty and charm. Includes index, and is illustrated.

852 _____. The Collier Quick and Easy Guide to Etiquette. New York: Collier Books, 1963.
Describes introductions and greetings, the use of names and titles, and the art of conversation. Calling cards and writing paper, letters, invitations, announcements and acceptances are included. Tells how to plan a party with a theme, and describes wedding procedures. Etiquette at dances, in the sickroom and on the telephone, for smoking, at the club and when travelling is outlined. There is a chapter for business and professional manners. Funerals, mourning and flag etiquette are included.

853 "Scattergood Says." American Magazine, 131:50, May, 1941.
Describes manners: "Manners is cream risin' milk of human kindness, but etiquette is a bo'quet of artificial flowers in a house without a garden."

Schleman, Helen Blanche, joint author See Stratton, Dorothy Constance.

854 Schrader, Constance. Nine to Five; A Complete Looks, Clothes, and Personality Handbook for the Working Woman. Englewood Cliffs, N.J.: Prentice-Hall, 1981.
Offers advice on what to wear for the job interview, how to care for skin, office protocol, work stresses and preparation for parties.

855 Schraub, Susan Hope. "Of Tea and Tables; A Nostalgic Look at Changing Etiquette." House Beautiful, 110:66, Nov., 1972.
Compares etiquette found in Emily Post's 1922 edition of Etiquette with that of today, focusing primarily on dinner parties and teas.

Schulze, Frederick, joint author See Schutz, Jacob Hubert.

856 Schutz, Jacob Hubert, and Schulze, Frederick. A Little Book of Church Etiquette; Or How to Behave Before Our Lord in the Blessed Sacrament and at Devotional Exercises in General. St. Louis, Mo.: B. Herder, 1929.
Intends to "help to open the eyes of such careless Catholics, that they may see the impropriety of their conduct." Describes the rubrics as the official rules of etiquette of the Catholic Church. Details proper decorum for sacristan, acolytes, ushers, collectors, organists and singers. Special acts of reverence and decorum, genuflections and bows and rules for communicants are set down. Correct behavior in church is detailed as is that for processions, funerals, The Angelus, visiting churches and sick calls.

857 Schwartz, Eleanor. "Closed Minds About Opening Doors." Psychology Today, 18:66, Feb., 1984.
Results of a study conducted by J.C. Ventimiglia of Memphis
State University on 479 instances in which one person opened
the door for another.
Schwartz, Marla Schram, joint author See Goss, Dinah Braun.
858 Scott, Judith Unger. Manners for Moderns. Illustrated by Ruth
K. Macrae. Philadelphia: Macrae-Smith, 1949.
Offers advice on everyday etiquette and travel etiquette,
as well as advice on clothes selection, personal grooming and
the etiquette of dating.
859 Scott, Miriam Finn. "Your Children's Manners." Woman's Home
Companion, 42:31, May, 1915.
Contends that in training children parents should recognize
that manners "should be a sincere expression of the child's
character..." and not a superficial act.
860 "Scourge of the Airlines." Flying, 40:39-42, June, 1947.
Pictorial essay features Prof. Jerry Colonna portraying boorish
behavior on an airplane.
861 Sedgwick, Henry Dwight. "Vanishing Gentlemen." Atlantic,
155:419-28, April, 1935.
Author reacts to the "general consensus of opinion..." that
the gentleman best be "poked away in our ancestral garret..."
and he specifically addresses "democrats, humanitarians, and
men of scientific attainments."
862 _____. "What a Gentleman Was." Atlantic, 155:259-68, March,
1935.
Defines the qualities of the gentleman as defined by the past,
and contends there is "the elimination of the gentleman that
is and for some time has been taking place under the stress
of alien forces."
863 Seeds, Charme. "You Get What You Expect from Men." Pictorial
Review, 28:2, March, 1927.
Relating her world-wide encounters with men, Seeds says that
"women may expect courtesy everywhere...," and if it is not
received, perhaps it is because "she gets what she invites."
864 Segal, Julius, and Segal, Zelda. "Kids Are People, Too." Parents
Magazine, 158, June, 1986.
Encourages parents to follow their own advice before trying
to teach children manners, and that parents should criticize
the behavior, not the child, and remember that the Golden
Rule applies to everyone.
Segal, Zelda, joint author See Segal, Julius.
865 Seligson, Marcia. "Who Needs Etiquette?" Life, 68:12, May
6, 1970.
The message is: "It's time for more honesty, less Etiquette."
866 Sellers, Edith. "Question of Good Manners." Living Age, 276:350-8,
Feb. 8, 1913.
The author recalls a Finnish town meeting, where the topic
for debate was a question of manners.
867 Sellers, Kenneth. "Can We Cope with Comfort?" American
Mercury, 83:17-20, Nov., 1956.

Discusses the "growing cult of 'informalism'..." which tends to rate commonly accepted manners as old-fashioned and out- moded, and equates "sloppy manners" with "modern." Suggests one way to recognize the informalist is the traits they exhibit, such as "cultural awareness."

868 "Sensible Shaper of U.S. Manners; With Excerpts from 1960 Edition of Etiquette." Life, 49:163-4, Oct. 10, 1960.
Eulogy to Emily Post, who died at the age of 86, traces a few of the changes in her advice. Illustrated with photos.

869 Seymour, Anne. A-B-C of Good Form. With introduction by Maud Howe. New York: Harper and Brothers, 1915.
Small book of advice covering the "essentials of good form." Describes the spirit of hospitality in detail, with specifics for proper and efficient entertaining. Advice also covers intro- ductions, invitations, calls, afternoon teas, luncheons, dinners, weddings, dances, table etiquette, hostess, guest and correspon- dence.

870 Shafto, Mary. "Social Forms of Oral Language." National Educa- tion Association Journal, 31:25, Jan., 1942.
Outlines techniques utilized by educators at the Bradley Park School in New Jersey, to teach proper etiquette to students, and then apply their knowledge to a life use situation.

871 Shames, Laurence. "What Every Man Should Know: How to Apolo- gize." Esquire, 101:40, March, 1984.
"An apology flatters; an apology condoles...." Lists requirements for a graceful apology.

872 Shand, Alexander Innes. "Memories of Manners." Living Age, 254:688-90, 763-5, Sept. 14-21, 1907; 255:177-9, Oct. 19, 1907.
Three part discussion covers dress, deportment and conversation. In the first part, dress, Shand reminisces about the dress of his boyhood, and changes from then to now. Deportment brings to mind when there were social spheres and circles which were not to be penetrated by outsiders. Of earlier days he says, "there might be scandals as to morals, but manners almost touched severity." Of conversation he laments it is no longer "cultivated--where serious talk used to be something of a social mania."

873 Shapiro, Norman Zalmon, and Anderson, Robert Helms. Toward an Ethics and Etiquette for Electronic Mail. Santa Monica, Ca.: Rand, 1985.
Presents a set of guidelines which are intended to help make the use of electronic mail effective; "the authors hope to accel- erate the process by which social customs and behavior appropri- ate to electronic mail become established." Describes two phenomena in electric mail systems, one is the likelihood that the recipient will react negatively in reading material that might have been misinterpreted. The second is the lack of control of who will see the message. Contents include a description of electronic mail as a new medium, the etiquette of sending, receipt and response of messages, acting as coor- dinator/leader of an interest group and the phenomenon of flaming. Includes list of Network Interest Groups, and glossary.

874 Sharpe, Helen S. "How to Teach Your Child Good Table Manners."
     Parents Magazine, 28:40-1, July, 1953.
     Traces what to teach children at each age ranging from ages
     five to ten and what to expect from your children's behavior.
     Lists ten points which are meant to help children understand
     parents' teachings at each age.
     Shaw, Adelaide, pseudonym See O'Shaughnessy, Marjorie.
875 Shaw, Carolyn Hagner. "McCall's Book of Family Manners." Mc-
     Call's, 84:sup 1-12, April, 1957.
     Author believes that manners should be taught at home by
     example and repetition. Outlines how to teach table manners,
     introductions, travel etiquette, and more.
876 _____. Modern Manners; Etiquette for All Occasions. New
     York: E.P. Dutton, 1958.
     Arranged in question/answer format. Topics include advice
     about wedding etiquette, birth announcements, anniversaries,
     and funerals. Business, telephone, and club etiquette is outlined
     as well. Procedures for entertaining, for the debutante and
     for giving a dance are given. "Courtesy in the Armed Services"
     and "Protocol--Social Official Procedures in Washington" are
     included. Illustrated, includes index.
877 Shea, Nancy Brinton. The Army Wife. New York: Harper and
     Bros., 1941.
     Army etiquette for the young girl marrying into the service.
     Contents include in part: engagements, "Kaydet" girl at West
     Point, weddings, the Army household, Army children, service
     in Washington, illness, and Army hospitalization. Death, military
     funerals, foreign service, etiquette for civilians visiting on
     post, and camp followers of the U.S. Army are additional topics
     addressed. Includes bibliography and index.
878 _____. The Army Wife. New York: Harper and Bros., 1948.
     Postwar edition includes information on Army life in occupied
     land and on foreign bases.
879 _____. "Call to Arms; What's What for Military Weddings."
     Woman's Home Companion, 69:96-7, June, 1942.
     Answers questions about military wedding etiquette, including
     the walk under the arch of swords, dress, and getting married
     at camp.
     Shea, Nancy Brinton, joint author See Pye, Anne Etheldra Briscoe.
     Navy Wife (1942).
880 Sheehan, Robert. "Business Manners." Fortune, 55:106-8, Jan.,
     1957.
     Uses examples of executive's manners, with detailed information
     on how to use the telephone, how to greet visitors saying,
     "good manners...constitute a necessary lubricant to business.
     A few moments spent on the amenities erase doubts and hos-
     tility...."
881 Sheldon, L.W. Sheldon's Twentieth Century Guide to Etiquette;
     An Accurate and Up-to-date Guide to Modern Etiquette. Phila-
     delphia: David McKay, 1901.
     Defines natural and formal etiquette in terms of the Golden
     Rule. Suggests early training in manners as necessary to be

instilled "precept upon precept and example upon example."
Other topics included are temperance, self-control, gallantry
versus coquetry, hospitality, politeness to servants, and behavior
in public. "Foolish disregard of public opinion has been the
secret of non-success in so many cases...." Advice about proper
deportment in the theater, opera, church and when travelling
is also included. Also discusses the visiting card, invitations,
introductions and conversation.

882 Sherwin, M.R. "How About Neatness and Manners?" Parents
Magazine, 25:38-9, March, 1950.
Contends neatness and manners are important and can best
be taught by setting an example to youngsters in the home.
This is done by making sure children are happy and respect
themselves.

883 Sherwood, Mary Elizabeth Wilson. Manners and Social Usages.
New York: Harper and Bros., 1918.
Details the custom of cards and calling and describes cards
of courtesy. Introductions as American customs are examined,
invitations and answers are discussed. Outlines wedding etiquette, and advises on formal and informal dining. Chaperones
and their duties are highlighted, and there is a chapter called
"Etiquette for Spinsters." Defines "Good and Bad Society"
and "Society's Small Talk." Considers "The Awkward and the
Shy," and "The Etiquette of Towns and Villages," as well as
"English Social Usage" and "How to Treat the English." Much
comparison is made between American and foreign social custom.
Illustrated with photos.

884 Shor, Jean. "Take Along an Open Heart." Rotarian, 90:8-11,
Jan., 1957.
Says that the smile, along with patience and courtesy are the
universal mediums of exchange, and that premise is supported
by different traveler's experiences. Also gives advice to tourists.

885 Shultz, Gladys Denny. "Polish for Little Diamonds." Better
Homes and Gardens, 16:34, May, 1938.
Suggests that by exposing children to social situations, they
take on a special grace. Parental guidance should put emphasis
on friendliness and thoughtfulness. Lists books to guide children,
and some manners even very young children can be taught.

886 "Sidestepping Ms. takes." Time, 124:33, July 30, 1984.
Determines how to address vice-presidential candidate Geraldine
Ferraro, a married woman who uses her maiden name profes-
sionally.

887 Sidey, Hugh. "A Season of Bad Manners." Time, 17, May 6, 1985.
Cites numerous examples of the "lapse from civility" in "the
general melee of partisan politics in Washington, D.C."

888 Siedentopf, A.R. "Bring Grace to the Table." American Home,
36:102, Nov., 1946.
Encourages readers to practice those graces of mind and manners
so that mealtime is "a restoration of the soul as well as body."

889 Sims, L. "Let's Put Napkins Under Our Chins." Coronet, 39:138,
Dec., 1955.
Looks at table manners.

890 Siple, Molly. "Manners; Elizabeth Post Rounds Off the Rules."
    House Beautiful, 117:10, Aug., 1975.
    A Chat with Elizabeth Post compares the modern adaptable
    manners to those of her grandmother-in-law's (Emily Post)
    day, illustrating changes with specific examples.
891 Skinner, Cornelia Oats. "If You're Going to Go, Go!" Ladies'
    Home Journal, 75:92, July, 1958.
    "It's simple, really: stand up, put on your coat, say good-bye—and
    leave." Gives situations in which lingering good-byes are exam-
    ined and discouraged.
892 Slocombe, Lorna. "Nice Girls Don't Chase Men." Woman's Home
    Companion, 66:47, March, 1939.
    Strategies for getting a man interested in one, without going
    after him.
893 Smallenburg, Carol, Smallenburg, Harry, and Piers, Maria W.
    "Social Graces and Disgraces; With Study Discussion Program."
    PTA Magazine, 59:7-9, 35-6, Dec., 1964.
    Description of teen-agers' "social graces and disgraces..." with
    study questions for educators to use, and guidance for coordinat-
    ing school effort with home life.
    Smallenburg, Harry, joint author See Smallenburg, Carol.
894 "Smarten Up Your Party Manners." Glamour, 83:48, Sept., 1985.
    List of do's and don'ts covers invitations, dinner and cocktail
    parties and post-party manners.
895 "Smile School: Teaching Courtesy and Service to Railroaders."
    Literary Digest, 123:5, May 29, 1937.
    Description of elaborate courtesy system designed to teach
    employees of Union Pacific railroad, which was the brainchild
    of W.M. Jeffers, president of U.P.
896 Smith, Elinor Goulding. "Rebel." Atlantic, 177:144, May, 1946.
    Tongue-in-cheek article about the discourtesy the author encoun-
    tered when dealing with sales clerks, bus drivers and other
    service people.
897 Smith, Emma R. "Easy Manners." Hygeia, 24:844, Nov., 1946.
    Children should learn manners from the people with whom
    they live. Tips on teaching children manners include the reminder
    that kindness and consideration for others are recognized
    principles of good manners.
898 Smith, F. Hopkinson. "Insolence of New York." Ladies' Home
    Journal, 26:9, Oct., 1909.
    Citing various discourteous behaviors to be found among New
    Yorkers during interaction with one another and out-of-towners
    Smith says, "I have no hesitation in saying that we have more
    solid chunks of insufferable insolence in New York than can
    be found in any other city in the world."
    Smith, Gregory White, joint author See Naifeh, Steven W.
899 Smith, H. Allen. "Why Didn't Somebody Tell Me?" Reader's
    Digest, 70:79-81, Feb., 1957.
    Tongue-in-cheek article about the difficulties encountered
    by the author because introductions were not complete, with
    a person's likes and dislikes, occupation and other pertinent
    information.

900 Smith, Helena Huntington. "Burning Question: Our Deplorable
Cigar-Etiquette." Reader's Digest, 28:55-8, March, 1936.
Laments lack of manners among smokers who destroy public
and private property with their carelessness.

901 Smith, Wendell. "How Are Your Fireplace Manners?" American
Home, 21:10, Feb., 1939.
Correct social conduct around the fireplace elucidated by
an authoritative fireplace fanatic.

902 Snowden, Sondra. "Doing Business Over Sushi or Enchiladas."
ABA Journal, 138, Oct., 1985.
Lists mistakes in protocol which cause Americans to lose international business. Says it's worth the effort to learn proper
protocol.

903 _____. The Global Edge; How Your Company Can Win in
the International Marketplace. New York: Simon and Schuster,
1986.
How to do business in 25 major-market countries. Includes
information on culture and local protocol, proper dress, entertainment, and advice on initiating contacts. Includes listing
of documents needed, customs allowances, tipping and hotels
and restaurants.

904 "Social Spot Cash." Atlantic, 111:143-4, Jan., 1913.
The responsibility of a guest is great, so that the pay-back
to a hostess should be immediate, "in the coin of agreeable
good fellowship."

905 "Social Training for High School Students; A Symposium." Journal
of Home Economics, 23:427-36, May, 1931.
Papers presented to illustrate how home economics departments
in various schools are approaching the social training students
need in order to be successful in the business and social worlds.

906 "Softening of Street Manners." Living Age, 290:61-3, July 1,
1916.
Says that the manners of the world which "lies outside the
front-door have changed for the better, thanks largely to
women."

907 Sokolov, Raymond. "Behind the Times; Effect of the Fork on
Table Manners." Natural History, 87:22, Aug., 1978.
Historical essay on the fork saying that "the history of its
spread from Italy northward parallels fundamental changes
in the history of Western manners...." Discusses the difference
in consciousness between pre- and post-fork cultures. Concludes:
"The best rule is: Get fed, stay as clean as you can, and attract
no attention."

908 _____. "Buzz Off Ms. Post, It's Time for the New Etiquette."
Saturday Review, 55:33-41, Dec. 16, 1972.
Contends since morals have changed, the new etiquette calls
for nonintervention, and uses eight situations such as "Bedding
the Unwed," to illustrate this point.

909 "Spaghetti: How to Eat It." Changing Times, 10:46, Nov., 1956.
Compares Amy Vanderbilt's and Emily Post's opposing views
on the spoon method of spaghetti eating.

910 Spangler, Douglas W. "Reviving Common Courtesy." USA Today, 111:28-9, May, 1983.
Smart businesses should reduce the discourtesy their workers show to customers. Lists specific advice such as return phone calls, answer letters, avoid putting people on hold and revive the words "please" and "thank-you."

911 Spock, Benjamin. "Doctor Spock Talks with Mothers." Ladies' Home Journal, 73:81, Feb., 1956.
Dr. Spock elaborates and clarifies his views on manners.

912 Sprackling, Helen M. Courtesy, A Book of Modern Manners. New York: M. Barrows, 1944.
Comprehensive volume begins advice with the everyday essentials, such as using "please" and "thank-you." Introductions, proper use of names, greetings, and speaking voice are some of the topics covered. Also advises on conversation, correspondence, calling cards, and smoking manners. Table manners, manners in public places and telephone courtesy are considered. Tells how to teach children manners and details proper deportment of manners. Includes index.

913 _____. The New Setting Your Table; Its Art, Etiquette and Service. New York: M. Barrows, 1960.
Advises on all types of dining, including everything from china, dinnerware, glass and the utensils to "Creating the Picture" and the "Technique of Setting Your Table." Correct forms of invitations are illustrated. Directions for serving with and without a maid are included. Also suggests different ideas for different types of parties. Includes numerous diagrams and photos.

914 _____. Setting Your Table, Its Art, Etiquette and Service. New York: Barrows, 1941.
Includes advice on how to create the picture with table setting, and describes everything about selecting and using china and glass. Includes advice on invitations, mistress/maid relationships, and maid's night out. Tells what to do for Sunday night supper, breakfasts and buffets, as well as after dinner coffee. Includes index and illustrated with photos.

915 Springer, Thomas Grant. "Veiled Politeness." Lippincott, 94:507-8, Oct., 1914.
Tongue-in-cheek approach to the "indignities in our public conveyances." Asks why people crowd onto the cars, and why men remain seated while women stand.

916 Squire, Anne. Social Washington, Washington, D.C.: Press of B.S. Adams, 1923.
Intends to aid people in learning "a code of manners that has resulted from years of adaptation to peculiar conditions." Outlines White House protocol, including how to address the President, and advice on invitations to and from the President as well as receptions and garden parties. Also tells who makes calls on the Vice-President, and protocol particular to that office. The protocol of the members of the Supreme Court is detailed, including the relative rankings of justices. Discusses in detail the protocol of seating at dinners, and ranks and proper

addresses for members of the Diplomatic Corps, the Cabinet, the Senate, the House of Representatives and the Army and Navy, and other officials. "Don'ts in Washington" are listed as well.

917 _____. Social Washington. Washington, D.C.: Press of B.S. Adams, 1941.
"In this revised edition no effort has been made to add to old customs except where changes have been definitely settled."

918 Stamm, F.K. "Courtesy." Good Housekeeping, 104:12, Jan., 1937.
Philosophical discussion of raising children to be courteous.

919 Starrett, Helen Ekin. Charm of a Well-Mannered Home. Philadelphia: Lippincott, 1923.
Discusses aspects of home-making on a philosophical level, touching upon etiquette in more general terms, but does include some specific instruction, for example, on the domestic service problem.

920 _____. The Charm of Fine Manners; Being a Series of Letters to a Daughter. Philadelphia: J.B. Lippincott, 1907.
Ten letters relate mother's advice on the relationship between behavior and manners, self-control and self-culture, aims one should set, personal habits, conversation, friends and associates, tact, the cultivated, religious culture and duties, and "The Finest Feminine Art—The Making of a Home." Letters include many anecdotes as a means of example.

921 Statler, E.M. "How We Practice Business Good Manners." System, 31:369-77, April, 1917.
Statler, president of Hotels Statler Co., tells what he means by service, which he considers a commodity. Defines service, and tells why he hires men who know how to smile and be pleasant. He considers their constant purpose to train employees in tact, and tries to do everything possible "to see that it is made easy for them to be pleasant in their dealings with our guests."

922 "Steady Company." Nation, 84:217, March 7, 1907.
An editorial outlines the virtues of steady company, "yet our 'upper circles'...will no doubt refuse to consider the reforms we have suggested, and steady company will be left as the solace and joy of what is known as the 'lower middle class'."

923 Stephenson, Margaret Bennett, and Millett, Ruth. As Others Like You. Illustrated by Barbara Carr. Bloomington: McKnight and McKnight, 1957.
Lists pointers for living with other people, and outlines the rules for making introductions. Different types of correspondence are described, and the etiquette at receptions, teas and different kinds of parties is given. Also includes advice on table manners, public manners, and travel etiquette. Discusses appearance as the means by which others will judge you. Illustrated, with index.

924 Stern, Barbara Lang. "Courtesy; It's Good for You; Views of Richard Corriere." Vogue, 169:84, Oct., 1979.
Views of Richard Corriere, says people need to learn skills

to cope with rudeness, "you discharge your stress by notifying
another person of your needs..." in a neutral way. "Dr.
Corriere points out that manners are a valuable, ritualized way of making
contact, which human beings absolutely need in order to survive."

924a Stern, Barbara Lang. "Situational Etiquette: When Speaking
Up for Yourself Can Mean Breaking the Rules." Vogue, 176:350,
May, 1986.
Defines "situational etiquette" as the "unwritten, agreed upon
rules that regulate people's behavior in social situations." For
example, the respect for an authority figure's space. Lists
specific suggestions for use in asserting oneself in socially
awkward situations.

925 Stern, Edith M. "Manners Go to School." School and Society,
50:52-5, July 8, 1939.
Review of programs in different schools throughout the country
which are teaching good manners. Suggests that pupils and
teachers have come to realize that knowledge of etiquette
is not the exclusive necessity of young ladies at finishing school,
but a part of daily life.

926 Stern, Renee Bernd. Standard Book of Etiquette, Social Forms
and Good Manners for All Occasions. Chicago: Laird and Lee,
1924.
"The war brought a certain disregard for good manners. We
are now on the return swing of the pendulum...and because
of this widening interest the following volume has been written...." Begins by defining etiquette, and outlines procedures
for greetings and salutations, introductions, conversation,
cards and visits and behavior in public. All types of correspondence, dining, table setting, and entertaining are covered, as
are ceremonies such as weddings and funerals. Includes index
and is illustrated.

927 Stevens, Carilyn. Etiquette in Daily Living. Chicago: Associated
Authors Service, 1934.
First appeared as a series of articles in the Christian Science
Monitor. Chapters included are "What and Why of Etiquette,"
"Good Manners in Speech" and "Slang and Some Don'ts." Subject
matter encompasses those aspects of etiquette usually found
in the books such as table manners, public deportment and
business meetings, as well as entertaining, teaching children
manners and "Courtesy in the Home." Includes bibliographical
essay.

928 Stevens, William Oliver. The Correct Thing; A Guide Book of
Etiquette for Young Men. New York: Dodd, Mead, 1934.
Dress, table manners, dances, calls, letters, public places,
travel, sports, automobiles, fraternities, business and numerous
miscellaneous suggestions are among the subjects covered
in this volume. Concludes with advice to young man that if
he forgets etiquette under a particular circumstance he can
always fall back on the lesson of the Golden Rule.

929 Stevenson, R. Helen. "Social Relationships of Workers in Business." National Education Association. Proceedings and Addresses, 1926:377-8.

Suggests teaching school age children manners and business etiquette which would become an asset in business throughout their lives. Early training in business manners "will in itself automatically bring into existence a good social relationship between the individuals who have been so trained, and, through them, between the organization of which they are members and the public."

930 Stewart, Donald Ogden. _Perfect Behavior, A Parody Outline of Etiquette._ New York: George H. Doran, 1922.
This parody outline covers all the topics found in traditional etiquette books, but in a different light. For example, in the chapter on correspondence, a sample letter from a debutante to a taxidermist is included, in which she thanks him for having stuffed her pet, Alice. Under the etiquette of travel he gives this advice: "An elderly lady with a closed umbrella, desiring to take a street car, should always stand directly under a large sign marked 'Street Cars Do Not Stop Here.'"

931 Stewart, Marjabelle Young, and Faux, Marian. _Executive Etiquette; How to Make Your Way to the Top with Grace and Style._ New York: St. Martin's Press, 1979.
"There is little doubt that good manners can smooth the path to success." Tells how to establish daily goodwill in the workplace, how to handle sexual harassment, and how to form friendships. Advice covers "The Etiquette of Handling Your Boss," the job hunt, the interview, travel and convention etiquette, and there is a chapter "For Women Only," examining questions peculiar to women in business. Describes the unwritten laws and unspoken rules, tells how to communicate effectively, and lists tactics for the business lunch. Comprehensive in scope.

932 _____. _Marjabelle Stewart's Book of Modern Table Manners._ Illustrated by Lauren Jarrett. New York: St. Martin's Press, 1981.
Explains how to have perfect table manners on any occasion, and anywhere in the world. Outlines correct use of utensils, and china, describes different styles of eating, i.e., American and Continental. Sets down rules for gracious eating, and tells how to dine in a variety of places, i.e., home, restaurant, or White House. Describes eating customs around the world. Outlines teaching children table manners in two easy lessons. Includes advice on entertaining, with a record book that includes check-lists for what was served, and guests invited. Illustrated with numerous diagrams and has index. There is historical information given throughout.

932a Stewart, Marjabelle Young. _The New Etiquette. Real Manners for Real People in Real Situations—An A-to-Z Guide._ Illustrated by Lauren Jarrett. New York: St. Martin's Press, 1987.
Encyclopedia format is designed to be used for quick reference and convenience. Stewart has "chosen to write about practical, everyday manners—situations and events the way they are likely to happen as well as the way they ought to happen." The author also attempts to reflect in her advice current trends in entertaining, and to play down situations "that the average

person is unlikely to encounter." Comprehensive in scope, offers advice under the general categories of ceremonies, entertaining, protocol, family manners, business manners and the single life. Elucidates proper deportment for topics ranging from adoption, alimony and how to eat bacon to business dress, cohabitation and dishware. Tells how to cope with food stuck in teeth, an open fly, telephone answering machines and an unintentional snub. Traditional topics such as table manners, weddings, entertaining and business etiquette are also covered. Contains numerous cross references and is illustrated. Appended with a party checklist, a checklist for the bar, a wine chart and a host and hostess dinner party record.

933 _____. The New Etiquette Guide to Getting Married Again. New York: St. Martin's Press, 1980.
Written to describe the "ways of remarrying that reflect tact and good taste." Initial planning, a church wedding, receptions, advice on working out relationships, and setting up a household are some of the topics addressed. Final chapter answers the most frequently asked questions about remarrying.

934 _____. Your Complete Wedding Planner; For the Perfect Bride and Groom to Be. New York: David McKay, 1977.
The thought and planning needed for every phase of the wedding, the engagement party, showers, rehearsal dinner, receptions and honeymoon is elucidated. There are schedules and appointment sheets for use in planning. Tells how to handle particular family problems which may occur. Lists steps to take in organizing the reception, including how to have a Do-It-Yourself-Reception. Includes an "Organizer" with blank forms and charts and lists for the bride-to-be to use in planning.

935 Stinnett, Caskie. "Guestmanship; Houseguests." Atlantic, 240:28, Dec., 1977.
General discussion of guest offenses, such as failing to come to meals promptly, or being publicly untidy.

936 Stockwell, Herbert G. "Business Manners." Outlook, 99:776-8, Nov. 25, 1911.
Discusses the theory that pleasing manners open doors of opportunity, and discusses particular traits such as the "wooden face," or curtness, and relates these traits to success in business.

937 Stoddard, Maynard Good. "Bed Etiquette." Saturday Evening Post, 255:56-7, March, 1983.
Bed etiquette includes not moving the bed on unsuspecting husbands. The right to snore is examined: "proper etiquette... calls for the snoree to shake the snorer gently by the shoulder...." Bed etiquette also takes into account the temperature of the sleeping partner's feet.

938 _____. "Etiquette: From Soup to Nuts." Saturday Evening Post, 52, Sept., 1986.
Humorous article looks at the changing rules and "situations...for which no rules of etiquette have been established...," and cites humorous examples to support this statement. Outlines rules for the formal dinner party.

939 _____. "Waiter, There's a Glass Eye in My Tapioca." Saturday
Evening Post, 252:80-1, Sept., 1980.
Humorous article about Stoddard's antics at a fund-raiser dinner
and what the etiquette writers don't tell you.

940 Stokes, S.J. "Easy Guide to Table Etiquette." Essence, 12:105,
Sept., 1981.
Guide to basic table etiquette with diagram of table setting,
says the most important thing to remember is that table etiquette provides the guidelines to prevent embarrassment.

941 Storipan, Alison. "Test Your P's and Q's; Table Manners." Seventeen, 36:32, Feb., 1977.
Multiple choice situations outlined for reader test. Also has
test for dating eitquette.
Strait, Suzanne Hart, joint author See DeShan, E.J.

942 Strang, Ruth. "Knowledge of Social Usage in Junior and Senior
High Schools." School and Society, 34:709-12, Nov. 21, 1931.
Summary of the results of a test of social usage given to 1,614
pupils, with the hope that it would prove useful in measuring
"the results of incidental and systematic instruction in social
usage; and in discovering deficiencies in knowledge of social
usage...."

943 Stratton, Dorothy Constance, and Schleman, Helen Blanche.
Your Best Foot Forward. New York: McGraw, 1940.
For college students, contents include discussion of introductions, table manners, dining in public places, dating, social
communication, "Extending and Receiving Courtesies," travelling
and personal appearance. Material is adapted from a survey
of students in nine co-educational institutions and is supple-
mented by opinions of college student leaders on 59 campuses.
Illustrated and has bibliography.

944 Street, G.S. "Pavement Reflections." Living Age, 277:373-5,
May 10, 1913.
Considers manners of people in the street, which have "become
more slovenly than they used to be and require admonishment."

945 _____. "Social English." Living Age, 272:195-204, Jan.27,
1912.
Focuses on English manners, and says that the traits found
among those considered showed them to be true models of
the better-mannered, thereby taking exception to the notion
that in earlier ages people were better behaved. Attributes
changes in conversation to a greater fluidity among the classes,
and a view of women with sincere respect as a cause for a
very great improvement in English manners.

946 Sullivan, Alan. "Manners." Harpers, 133:454-8, Aug., 1916.
Contends that Americans have lost the "facon de vivre," and
that they have become ruthless, arrogant and impatient, so
that perhaps "one should not expect manners in a democracy."

947 Sutherland, Douglas. "How to Be a Gentleman—An Authoritative
Short Guide." Esquire, 90:92-3, Dec. 19, 1978.
Parodies those attributes frequently associated with gentlemen,
saying, for example, that "gentlemen do not use napkin rings
or the word toilet."

948 Suthers, Albert E. "Some Comments on Courtesy." Asia, 41:101, Feb., 1941.
   Three incidences of courtesy encountered by the author from children on a trip from Medan to Phnom-Penh.

949 Sutton, J. Laurance. "Living Room Eatiquette." American Mercury, 84:22-4, March, 1957.
   Tongue-in-cheek advice on how to "get through a refreshment period in the living room without incident."

950 Swadley, Elizabeth. Your Christian Wedding. Nashville: Broadman, 1966.
   Tells who to tell first when engaged and outlines decisions to be made in order to proceed with wedding plans, i.e., where, what kind of wedding, and who pays for what. Suggests consulting with the minister, and tells who does what in the wedding ceremony. Advice also covers invitations, flowers and pictures for the wedding. Includes a wedding checklist, and samples of correspondence.

951 Swain, Sana. Sana Swain's Dictionary of Advice. New York: Sana, 1923.
   Question/answer format. Author hopes "you, dear reader, will profit by my long experience with heart affairs—experience which has been crystallized in this valuable book—the only one of its kind." Chapter One is called, "Problems of Young Men and Women," advises on young people's problems from school period into the business world. Chapter Two is "Problems of Love's Awakening," which addresses that important period of the awakening of love and covers the countless questions of behavior, manners, social etiquette and convention. Chapter Three addresses "Problems of Courtship" and advises how to choose the lifemate. The last chapter, "The Problems of the Proposal and the Engagement" answers the "many perplexing problems of the engagement period."

952 Swartz, Mimi. "Saving Face; Life's Little Embarrassments Call for Wit, Tact—and Sometimes an Outright Apology." Savvy, 84, Feb., 1985.
   Offers advice to those having committed a social blunder, tells how successful and powerful women have recovered from embarrassing situations.

Swartz, Oretha D., joint author See McCandless, Bruce.

953 Sypher, Wylie. "Mrs. Post May I Present Mr. Eliot." American Scholar, 45:250-2, 1986.
   Analyzes T.S. Eliot's and Emily Post's "quest for tradition, for ritual, for a usable past in society where the middle class had established itself economically but had the uncomfortable sense that it lacked 'culture'."

954 "Table Manners." Coronet, 31:19a, March, 1952.
   Six pictures with captions illustrate points of etiquette from the "boarding house reach" to blowing on soup.

955 "Table Manners; How to Simplify Your Service." House and Garden, 19:106, May, 1947.
   Suggestions on how to make serving dinner to guests easier, particularly for those who don't have a maid.

956 "Table Manners in Paris." Living Age, 335:282, Dec., 1928.
Describes a variety of etiquette practices in a variety of places
including Paris, Singapore and Constantinople.
957 Taintor, Sara Augusta. Handbook of Social Correspondence;
Notes, Letters and Announcements for Various Occasions. New
York: Macmillan, 1936.
Gives examples of correspondence such as invitations, acceptances, regrets and notes of condolence, appreciation and congratulation, with examples of announcements and invitations for
clubs, committees, associations and academic and civic occasions. Advice also covers forms of address and correct stationery.
958 Tait, Eleanor Gibson. "What Not to Do in Society." Harper's
Bazaar, 42:1044-5, Oct., 1908.
Describes what is unacceptable behavior, and encourages the
woman who is "bent on social success..." to "cultivate her
personality."
959 Taves, Isabella. "Memo to the Manless." Good Housekeeping,
149:24, Oct., 1959.
Advice to the extra woman to insure they are welcome guests
at parties, as well as how they should give parties.
960 "Teacher of Courtesy." Outlook, 89:362, June 20, 1908.
Applauds the President of the Delaware, Lackawana and Western
Railroad for appealing to its employees "to study and practice
the art of courtesy in dealing with the public."
961 "Telephone Temper." Literary Digest, 77:76-7, April 14, 1923.
Includes instructions for telephone users to make life for the
telephone operator easier.
962 Terhune, Mary Virginia (Hawes). "Are Our Women Ruder than
Our Men?" Independent, 77:738-41, April 8, 1909.
Addresses the question "Have we American women grown
arrogant by reason of the deference we have always had from
our big brother?" Relates personal experiences to illustrate
her discussion.
963 _____, and Van de Water, Virginia. Everyday Etiquette, A
Practical Manual of Social Usages. Indianapolis: Bobbs-Merrill,
1905.
Classic etiquette book of the era. Instructs readers in all aspects
of social life. Chapters on cards and calling, the chaperone,
mistress and maid, self-help and observation may be of particular
interest. There are chapters called "Mrs. Newlyrich and Her
Social Duties" and "Of Mistress and Maid." Advice to Mrs. Newlyrich includes, "Purse-pride is contemptible in its meanness
and folly. You are safe from ridicule if you keep this fact
in mind."
964 _____. Marion Harland's Complete Etiquette. Indianapolis:
Bobbs-Merrill, 1914.
Comprehensive in scope, encompasses all aspects of etiquette
in America. Proper deportment between men and women is
detailed, and one chapter is called "Coeducation Socially Considered," which examines the development of social relationships
in coeducational environments. Discusses the chaperone, "Hos-

pitality as a Duty," and "Courtesy from the Young to the Old."
Also has advice for the shy: "forget yourself and your affairs
in interest in others and their affairs." Also tells how to get
off a street-car, and how to learn to talk well. Closes with
a description of self-help. Includes index.

965 _____. "Minor Table Manners." Good Housekeeping, 49:525-8,
Nov., 1909.
Examines the necessity of the mother to stamp "the trademark
of breeding upon the child at an incredibly early age...."

966 Tessendorf, K.C. "Random Resume of Manners at Table." Mankind, 6:32-5, Feb., 1978.
Looks at table customs of ancient times, from Greeks and
Romans to English nobility, with the premise that: "eating
preceded dining, and may well succeed it."

967 Theodoracopulos, Taki. "Manners Make the Man." Esquire, 99:120,
Jan., 1983.
Suggests that good manners mean putting others ahead of
oneself, and to beware of contrived manners which are a substitute for common sense. Contends that the commercializing
of etiquette classes means that "etiquette is making a rude
comeback."

967a Theroux, Phyllis. "Minding Our Manners." Parents Magazine,
82-4, Dec., 1986.
Focuses upon teaching children to acknowledge gifts received,
placing as much emphasis on why this is an important function
as how the author gets her own children to write notes.

968 _____. "Party Time." Parents Magazine, 60:56, June, 1985.
Encourages the use of parties to teach children skills and to
help expand their vistas.

969 Thomas, Ethel Dodd. "Manners in the Garden." House and Garden,
76:56, Dec., 1939.
An assortment of do's and don'ts for both the owner of a garden,
and the visitor to the garden.

970 Thornborough, Laura. Etiquette for Everybody; A Guide to Social
Usage for Old and Young. New York: Barse and Hopkins, 1923.
Defines the purpose of an introduction as well as how to make
one. The rules for calling are given. Formal and informal social
functions are examined, and proper deportment at either is
outlined. There are do's and don'ts for games such as bridge,
golf, tennis, football, baseball and motoring. Answers the question of street salutations, and considers the ideal chaperone
"the one who is not regarded as such by the young people."
Lists etiquette for ceremonies, and for the home. Concludes
with discussion of the guiding principles of a code of conduct.

971 _____. Etiquette of Letter Writing. New York: Barse and
Hopkins, 1924.
Defines the rules of good taste in letter writing, and lists the
first principles of letter writing. Details of different kinds
of letters are given, and different parts of the letter are illustrated and specimen letters are included. Outlines proper choice
of words and proper use of punctuation and paragraphs. Includes
numerous samples.

972 "Thoughts on Declining Manners." Bookman, 36:126-7, Oct., 1912.
     Contends that the outcry against the lack of manners among Americans is nothing new, as evidenced in American literature in the past fifty years.

973 "Thumbing a la Emily Post." Newsweek, 21:71, Feb. 22, 1943.
     Brief biography of Emily Post, and discussion of her wartime advice, particularly hitchhiking etiquette.

974 Tidwell, Barbara Guinn. Finishing Touches for Success; (Manners to Money). Dubuque, Iowa: Kendall/Hunt, 1983.
     "There is no way to be a truly successful person in life until you attain the basic fundamentals of manners...." Discussion begins with defining proper conversation, and offers advice on table manners, difficult-to-manage food, introductions and travel. Tells how to best present oneself by developing proper posture, poise and grooming. Tells how to develop good personality traits and how to achieve success. Illustrated with numerous photos.

975 Towne, Charles Hanson. Gentlemen Behave; Charles Hanson Towne's Book of Etiquette for Men. New York: Julian Messner, 1939.
     Proper decorum at school and college is defined. Comprehensive coverage of etiquette topics generally found, of interest may be the discussion of driving manners, and a chapter called "Some Inexcusably Bad Manners," as well as one for "Wines, Liquors and Cigars." Includes index.

976 Train, Arthur. "Going to the Dogs." Saturday Evening Post, 201:14-15, June 8, 1929.
     Views etiquette books "with the distinct conviction that almost without exception such books are and always have been catch-penny contrivances written by hack writers in dusty libraries and compiled from all preceding lore since the days of Ptolemy Philadelphus." Continues to examine the value of etiquette books as a true reflection of the society they purport to arbitrate.

977 "Transplanting Manners." Independent, 75:300, Aug. 7, 1913.
     Description of the course in "Americano" manners initiated into the Filipino school system, described as "a curious task, the codification of the social ideals of a fairly civilized people for application to a generation just arriving from barbarism."

978 Trueblood, D. Elton. "Courtesy of Jesus." Christian Century, 48:678-9, May 20, 1931.
     Tells how Jesus looks, as He is described in the Bible, by His actions rather than a physical description. The recording of His words and deeds provides any description needed.

979 Tunis, John R. "What a Difference If More Businessmen Answered Their Own Telephones." Rotarian, 51:17-19, Nov., 1937.
     Illustrates the importance of courteous telephone manners to business. The author makes a plea for "taking the 'curt' part out of courtesy."

980 Udell, Rochelle. How to Eat an Artichoke and Other Trying, Troublesome, Hard-to-get-at Foods. Illustrated by Marilyn

Schaffer. New York: Putnam, 1982.
Illustrated volume advises on how to eat foods such as lobster,
artichokes, corn-on-the-cob, pizza, pasta and more.

981 Ufford, Helen. "Popping the Etiquette Question." Delineator,
123:38, Aug., 1933.
Answers questions about fork shifting, signatures of married
women, wedding recessionals, introductions and birthday parties.

982 _____. Weddings; Modes, Manners and Customs of Weddings.
New York: Delineator, 1927.
Outlines all the details to be attended to in preparation for
a wedding, such as the decisions to be made. Includes suggestions
for wedding invitations and announcements. Tells how to choose
the attendants, their costumes and what their duties are. Lists
wedding expenses and who pays for what. Concludes with answers
to miscellaneous questions. Illustrated.

Ufford, Helen See King, Mrs. John Alexander.

983 Underwood, Isabel. "Manners of Table Ten." Good Housekeeping,
53:596-9, 817-8, Nov., Dec., 1911.
Narration by "Ethel May," the censor," who instructs the girls
at Table Ten in proper table etiquette. She sets forth the proper
dress and posture at the dinner table, and the various uses
of the cutlery, china, and glassware.

984 Universal Golf Dictionary, Summary of Golf and Golf Etiquette.
Springfield, Mass.: Universal Golf Company, 1934.
Lists twenty rules of etiquette, introduction gives the history
of the origin of the game, and a dictionary of golf terms.

985 Urban, Louise. "Man Who Makes Courtesy Pay." American Magazine, 84:56-8, July, 1917.
Biographical sketch of William V. Backus, founder of the Appreciation League. Members of the League report the good manners
of workers to their employers, choosing to emphasize the positive actions of service people.

986 Uris, Auren. The Blue Book of Broad-Minded Business Behavior.
New York: Thomas Y. Crowell, 1977.
Book addresses the "complex and urgent need..." for policy
guiding behavior in "the new world created by recent social
upheavals...." Introduction discusses the relationship between
good management and etiquette, and etiquette as it relates
to the world of business. Chapters cover "Money and Ethics,"
"Your Company and the World," "Sex on the Workscene--The
New Look," "Special Problems in Dealing with People," "Status,
Status Symbols, and Politics," as well as gift-giving, luncheons
and meetings. Includes index.

987 Vanderbilt, Amy. Amy Vanderbilt's Complete Book of Etiquette;
A Guide to Gracious Living. Drawings by Fred McCarroll. New
York: Doubleday, 1952.
Comprehensive in scope, topics encompass virtually all aspects
of etiquette, including the ceremonies of life, dress, home,
entertaining, household management, correspondence, the
family and social education of the children, public life, travel
etiquette and more. That there are nine sections and seventy-
five chapters attests to the detail in which topics are elucidated.

Includes samples of correspondence, invitations and replies, and has diagrams, line drawings and an index. Touches upon virtually every aspect of life--from adopting a child to selecting a car.

988 _____. Amy Vanderbilt's Complete Book of Etiquette; A Guide to Gracious Living. Illustrated by Fred McCarroll, Mary Suzuki, and Andrew Warhol. Garden City, N.Y.: Doubleday, 1954. Remains essentially same as first edition.

989 _____. Amy Vanderbilt's Complete Book of Etiquette; A Guide to Gracious Living. Illustrated by Fred McCarroll, Mary Suzuki, and Andrew Warhol. Garden City, N.Y.: Doubleday, 1956. This edition expanded under weddings, to advise when the bride (new) or groom has been married before. Under funerals, the topic "Resumption of Dating" has been added.

990 _____. Amy Vanderbilt's Complete Book of Etiquette; A Guide to Gracious Living. Illustrated by Fred McCarroll, Mary Suzuki, and Andrew Warhol. Garden City, N.Y.: Doubleday, 1958. This edition has the addition of a thumb-index.

991 _____. Amy Vanderbilt's Complete Book of Etiquette; A Guide to Contemporary Living. Rev. and expanded by Letitia Baldrige. New York: Doubleday, 1978. Suggests that the content is different from what Amy Vanderbilt wrote, but that her spirit "is here." Part One discusses the importance of home and family, advising on problems such as drugs, alcohol and tobacco as well as manners in the family. Part Two describes proper conduct for the ceremonies of life such as weddings and funerals. Part Three is devoted to the etiquette of entertaining, including table manners. Part Four advises on business etiquette. Part Five discusses all aspects of stationery as an important communication tool. Part Six is "Your Official Self" and is concerned with protocol. Part Seven discusses dress, and aspects of the public person. Part Eight is concerned with gift giving and Part Nine deals with the etiquette of travel on all modes of transportation. Includes index, samples of correspondence, and illustrations.

992 _____. Amy Vanderbilt's Etiquette. Drawings by Fred McCarroll, Mary Suzuki, and Andy Warhol. Garden City, N.Y.: Doubleday, 1972. "This major revision has been much more difficult...because the sixties and early seventies have been a period of social upheaval." The wedding section includes a new topic called "Modern Weddings," and there is a new chapter called "Second and Subsequent Marriages." The turtleneck is included as a new item under men's clothing. Still includes advice on employer-servant relations, but dropped the advice on household finances and religious education for children.

993 _____. Amy Vanderbilt's Everyday Etiquette. Answers to Today's Etiquette Questions. New York: Bantam Books, 1974. Covers a variety of topics, including the social graces, entertaining, weddings, funerals, correspondence, children, divorce and dress. Compiled from questions asked in Ladies' Home Journal. Includes index and drawings.

994 _____. Amy Vanderbilt's Everyday Etiquette. Completely revised and updated by Letitia Baldrige. New York: Bantam Books, 1981.
Same as Amy Vanderbilt's Complete Book of Etiquette; A Guide to Comtemporary Living. New York: Doubleday, 1978.

995 _____. Amy Vanderbilt's New Complete Book of Etiquette; A Guide to Gracious Living. Drawings by Fred McCarroll, Mary Suzuki, and Andrew Warhol. New York: Doubleday, 1963.
Substantially revised over the 1952 edition. Section on wedding customs expanded to include new ones. Sports chapter changed to reflect changes in clothing and the addition of the sport of bowling. Protocol is not as rigid, and the section on men's clothing changed substantially. There is more information on informal entertaining. A new chapter is addressed to young college students. However, still contends, "Chaperones still have their place...."

996 _____. "Children's Manners." Ladies' Home Journal, 82:52, June, 1965.
Answers questions on children at the table, whispering, and adults' names.

997 _____. "Manners for Children Haven't Changed." Better Homes and Gardens, 30:220-3, May, 1952.
Says that children's manners have always been considered atrocious by the older generation, and includes 36 rules for parents to use to teach their children manners.

998 _____. "Modern Manners, The Newest Status Symbol." Coronet, 48:113-19, Oct., 1960.
Describes acceptable changes in etiquette for contemporary readers, contending that the forms change constantly.

999 _____. "Twelve Keys to Courtesy." Parents Magazine, 29:38-40, July, 1954.
In order to teach manners, parents must find time for courtesy and consideration within the home. Lists twelve requirements for success, i.e., "Parents should explain to children very early that etiquette rules are important because they make our lives more comfortable."

1000 Van de Water, Frederick F. "My Son Gets Spanked." Harper, 157:429-34, Sept., 1928.
The author's ponderings on "over-emphasizing standards of chivalric forbearance..." as instigated by his son's behavior towards a girl.

1001 Van de Water, Virginia. "Manners and Tempers." Woman's Home Companion, 37:50, March, 1910.
Courtesy outside the home is no more important than that practiced in the home, particularly the courtesy of controlling one's temper.

1002 _____. Present Day Etiquette, Including Social Forms. New York: A.L. Burt, 1924.
Begins with advice on sending and receiving invitations, followed by details on cards and calling. Chapters also offer advice on letter writing and the proper format for making

introductions. Different types of social functions are described and include photos of properly set tables. The roles of the debutante, chaperone and bachelor in society are defined. Also advises on engagements, weddings, courtesy from the young to the old, neighbors, church etiquette, newly arrived members of society, business etiquette and clubs. Details manners in sport and at home. Includes index and photographs. Van de Water, Virginia, joint author **See** Terhune, Mary Virginia (Hawes).

1003 Vane-Tempest, F. Adolphus. "Decay of Manners." Living Age, 252:731-5, March 23, 1907.
Traces decline of manners from the grand manner of the Regency, through the Victorian era to the fall. Lists the age of rush, the first steam engine, and the decline in dress as contributing factors in this decline. Informality in address and conversation "is slipshod, curt, and ugly." And the final factor contributing to this decay is the loss of dignity, grace and repose brought about by the hustle of life in the metropolis. Van Hoomissen, George, joint author **See** Rachlin, Seth.

1004 Van Rensselaer, Mathilde. "Seven Ages of Manners." Good Housekeeping, 89:130, July; 120, Aug.; 114, Sept.; 108, Oct.; 104, Nov., 1909; 90:106 Jan., 1930.
Correlates the seven ages of a girl growing into a woman with particular points in etiquette she should learn at each age. For example, at the very young age the child should be taught the value of good manners, and includes instructions on methods to use to do so. Continues through the seven ages covering wedding etiquette, hostess duties, etc.

1005 Varney, Ronald. "How to Take a Meeting." Esquire, 102:50, Oct., 1984.
How to behave when attending a business meeting, with the basic premise that bad manners can be bad for business.

1006 Vermes, Jean Campbell. Complete Book of Business Etiquette. New York: Parker, 1976.
Contends that money may be the driving force behind the wheels of commerce, but etiquette "is the oil that lubricates them." Includes advice on how to introduce people of varied business status, and gives techniques for placing, receiving, screening and transferring phone calls. Describes proper deportment for visiting and receiving visitors, and waiting room etiquette. Other subjects include firing and being fired, customs for dining in business related situations, parliamentary rules, business meetings, correspondence, and even etiquette in the office elevator. There is a chart for specific forms of address.

1007 _____. Etiquette Made Simple. New York: Doubleday, 1962.
The rules of etiquette are presented in a progressive pattern, which begins at home and moves outward to describe manners applicable at work and play. Advice covers children's manners, teen-ager's manners, and adult's manners, as well as speech usage, personal correspondence and being a good hostess. There is advice on office manners, sports, theater, visiting,

dining out, weddings, funerals and much more. Comprehensive in scope, covers each topic in detail, with a chapter review at the end of each chapter which is intended to review the essence of each chapter. Includes index.

1008 _____. Key to Etiquette for Everyone. N.Y.: Imperial, 1959.
"Intended as a key to good manners and correct behavior...." Scope is comprehensive, covering much the same topics as in Etiquette Made Simple. There is a chapter on divorce, treatment of the sick is discussed and how to behave at funerals is described. Also covers in part: table manners, introductions, dress, entertaining, weddings, and travel.

1009 Vespa, Mary. "Horrified? Insulted? Relax, Advises Judith Martin, Good Manners Are the Best Revenge." People Weekly, 18:38, Aug. 9, 1982.
Interview with Judith Martin in which she answers questions such as "Isn't etiquette outdated?" and "How does one deal with a rude person?"

1010 "Vive l'Amabilite." Time, 65:34, May 16, 1955.
Discourse on the state of French manners.

1011 Vogue's Book of Etiquette; A Complete Guide to Traditional Forms and Modern Usage. Edited by Millicent Fenwick. New York: Simon and Schuster, 1948.
Eight sections are preceded by an introduction. They cover manners in general, ceremonies and events, weddings, furnishing a household, entertaining, correspondence and clothing. Covers all aspects of etiquette within these topics in great detail. Illustrated. "Etiquette is a forum for citizens, open to anyone who cares about the amenities of living."

1012 Vogue's Book of Etiquette and Good Manners. New York: Conde Nast in association with Simon and Schuster, 1969.
"Here is an up-to-date reference book that is designed to be just as useful in one's everyday life as upon special occasions." Arranged differently from 1948 edition, although coverage of topics is just as comprehensive. Gives advice on manners in general, i.e., smoking, table manners, introductions, and on particular manners such as restaurant manners. Etiquette of pregnancy to the etiquette of funerals is determined. Describes "Great Happy Occasions," and "Entertaining." Details correspondence and cards, business manners and public speaking. Illustrated, has charts, diagrams, lists, and samples of correspondence. Indexed.

1013 Vogue's Book of Etiquette, Present-Day Customs of Social Intercourse with the Rules for Their Correct Observance. New York: Conde Nast, 1923.
Offers advice on children's manners, conversation, divorce, engagements, arriving and leaving, forms of address, and air travel ("into small planes no woman should step without a leather helmet, a leather coat, warm, short skirts and thick stockings..."). Maintains that in order to be a good conversationalist one must have character. Letter-writing, table service, entertaining, protocol in Washington, etiquette in other countries and family events are additional topics covered.

1014 Wade, Margaret. Social Usage in America. New York: Thomas
Y. Crowell, 1924.
Includes traditionally covered topics such as table manners,
speech, correspondence, introductions and business etiquette.
There is a discussion of social usage in Washington, D.C.,
and instructions are interspersed with anecdotes about the
social life of Washington, D.C. Her approach is broad, and
concludes with a numbered list of "What Not to Do's."
1015 Waele, Harriet de. "Manners Aren't Sissy." Country Gentleman,
123:50-1, Jan., 1953.
Advises that families should make their company manners
everyday manners as well, so that manners come easily.
1015a Waggoner, Glen, and Moloney, Kathleen. With the editors
of Esquire. Esquire Etiquette. The Modern Man's Guide to
Good Form. New York: Macmillan, 1987.
"In a rapidly changing world, we think it is important to bring
to any discussion of social conduct a healthy skepticism,
a strong sense of one's own values, and a generous sense of
humor." Topics are arranged in dictionary form, ranging from
answering machines and apologies to children and Christmas
cards. There is advice for the man "who always wants to
appear in good form..." whether breaking up, grooming, smoking, eating or getting married. Additionally, apologies, toasts,
dutch treats, friendly wagers and when it is appropriate to
stand up or sit down are topics included. Arrangement is
significantly different from previous editions, advice is general
rather than specific.
1016 Waggoner, Glen. "Mind Over Manners." Esquire, 103:40, May,
1985.
How-to for etiquette problems presented by answering machine
messages, saloon payment methods, and other little "etiquette
things" that sometimes trip people up.
1017 Walker, H. "O Mores!" Forum, 75:467-72, March, 1926.
Compares points of etiquette from an old etiquette book,
Peale's Popular Educator, by R.S. Peale, with similar points
from Emily Post's Etiquette.
1018 Wallace, Lily Haxworth. New American Etiquette. New York:
Books, 1941.
Gives proven methods for making and keeping friends, developing poise, and for the elimination of all awkwardness. Offers
advice to Mr. and Mrs. Average American, including how
they should behave in their homes, neighborhoods, clubs,
and when travelling. Tells how to greet people, and make
introductions. Describes proper conduct for children from
babyhood through college. Also advises on the etiquette of
correspondence, invitations, announcements, dances, chewing
gum and smoking. Elucidates the etiquette of sport, as well
as that of the telephone, telegraph and radio. There is a chapter
on the sensible use of wines and liquors. Has many photos,
illustrations and an index.
1019 Washington, George. "Rules of Civility and Decent Behavior
in Company and Conversation." Congressional Digest, 11:47-9,

Feb., 1932.
Lists the classic rules set forth by Washington, such as "Sleep not when others speak" and "Spit not into the fire."

1020 Watrous, Peter. "Step-Etiquette." Psychology Today, 18:80, Jan., 1984.
Cites Emily Post, Judith Martin and Eve Drobot on their advice for situations not covered formally in the etiquette books, implying that contemporary etiquette writers are winging it like everyone else in regard to step-family situations.

1021 Watson, H.B. Marriott. "Men and Manners." Harper's Weekly, 55:21, June 17, 1911.
Comparison of British and American manners, and the effect upon manners which "the increased liberty of the one sex..." has had. Declares that "socially there is very little etiquette now."

1022 _____. "Passing of the Gentleman." Harper's Weekly, 54:20, Nov. 26, 1910.
Sets forth a definition of the gentleman and asks if he can "hold his place against the invasion of the cad with ideas?" Concludes "the question leaves one speculating, for the future does not belong to the gentlemanly virtues."

1023 Watson, Lilian (Eichler) The Customs of Mankind, with Notes on Modern Etiquette and the Newest Trend in Entertaining. New York: Doubleday, 1924.
Traces the origins of etiquette, in an attempt to "search the sources of modern customs...." Speech, introductions and the debutantes of yesterday are examined to determine their origins. There is a short history of courtship and marriage customs, writing customs, and gift giving. Calling customs are described with an historical perspective, as are hospitality and entertainment customs. There is a "Tale of Table Manners," and a description of "Holidays and Their Customs." Dance, dress and funeral customs are examined. Treatment of topics is world-wide in scope and is related to contemporary etiquette. Includes numerous photos and index.

1024 _____. The New Book of Etiquette. Illustrations by George Wescott. Garden City, N.Y.: Garden City, 1924.
Divided into two parts, the first beginning with an outline of the development of social life, from cave dwellers to the present, with an historical outline of etiquette. The second part is a discussion of the new etiquette with advice to readers to "cultivate a true sense of values." Encompasses tradtionally covered topics, i.e., correspondence, introductions, conversation, weddings, etc., and some not usually found, such as a chapter on self-consciousness. Discusses the passing of calling customs. Appendix has questions and answers, and a list of reminders.

1025 _____. The Standard Book of Etiquette. Garden City, N.Y.: Garden City, 1948.
Up-dated edition is meant to address the far-reaching changes which have taken place in society. Information included in earlier editions is included here, and there is a comparison

drawn between the traditional usage and the modern. This edition includes a chapter called "The Staff of a Big House," and tells how to address, employ, get-along-with and fire a maid. Includes lists of frequently asked questions and answers to them at the end of many chapters, and an appendix lists correct forms of address.

1026 Weber, Bruce. "My Life Is a Wrong Number." New York Times Magazine, 28, Jan. 6, 1986.
Describes difficulties the author has had because he shares the same name as a famous photographer.

1027 Weissbourd, Bernice. "Eating as Adults Do." Parents Magazine, 57:98, Feb., 1982.
Tips for parents of a two-year-old tells how to manage the messiness at mealtime and how to teach him manners at the table. Contends there is an advantage of learning manners from the family gathering at mealtime.

1028 Weitz, John. Man in Charge; The Executive's Guide to Grooming, Manners and Travel. New York: Macmillan, 1974.
In order to be in charge, one must be confident and comfortable, giving the appearance of "poshrich" as opposed to "showjocks." Advice covers dress and grooming, social and business etiquette, travel, and international business customs.

1029 Werner, Marilyn. The Bride's Thank-You Note Handbook. New York: Essandess, 1968.
Contains extensive collection of sample thank-you notes arranged alphabetically by type of gift. Gives advice on establishing a routine for prompt writing and guidelines for appropriate tones, openings and closings. Also describes best stationery to use.

1030 Wertheimer, Leopold. "It Pays Me to Do It Different." System, 36:42-6, July, 1919.
Owner of a successful chain of department stores tells why his business grew. Gives the step-by-step account of how he built his business using small courtesies such as lending merchandise to charitable causes, giving special courtesy to maids and children, providing a shopping service, and ascribing to the philosophy that the customer is always right.

1031 West, Mrs. G. C. "Modern Manners and the Unmannerly Age." Cosmopolitan, 37:394-400, Aug., 1904.
Using a country house party as her base of reference, the author compares manners past and present. Discusses greeting guests and proper dinner hours.

1032 Weston, Elizabeth Stewart. Good Housekeeping's Complete Wedding Guide. Illustrated by George Wiggins. Floral decorations by Ann Hogan. Garden City, N.Y.: Hanover House, 1957.
Comprehensive volume covers all aspects of planning a wedding. Details traditions and customs of engagements and weddings. Defines an official engagement and tells how to announce it. Offers advice on showers, invitations and announcements, dress, wedding gifts, the trousseau, attendants and their duties and professionals who can help. Also includes lists of specific instructions for the wedding, including floral arrangements,

music, beverages, wedding cakes, and wedding guests. Indexed, has illustrations.

1033 "What a Thoughtful Guest Should Know." Good Housekeeping, 155:161, Dec., 1962.
Brief discussion of the etiquette of attending a party, focusing on invitations, gifts, and saying thank-you.

1034 "What Are Good Manners?" Golden Book, 2:55-60, July, 1925.
Pot-pourri of anecdotes and poems about manners.

1035 "What Courtesies Do You Expect from Men?" Woman's Home Companion, 77:7, March, 1950.
Results of a poll answer the question whether Americans should preserve or abandon customs such as men standing when a woman enters the room, giving up seats in public conveyances, or allowing a woman to precede him through a doorway.

1036 What Do You Know About Etiquette? The Etiquette Question and Answer Book. New York: Ready Reference, 1927.
Quiz game format asks etiquette questions. "The five hundred questions in this book deal with all phases of social conduct...." Includes 20 quizzes each with 25 questions.

1036a "Whatever Happened to Common Courtesy?" Reader's Digest, 131:168-70, July, 1987.
Contends that common courtesy has become a contradiction in terms. Examines sociological factors which have contributed to a decline in courtesy, such as Women's Lib, and the influence of television.

1037 "What Manner of Men? Ill-mannered Americans." Newsweek, 66:92, Nov. 1, 1965.
Discusses bad manners exhibited at the New York World's Fair, saying this display is an "expression of a larger blight..." and contends that, in general, manners are declining in America.

1038 "What Would Emily Post Have Said?" Life, 49:46, Oct. 10, 1960.
Editorial concerned with bad manners of Americans at the United Nations, as well as those exhibited by Castro, and Khrushchev. Makes a connection between manners and politics. (Emily Post died this week.)

1039 "What You Can Eat with Your Fingers." Good Housekeeping, 161:163, Sept., 1965.
How-to's for eating problem food such as artichokes, bacon, squab, quail, chicken and more.

Wheeler, Blanche, joint author **See** McCrady, Marjorie Ellis.

1040 Wheeler, Robert L. "Emily Post of the Fifties." Forum, 104:233-5, Nov., 1945.
Highlights from an etiquette book written in the 1850's, called Behavior Book: A Manual for Ladies, by Eliza Leslie.

1041 White, H. "Realism in Etiquette; Dance Etiquette." Dance Magazine, 32:76-7, Jan., 1958.
Tells how dance teachers can help children learn dance etiquette, an experience which "should provide values which would carry over into every area of life...."

1042 White, Rose V. Mealtime Etiquette. New York: Pocket Books,
     1963.
     Good table manners should be automatic so that "we can
     enjoy the company of others." Examines the importance of
     early training and using good table manners as an everyday
     pattern of behavior. Proper seating arrangements for different
     occasions at the family table are diagramed. How to entertain
     at home, the responsibilities of the hostess and duties of
     the host are described. Lists specific behavior to be avoided
     when dining. Also tells how to eat awkward foods, and what
     to know when dining out. Includes numerous photographs,
     a wine chart and an index.
1043 Whittle, Ellen. "Manners Still Count." 50 Plus, 20:34-5, Oct.,
     1980.
     Biographical sketch of Elizabeth Lindley Post, granddaughter-
     in-law of Emily Post.
1044 "Who Pays for It?" Independent, 59:1238-9, Nov. 23, 1905.
     Scathing editorial about the smart set in society. "Far be
     it from us to take our four hundred to task for worthlessness
     and stupidity." The four hundred refers to the social register,
     the author continues contending that "the American people
     when it is once possessed of the facts...will not go on patiently
     paying the bills of a smart set that chooses to be both morally
     wanton and economically worthless. That is to say, we shall
     take away from its multi-millionaire husbands and papas
     the ownership of those vast worth-producing public utilities
     that rightfully are the property of the public."
1045 "Who Snubs Whom? Memo from Geneva." U.S. News and World
     Report, 36:54, May 7, 1954.
     Protocol problems presented when one country fails to recog-
     nize another are actually reflections of larger world problems.
     Discusses the problems encountered by the Swiss as a neutral
     country as well.
1046 "Who's Polite Now?" Woman's Home Companion, 73:7-8, April,
     1946.
     Results of a poll taken by the magazine which indicates the
     public perception is that in general men have better manners
     in public, teen-agers have no manners, and that parents have
     better manners than their off-spring.
1047 "Why Can't We Make Politeness the Fashion Once More?" Satur-
     day Evening Post, 233:10, Dec. 17, 1960.
     The thank-you offered by New Jersey toll collectors so astounds
     some motorists that they are clogging traffic!
1048 "Why Etiquette Vanished, Why It's Coming Back." U.S. News
     and World Report, 93:71-2, Dec. 6, 1982.
     Interview with Judith Martin includes her explanation for
     the decline in good manners in the past 20 years, as well
     as her advice on how to handle particular situations.
1049 Wier, Ester. Army Social Customs. Harrisburg, Pa.: Stackpole,
     1960.
     Intended to "set forth procedures and courtesies which smooth
     the way for the new Army wife...." Describes the Army custom

of calling, and describes the proper use of cards. Details
on the use of invitations and replies are supplied. The chapter
"Your Social Life as a Couple" describes proper deportment
at dinners, weddings, luncheons, teas and other functions.
There are notes for enlisted men's wives and for the bachelor
officer. Discusses the importance of tradition, and the relationship among "Sister Services." Army life in the Washington,
D.C. area is examined. Includes a collection of abbreviations
and terms widely used by Army personnel, and an index.

1050 _____, and Hickey, Dorothy Coffin. The Answer Book on
Air Force Social Customs. Harrisburg, Pa.: Military Service,
1957.
Question/answer format, discussion begins with social calls,
defining must calls, and what form of calling cards should
be used. Discusses different types of social occasions and
proper deportment in light of Air Force customs. Topics covered include breakfasts, coffees, dessert bridge, formal and
informal teas, formal dinners, bridal showers, weddings and
organized parties. Includes advice on the role of the Air Force
wife in supporting her husband in overseas duty. Miscellaneous
Air Force customs are outlined, rules for living on base are
listed, and Air Force social life in Washington is examined.
Information on insignia and Air Force terms is included. Has
bibliography and index.

1051 _____. The Answer Book of Naval Social Customs. Harrisburg,
Pa.: Military Service, 1956.
Encompasses same subjects covered in the Air Force edition,
from the Naval perspective. The etiquette of going aboard
ship is outlined, and gives an overview of miscellaneous Naval
customs. Insignia is described, and Naval terms are defined
for the civilian. Includes index, illustrated.

1052 Wiessler, David A. "Why People Are Rude—How It Harms Society." U.S. News and World Report, 95:54-5, Aug. 22, 1983.
Examines the causes of rudeness, citing specific incidents.
Interviews Dan Baugher, Associate Professor of Management
at Pace University, who suggests that one reason for rudeness
may be crowding. Baugher says the best way to respond to
rudeness is not to respond in kind, and the best way to prevent
it is to reduce aggression in society.

1053 Wilcox, Bettina. A Simplified Guide to Table Setting. New
York: Homecrafts, 1951.
Includes fundamentals because "in matters of table service
there is a certain justification for following a group of more
or less constant rules...." Tells how to make the dining place
a pleasant one using dishes, glassware, linens and decorations.
Suggests different types of settings for different occasions.
Advises on wine selection. Numerous photos.

1054 Wilde, Merida. "Can It Be Taught?" Bookman, 61:656-60, Aug.,
1925.
Relates difficulties encountered because of a lack of social
education as a child, and encourages public schools to teach
the social amenities.

1054a Willens, Michele. "The Six Rudest Restaurants in America."
Money, 16:115-16, Oct., 1987.
Maintains that a number of major American cities "have
spawned a class of restaurant that shamelessly favors the
elected elite to the point of barely tolerating the rest of
us." Cites stories from disgruntled diners, and lists six restaurants which are the rudest, in descending order of outrageousness. (Outrageousness is defined as rudeness plus cost.) Includes
advice on how to fight back, such as not tipping, or writing
a letter of complaint.

1055 Willson, Nina Cotton, and Rogers, Lois V. "Improve Your Pupils'
Cafeteria Manners; Good Manners Club." National Education
Association Journal, 42:108, Feb., 1953.
Teachers relate their experience in establishing a Good Manners
Club in the public schools of Arizona. The program provides
"an opportunity for voluntary participation by all the children
in a school and the development of poise and confidence...."

1056 Wilson, Barbara. Bride's School Complete Book of Engagement
and Wedding Etiquette. New York: Prentice-Hall, 1959.
Encompasses wedding customs, engagements, budgets, showers,
ceremonies, receptions, honeymoons, military weddings and
guests. Question/answer format. Includes bibliography and
index.

1057 _____. Complete Book of Engagement and Wedding Etiquette.
New York: Hawthorne Books, 1970.
Answers questions ranging from what to serve at a wedding
reception to what the groom pays for. Provides guidance
for various religious customs, tells what to pack for the honeymoon, and how to elope. Covers virtually all aspects of planning
before, during and after the wedding.

1058 Wilson, Margery. The New Etiquette; The Modern Code of
Social Behavior. New York: Frederick A. Stokes, 1937.
Arranged by subject includes the etiquette of doors, chairs,
tables and the body. There are chapters on introductions,
weddings, entertaining, cards, calls and callers and servants.
Three chapters are devoted to teaching manners to children,
from infancy to teens. Occasionally illustrated with photos.

1059 Wing, Joan E. "Courtesy Is My Business." Nation's Business,
25:19, Nov., 1937.
Wing describes how she became established as a teacher of
courtesy to businesses.

1060 "Winning with Savoir-faire." Industry Week, 33, July 8, 1985.
Suggests that American businessmen in the global market
must develop an understanding of international business protocol in order to be competitive.

1061 Witan. University of Kansas. Lady Lore; A Swingtime Handbook
of Etiquette for Girls—Young and Old. Edited by James W.
Putnam. Lawrence, Kan.: Witan, 1939.
Addressed to the "thousands of American girls now in high
school and college, at work, or starting their own homes. Written for women, by men, includes advice on the home, dating,
"Autoetiquette" and personal cleanliness. Smoking in public,

dances, conversation, sports and sororities are topics discussed. Also includes a discussion of the teaching profession, how teachers should behave, how the business girl acts and marriage. There is an examination of whether a girl should choose marriage or career.

1062 Witan. University of Kansas. <u>Manners Make Men</u>. Lawrence, Kan.: Witan, 1940.
Offers advice on manners in general, as well as "What Your Best Friend Won't Tell You." There is advice on how to dress, dance and date. Outdoor sports, driving, conversation, receptions, "cigaretiquette," introductions, table manners, and business relations are all subjects addressed in this little book. Appendix has George Washington's <u>Rules of Conduct</u>, and other musings about etiquette from famous people.

1063 Withers, A.M. "First Name Mania." <u>School and Society</u>, 58:27-8, July 10, 1943.
Withers feels that "first-naming is a precious privilege, an especially intimate form of intimacy..." which is currently being abused by Americans who insist upon a less formal approach to addressing one another.

1064 Wittenberg, Ernest. "How You Gonna Keep 'em Down in Upper Volta After They've Met Lloyd Hand?" <u>Esquire</u>, 64:24, Dec., 1965.
Biographical sketch of President Johnson's Chief of Protocol, Lloyd Nelson Hand, and some examples of his on-the-job performance.

Witting, Clifford, joint author **See** Purnell, Max.

1065 Wodehouse, P.G. "Pile 'em in Politely, George." <u>Vogue</u>, 123:112-13, May 1, 1954.
Talks about the manners of New Yorkers with humor, with numerous examples.

1066 Woods, Marjorie (Binford), and Flynn, Helen. <u>Marriage Manners; A Set of Etiquette Pointers to Help Keep Magic in Your Marriage</u>. Indianapolis: Bobbs-Merrill, 1955.
Written specifically for young, married people, advises on how to get along with each other, neighbors, and in-laws. Offers advice on how the wife can boost her husband's career. Discusses running a household and being a good hostess, and gives advice on family finance, including practical pointers for those just starting off. Tells how to adjust to each other's friends, and how to fit them into the marriage.

1067 Woodward, Elizabeth S. <u>Personality Preferred!</u> New York: Harper and Bros., 1935.
Opens with a discussion of personal grooming, and continues with advice on how to meet people. Table manners, manners at the movies, manners on the street, travel etiquette, and dating manners are subjects covered. Also advises on the proper way to write letters, visit and do business. Telephone etiquette, dance etiquette and proper deportment for a young lady in the company of a young man is outlined. Concludes by saying: "The girl who knows how to behave anywhere and anytime is clever."

1068 Woodward, Frederick A. Courtesy in Public Service; Why, Where and How to Come by It. New York: Exposition Press, 1954.
Areas of consideration include defining the earmarks of courtesy, courtesy as an aspect of personality, and developing and using a courteous manner. Deals specifically with courtesy in government agencies, with advice on what management can do to aid visitors, thereby providing courteous service. Concludes with discussion of the benefits of a systematic study of human behavior.

1069 Woodward, Stanley. "Protocol; What It Is and What It Does." U.S. Dept. State Bulletin, 21:501-3, Oct., 1949.
Protocol is the rule book by which international relations are conducted. A prime purpose is to create an atmosphere of friendliness in which the business of diplomacy may be transacted. Outlines specific functions and duties of the Protocol Office, although "the implicit functions of protocol are unlimited."

1070 Wright, Helene. "Smart Girl in a Smart Restaurant." Good Housekeeping, 147:4, Dec., 1958.
Advice for dining in a restaurant includes what to do about coats, tips, etc.

1071 Wynkoop, Eliza. "Bad Times, Better Manners." Atlantic, 150:380-2, Sept., 1932.
The author contends there has been a change of atmosphere in service people's manners, citing examples from personal experience, and attributing the change to economic hard times.

1072 Wyse, Lois. Company Manners; An Insider Tells How to Succeed in the Real World of Corporate Protocol and Power Politics. New York: McGraw-Hill, 1987.
Part One discusses the element of style in an office, for example, Maverick, Entrepreneur and Executive are all styles of company manners. The second part describes leveraging through use of the power lunch, in meetings, and by use of star power. Part Three discusses power people, spousemanship, "Working the Party," "Is There Life After Work?," and "The Five Key" to company manners. Addressed to the boss, includes very specific do's and don'ts, and uses examples from life experiences of "power people."

1073 Zemke, Ron. "Is Good Management Just Good Manners?" Training; The Magazine of Human Resource Development, 6, July, 1986.
Parallels etiquette with contemporary management theories, using comparisons of the workplace and social situations.

1074 Zinsser, William K. "Tragi-Comedy of No Manners." New York Times Magazine, 22-3, Jan. 29, 1961.
"The subway is the supreme test of manners, and the average rider rarely passes the test." Suggests that the lack of manners is in part due to the system itself, because "rush hour turns lambs into lions, gentle people into fiends and fullbacks."

1075 Zoebel, Louise Purwin. "Guide to Good Manners for Swimming
     Pool Guests." <u>Parents Magazine</u>, 34:78, July, 1959.
     Lists 15 pointers for pool guests, such as not dropping in un-
     announced.

For Further Reading

Aresty, Esther. The Best Behavior. New York: Simon and Schuster, 1970.

Babbitt, M.R. Bibliography of Etiquette Books Published in America Before 1900. New York: New York Public Library, 1947.

Carson, Gerald. The Polite Americans: A Wide-angle View of Our More or Less Good Manners Over 300 Years. Westport, Conn.: Greenwood Press, 1966.

Mason, John Edward. Courtesy Through the Ages; An Introduction to the History of Manners. Philadelphia, 1937.

Post, Edwin. Truly Emily Post. New York: Funk and Wagnalls, 1961.

Schlesinger, Arthur M. Learning How to Behave: A Historical Study of American Etiquette Books. New York: Macmillan, 1946.

Van Arsdale, May Belle. Manners Now and Then. New York: Harcourt, Brace, 1940.

Van Rensselaer, May (King). The Social Ladder. New York: Henry Holt, 1924.

Index

Boldface *entries signify books, entries in quotation marks are articles,*
and ALL CAPS *entries refer to subjects.*